The Private Secretary's Complete Deskbook

By the same author:

The Office Junior in Training

Office Correspondence Guide

The Private Secretary's Complete Deskbook

CAROL E. FISHER

Formerly Principal of Fisher's Secretarial College, Ayr
Fellow of The Society of Commercial Teachers
Fellow of The British Society of Commerce
Holder of Pitmans College Higher Secretarial Diploma

HARRAP · LONDON

First Published in Great Britain 1972
by George G. Harrap & Co. Ltd
182-184 High Holborn, London WC1V 7AX

ISBN 0 245 50814 7

Text set in 9/10pt IBM Press Roman, printed by photolithography, and bound in Great Britain at The Pitman Press, Bath

To My Former Students

Acknowledgments

My grateful thanks are due to the Bank of Scotland and the Royal Society of Arts; to Mr. R. A. Kelly, B.A., for so kindly allowing me to quote from his book *English Exercises for Secretaries* (published by Harrap and Co., Ltd.); to the Oxford University Press for permission to quote from the *Authors' and Printers' Dictionary*, by F. Howard Collins; and to Methuen and Co., Ltd., for permission to use an extract from *The Wind in the Willows*, by Kenneth Grahame.

Thanks are due also to the following professional and business friends for their help in reading and criticizing various sections of the manuscript: Mr. J. S. Campbell, Mr. A. J. Ferguson, M.A., B.Ed., Mr. J. Arthur Haugh, Mr. W. McKean, Mr. J. T. Templeton, C.A., Mr. G. M. Wilson, and, in particular, Mr. J. W. Forsyth, F.L.A., F.S.A. (Scot.), for his helpful criticism and advice throughout.

1972 C. E. F.

Contents

Diagrams

1

The Private Secretary—Deportment and Duties

Letter of Application – The Interview – Qualifications – Personal Qualities – Appearance and Manner – Secretarial Duties.

Letter of Application

THE letter of application is usually your *first* introduction to a prospective employer, and you should do your best to ensure that it creates a favourable impression. Your letter should be carefully and neatly written (in ink) in your best handwriting – unless the advertisement calls for a typewritten letter – and should be phrased in good plain English, avoiding all commercialisms. It should be free from spelling and grammatical errors, and should be correctly punctuated and paragraphed.

In planning the letter careful thought should be given to the arrangement of the paragraphs, the following being the usual form:

(1) Reference to source of advertisement and formal application for the post.

(2) Age and education.

(3) Details of secretarial training and examination successes.

(4) Previous employment (if any).

(5) Any other experience or qualifications likely to be useful.

(6) Reference to testimonials enclosed, or names and addresses of referees.

(7) A statement expressing willingness to keep any appointment for an interview.

Be sure to give *all* the information asked for in the advertisement, and state why you are leaving your present firm, if this is the case.

If testimonials are asked for, neatly typed *copies* of the originals should be enclosed. Never part with originals, which may be produced at the interview if necessary. Where personal references are required you should obtain (in advance) your referees' permission to use their names.

Finally, if you are invited to attend for interview, be sure to reply immediately, confirming that you will be able to attend at the time stated.

NOTE. In the early stages of your career the relevant information may be given in the body of the letter, but as you gain experience (and perhaps additional qualifications) it would be advisable to enclose a typewritten statement giving brief details of your qualifications and experience.

The Interview

A little preparation in advance will not only prevent any sense of flurry or anxiety, but will also increase your confidence and help you to feel at your best when you attend for that all-important interview.

The following suggestions will be found helpful:

(1) Try to find out beforehand as much as you can about the post and about the firm itself.

(2) Dress smartly but simply for the interview, and see that your general appearance is neat and business-like.

(3) Be punctual in keeping the appointment. If any doubt exists as to the exact location, check the address (in advance) in a street guide or map.

(4) Be prepared to undergo a test, and take with you a pen or pencils, eraser, and notebook. Also have with you (in a separate envelope) your shorthand, typewriting, and other certificates; the originals of your testimonials; and your personal statement, giving particulars of education and training, details and dates of previous employment, if any.

(5) Enter the interviewer's room quietly but confidently, greet him with a pleasant smile, and wait until you are invited to sit down.

(6) Listen carefully to the questions put to you and answer clearly and fully (not merely "Yes" or "No"). Do not ramble but keep to the point, and answer truthfully and naturally. Look at the interviewer while you are speaking, and don't mumble!

(7) Show an intelligent interest in the work and a desire to accept the post if it is offered. Any doubts can be thought over afterwards and the post courteously refused if it is considered unsuitable.

(8) Remember that it is always better to take a reasonable view of salaries until you have proved your worth.

(9) If you are asked whether there is anything you wish to know about the post, do ask one or two appropriate questions; e.g., "Shall I be working with a number of other girls?" "Are there canteen facilities?" (These questions should be thought out beforehand.)

(10) At the close of the interview thank the interviewer for seeing you.

It is always helpful to prepare, in advance, answers to possible questions that you might be asked; e.g.:

(*a*) What is your present position? And your present salary? (*Or:* What schools did you attend? What were your best subjects?)

(*b*) Why are you leaving your present post?

(*c*) Why did you choose a secretarial career?

(*d*) Where were you trained? What subjects did you study?

(*e*) Why do you want this particular post?

(*f*) If appointed, how soon could you start?

(*g*) What, in your opinion, are the essential qualities of a private secretary?

(*h*) What are your hobbies?

(*i*) What books have you read recently?

(*j*) What is your ambition?

(*k*) What is your father's occupation?

(*l*) Are there any questions you wish to ask?

Qualifications

The basic qualifications of the private secretary may be briefly summarized as follows:

(*a*) *Good General Education.* A good education must necessarily include a sound knowledge of English, which in turn implies a thorough knowledge of English grammar and an extensive vocabulary, as well as the ability to spell and punctuate correctly.

(*b*) *Proficiency in Shorthand and Typewriting.* This implies not only good speeds in shorthand and typewriting but also the ability to transcribe one's shorthand notes with accuracy and intelligence.

(*c*) *Good Practical Grounding in Accounts.* Although it is seldom necessary for the secretary to keep a complete set of books, most secretaries will find that a certain amount of accounts work has to be carried out in the form of a bound ledger or card-index ledger system, bank accounts and reconciliation statements, cash and petty cash books, income and expenditure accounts, etc.

(*d*) *Knowledge of Secretarial Procedure.* This covers a wide field, but may best be described as a knowledge of general office practice and secretarial duties, including the ability to perform daily routine tasks efficiently; e.g., attending to correspondence, arranging appointments, handling telephone calls, etc.

(*e*) *Interest in Current Affairs and a Good Standard of General Knowledge.*

Personal Qualities

The personal qualities essential in a good secretary are as follows:

(*a*) *Discretion and Loyalty.* No matter what type of secretarial post is involved, these two qualities are of paramount importance. The private secretary will frequently, in the course of her duties, acquire a great deal of confidential information, some of which may be of especial interest to outsiders. She must at all times, however, keep a silent tongue, even at the risk of appearing stupid, and *never* discuss her employer or her work.

(*b*) *Tact and Courtesy.* A secretary requires tact in handling an awkward situation or a 'difficult' client. She needs courtesy in her dealings with all callers – both telephone and personal – and with other members of the staff.

(*c*) *Orderliness.* This implies both method and neatness in working – a tidy desk and a tidy mind!

(*d*) *Punctuality.* The importance of punctuality cannot be over-emphasized. The secretary's day is one of a thousand-and-one interruptions, and it is therefore essential for her to start the day in a calm, unflurried state of mind.

(*e*) *Common Sense.* The private secretary needs to exercise common sense in handling the unexpected situation as well as ordinary routine matters. If she is faced with a problem she will try to find the solution. She will be able to work on her own initiative, leaving her employer free to concentrate on more important matters such as management and organization.

(*f*) *A Good Memory.* Although the secretary is not expected to remember every little detail – dates and times of appointments, for example, being recorded in her diary or appointments book – she must, however, cultivate a good memory as this is a valuable asset to the private secretary.

(*g*) *Ability to take Responsibility.* It is probably this quality more than any other that distinguishes the private secretary from the shorthand-typist, who is concerned mainly with the routine work of an office but is not as a rule expected to take responsibility.

(*h*) *Enthusiasm for Work.* The private secretary's job is seldom an easy one, and may involve really hard work and uncertain hours. It is therefore imperative for her to take a keen interest in her work in order to acquire the genuine enthusiasm that is characteristic of the efficient secretary.

(*i*) *A Cheerful and Equable Temper.* The private secretary should not only be hard-working and efficient but must also possess the right temperament for a job that could otherwise prove exacting. To be able to remain calm and cheerful when things fail to run smoothly and to accept blame with a good grace, whether deserved or not, is an invaluable asset.

(*j*) *A High Personal Standard.* The efficient secretary is never guilty of careless, slipshod work, but takes a real pride in everything she does. No matter how busy she may be, she makes a point of checking all letters or documents she has typed before passing them through for signature – knowing that the quality of her work can do much to enhance the reputation of her firm.

Appearance and Manner

A well-groomed appearance plays an important part both in obtaining a secretarial post and in being singled out later for promotion. Common sense should be exercised about what is suitable wear for the office. A good, clear speaking voice is important, as is an easy and graceful deportment.

In general, the manner of the best secretaries may be characterized as pleasant, courteous, and helpful. They have that 'certain charm' which enables them to meet people and put them at their ease, and can display patience and tact when things go wrong in the office or when they are faced with awkward callers.

Secretarial Duties

The duties of a private secretary will, of course, vary with the type of post she holds; but the more important duties, which most secretaries are required to perform, are as follows:

(*a*) To deal with correspondence – either from dictation or by herself.

(*b*) To attend to the daily routine work of the office; e.g., opening and sorting of mail, filing, entering up account books, etc.

(*c*) To keep a diary of her employer's engagements, and to see that he keeps his appointments!

(*d*) To make his travel arrangements, hotel reservations, etc.

(*e*) To receive callers and handle telephone calls, and to shield her employer from unnecessary interruptions.

(*f*) To attend meetings (when necessary) and to carry out the duties relating to meetings; e.g., prepare agenda, take minutes, and write up minutes in Minute Book.

(*g*) To supervise junior secretarial staff.

(*h*) To take a keen interest in her employer's work; to see that he is relieved of minor routine business, so that he can concentrate on more important matters; and, in general, to do everything possible to contribute to his success.

2

English (1)

Spelling – Pronunciation – Punctuation.

THE importance of a sound knowledge of English in secretarial work cannot be too strongly emphasized. The private secretary must be able not only to spell correctly and punctuate intelligently but also to use the right word in the right place. She should never be guilty of grammatical errors, either in speech or in writing, and she must possess a good vocabulary.

Spelling

The following list contains words that are frequently misspelt. If your spelling is weak you should work through the list systematically, taking time and trouble to master all these words, knowing that as a secretary your spelling must be faultless.

abridgement (*or* abridgment)
abscess
absence
accede
accelerate
accessible
accessary (*involving complicity*)
accessory (*something additional*)
accommodate
achieve
acknowledgement (*or* acknowledgment)
acquaintance
acquiesce
acquire
acquitted
address
adherence
adjourn
adjustable
admissible
adolescent
advantageous
advice (*noun*)
advise (*verb*)
advisable
aerial
aeroplane
aforesaid
aggrieved
aghast
agreeable
alignment

allegiance
allotted
all right (*not* alright)
already
amateur
analogous
analogy
analyse
analysis
annihilate

anomalous
anomaly
anonymous
answer
antecedent
anxiety
appalling
apparatus
apparent
appraise

appropriate
apropos
arctic
argument
arrangement
ascend
asphyxiate
assassin
assessable
assessment

atrocious
autumn
auxiliary
awful
bachelor
bankruptcy
bargain
barrenness
battalion
beginning

believe
belligerent
beneficial
beneficiary
benefited
besiege
biased (*or* biassed)
bigoted
boycott
Britain (*country*)

Briton (*person*)
Britannia
Brittany
brochure
buoy
business
calendar
campaign
cancelled
casualty

catalogue
category
ceiling
cellar
cemetery
chancellor
chaos
chaotic
changeable
chargeable

chauffeur
circuit
clientele
coalesce
codicil
coerce
coercion
coincidence
collateral
colleague

colloquial
column
commemorate
commission
committee
comparatively
compatibility
competence
competitor
compulsorily

concede
conceit
concession
concurrence
confidant (*noun*)
confident (*adj.*)
connoisseur
conscientious
conscious
consensus

consistency
consistent
constituency
convalescence
convertible
corollary
correspondence
correspondent
corroborate
corruptible

council (*noun*)
counsel (*noun* and *verb*)
counterfeit
courteous
credentials
criticism
criticize
cuisine
debtor
decease

deceive
decision
defensive
deferred
deficiency
deficit
definite
dense
dependant (*noun*)
dependent (*adj.*)

descendant
deteriorate
develop
development
dilapidated
diphthong
disappear
disastrous
disappoint
discernible

discipline
discrepancy
discretion
disease
discreet (prudent, circumspect)
dispense
dispossess
dissatisfied
dissimilar
distinctive

eccentric
ecstasy
effervescent
efficacious
efficient
eighth
eligible
eligibility

embarrassment
emigrant

emphasize
endorsement
enrolment
enthusiasm
enumerate
epitaph
epithet
epitome
equanimity
equipped

equivalent
especially
essential
esteem
exaggerate
excellent
exemplary
exercise
exhaust
exhilarate

exigency
existence
exorbitant
expense
experience
explicit
extraordinary
extravagance
facsimile
familiar

fascinate
fatiguing
favourite
feasible
February
feign

fictitious
financial
fiscal
flexible

foreclose
foreign
forestall
forfeit
formally
formerly
forty
friend
fulfil
fulfilled

fulfilment
gauge
gauging
gazetteer
government
grammar
gramophone
grievance
guarantee
guarantor

handkerchief
harassed
height
heinous
hideous
honorarium
honorary
humorous (*but* humour)
hygienic
hypocrisy

hypothesis
identical
illegible
illiterate

immediately
immigrant
imminent
immovable
impassable
impervious

implicit
inaccessible
inaugurate
incidence
incidental
incipient
incite (*verb*)
incoherent
incomparable
incorrigible

incurred
indefensible
indemnify
independent
indictment
indispensable
ineligible
inexhaustible
infallible
inference

inflammable
influential
innocuous
insatiable
insistence
insistent
install (*or* instal)
installation
instalment
intelligent

intense
intercede
interim
intrinsic

inveigle
inventory
invigilate
irreducible
irrelevant
irreparable

irresistible
itinerary
jeopardy
judgement (*or* judgment)
keenness
knowledge
leisure
liaison
libellous
licentiate

lien
lieutenant
lightning
lik(e)able
livelihood
loose
lose
magnanimous
maintenance
manoeuvre

manageable
marriage
meant
medicine
Mediterranean
meteorological
miniature
minutes
minutiae
miscellaneous

mischievous
misdemeanour
misshapen
misspell
monotonous
mortgage
mortgagee
mortgagor
movable
murmuring

naphtha
nauseous
necessarily
negligible
neighbouring
niece
noticeable
nuisance
occasionally
occur

occurred
occurrence
omitted
onerous
opportunity
originally
oscillate
ostensible
ostracize
palate

palette
pamphlet
paraffin
parallel
paralysis
paraphernalia
parliamentary
paroxysm
pavilion
peaceable

perforate
perjury
permanent
permeate
permissible
persevere
personnel
phase
phenomenon
phenomena

physical
piece
plausible
pleasant
plebeian
pneumatic
poignant
possession
practice (*noun*)
practise (*verb*)

precedence
precedent
precede
preceding
precincts
precocious
predecessors
preferred
prejudice
preliminary

prevalence
primitive
principal (*adj.* and *noun*)
principle (*noun*)
privilege
procedure
proceed
proceeding
profession
proffered

proficient
promissory
pronunciation
prophecy (*noun*)
prophesy (*verb*)
proprietary
psychological
pursue
pursuit
quandary

quarrelled
queue
quiet
quorum
recede
receipt
receive
receptacle
recipient
reciprocal

reciprocity
recommend
recompense
reconnoitre
reference
referred
regrettable
reimburse
relevant
relieve

reminiscence
remodelled
repertoire
repetition
reprieve
rescind
reservoir
resistance
resources
resuscitate

reticence
retrieve
reversible
rhyme
rhythm
sagacious
scarcely
scene
schedule
scheme

sciatica
scrutinize
secede
secretarial
sedentary
seize
seizure
sense
sentence
separate

sergeant
serviceable
shield
siege
simultaneous
sincerely
skilful
singeing
solicitor
soliloquy

souvenir
sovereign
species
specious
speech
spontaneous
stationary (*adj.*)
stationery (*noun*)
statistical
statutory

stereotype
stupefy
subpoena
subterranean
succeed
successful
superfluous
superintendent
supersede
superstitious
suppress
survivor
susceptible
symmetry
symptom
syndicate
synonymous
synopsis
tacit
tangible
tariff
technical
temporarily
tenacious
tendency
traceable
transferable
transferred
twelfth
tyranny
tyrannical
ultimatum
undoubtedly
unique
unnecessary
unparalleled
until
utilitarian
vaccinate
vacillate
variegated
veracity
verbatim
vertical
veterinary
vice versa
vicissitudes
view
villain
vitiate
volatile
Wednesday
weird
wield
woollen
worshipped
yield
zealous

Pronunciation

A secretary must be able to speak well. Her pronunciation should therefore conform to what could be described as 'standard' pronunciation – that form of speech which is common to most educated people, whether they come from London, Edinburgh, Belfast, or Cape Town.

In the following list of words the accent is on the *first* syllable:

admirable
calumny
capitalist
comment (both *noun* and *verb*[1])
comparable
conjugal
conjure (kunʹjer) *But:* when this word means 'to beseech,' 'to implore earnestly', it is pronounced: konjoorʹ.
contrary
decade (dĕcʹade)
decadence (dĕcʹadence)

[1] *Chambers's Dictionary* gives as the alternative form of the *verb*: kom-entʹ.

decadent (dĕcˈadent)
deficit (dĕfˈicit)
desultory (dĕsˈultory)
elixir (ĕlixˈer)
equitable (ĕqˈuitable)
exigent (ĕxˈigent)
exquisite
flagrant (flāˈgrant)
forehead (fŏrˈĕd)
formidable
harassed (hărˈăssed)
inventory
lamentable
lethargy
mischievous
posthumous (pŏstˈūmous)
replica (rĕpˈlica)
reputable (rĕpˈutable)
respite (rĕsˈpit)
salutary (salˈūtary)
syncope (sĭnˈcopē)

The following words are pronounced with the accent on the *last* syllable:

artisan
artiste (artēstˈ)
assignee (assĭnēˈ)
chagrin (shăgrēnˈ) The B.B.C., however adopts shăˈgrin for the *noun* and shăgrēnˈ for the *verb*.
consols (abbreviation of 'consolidated annuities')

Each of these words admits of *alternative* pronunciation or accent:

accessory (accent on either first or second syllable)
acoustic (acowsˈtic *or* acoosˈtic)
adult (accent on either first or second syllable)
amateur (amˈater *or* amˈatūr)
amenity (amēnity *or* amĕnity)
applicable (accent on either first or second syllable)
aspirant (asˈpĭrant *or* aspīrˈant)
cognizant (kogˈnizant *or* konˈizant)
communal (accent on either first or second syllable)
contemplative (accent on either first or second syllable)

controversy (accent on either first or second syllable)
conversant (accent on either first or second syllable)
decorous (dĕcˈorous *or* de-cōrˈous)
despicable (accent on either first or second syllable)
environs (envīˈrons *or* enˈvĭrons)
evolution (ēvolution *or* ĕˈvolution)
exigency (ĕxˈigency *or* ĕxigˈency)
fascism (făˈshizm *or* făˈsizm)
fascist (făˈshist *or* făˈsist)
fetish (fĕtˈish *or* fētˈish)
gala (gāˈla *or* gahˈla)
garage (garˈahzh *or* garˈij)
gibberish (pronounced with either hard or soft *g*)
hospitable (accent on either first or second syllable)
inveigle (invēˈgle *or* invāˈgle)
laboratory (accent on either first or second syllable)
legislative (lĕgˈisla-tive *or* lĕgˈislā-tive)
legislature (legˈisla-tūre *or* legˈislā-tūre)
migratory (mīˈgratory *or* mīgrāˈtory)
patriot (pāˈtriot *or* păˈtriot)
peremptory (perˈemptory *or* perempˈtory)
pharmaceutical (pharmasūˈtical *or* pharmakūˈtical)
pianoforte (pronounced with or without the final ē)
precedence, precedent (the usual pronunciation of these words is: prĕssˈidence, prĕssˈident) The B.B.C., however, adopts for the former: prē-sēˈdence.
privacy (prīvacy *or* prĭvˈacy)
profile (prōˈfīl, prōˈfēl, prōˈfĭl – the *second* being probably the most common to-day)
quandary (kwŏndārˈy *or* kwŏnˈdăry)
recondite (rĕcˈondīte *or* rĕconˈdīte)
suave (swāv *or* swahv)
subsidence (subsīˈdence *or* subˈsĭdence)
surveillance (survālˈance *or* survālˈyance
tryst (trīst *or* trĭst)
valet (vălˈet *or* vălˈā)
vitamin (vītˈamin *or* vĭtˈamin)

Miscellaneous Words

acumen (acūˈmen)
administrative (adminˈistrative)
administrator (adminˈistrātor)
administratrix (adminˈistrātrix)

aerated (this word has *four* syllables: āˈer-ātˈ-ed)
alias (āˈlias)
alibi (ăˈlibī)
ally, allies (ăˈli, ăˈliz)
amenable (amēˈnable)
anaesthetist (anēsˈthetist)
apparatus (ăppărāˈtus)
archives (arˈkīves)
attorney (atterˈney)
centenary (sentēˈnary)
centrifugal (accent on the *second* syllable)
chicanery (shicāˈnery)
chimera, chimerical (kĭmērˈa, kĭmĕrˈikal)
chiropodist (kīrŏpˈodist *or* kĭrŏpˈodist)
clandestine (clandesˈtĭn)
clientele (klīentēlˈ)
condolence (accent on *second* syllable)
coup (koo)
courtesy (kerˈtesy)
culinary (kūˈlinary)
cynosure (sĭnˈō-shoor *or* sīnˈō-shoor[1])
decorum (accent on *second* syllable)
demoniacal (dēmonīˈacal)
deteriorate (pronounced with *five* syllables)
dishabille (disˈabēl *or* disabēlˈ)
dishevelled (dish-ĕvˈelled)
doctrinal (doctrīˈnal)
economic, economics (first syllable is pronounced: ē)
ennui (onˈwē)
envelope (ĕnˈvelōp)
ephemeral (ephĕmˈeral)
extempore (this word has *four* syllables: ex-tempˈor-ē)
facade (fa-sahdˈ)
fête (fāt *or* fĕt[1])
flaccid (flakˈsid)
forte (fort)
fracas (frăˈcah)
gesticulate (jĕstĭcˈulate)
gesture (jĕstˈure)
gibbet (jibbˈet)
heinous (hāˈnous)

[1] Adopted by *Chambers's Dictionary* as the alternative pronunciation.

illustrative (accent on the *second* syllable)
impious (im'pĭous)
inchoate (in'ko-āte)
indict, indictment (indīt', indīt'ment)
inexorable (accent on *second* syllable)
irrefutable (accent on *second* syllable)
irreparable (accent on *second* syllable)
irrevocable (accent on *second* syllable)
lichen (pronounced: līk'en)
longevity (lŏnjĕv'ity)
longitude (lŏn'jitūde)
machination (măkinā'tion)
medicine (mĕd'sin)
medieval (also spelt *mediaeval*) (pronounced: mĕdiē'val)
mediocre (mē'diōker)
memoirs (mem'wars)
mortgage (the *t* is silent)
naïve (nah-ēv')
naïvete (nah-ēv'tā)
naphtha (naftha)
nonchalant (non'shalant)
obligatory (oblĭg'ătory)
orgy (or'jĭ)
patent (pā'tent)
patron (pā'tron)
patronage (pă'tronage)
plebiscite (plĕb'ĭssĭt)
preface (prĕf'is)
psychiatrist (sīkī'atrĭst)
remonstrate (rĕmŏn'strate—accent on *second* syllable)
reredos (rēr'dŏs—pronounced with *two* syllables)
residuary (rezĭd'uary)
retail (*verb* —accent on *second* syllable) *But:* 'a retail dealer' has accent on *first* syllable
retailer (accent on *second* syllable)
sinecure (sī'necūre *or* sĭ'necūre[1])
skein (skān)
species (spē'shēz)
status (stā'tus)
sycophant (sĭck'ophant)
tortoise (tor'tus)
trait (trā)

[1] Adopted by *Chambers's Dictionary* as the alternative pronunciation.

treatise (trēˈtĭz)
untoward (untōˈerd)
vagary (văgārˈy)
vagrant (vāˈgrant)
vice versa (vīˈsė versa)
visa (vēˈza)
wrath (wrawth *or* wrahth[1])

Punctuation

The object of punctuation is to clarify the meaning of written language. Hard-and-fast rules cannot be laid down, as a writer will punctuate his work in the manner that he considers will convey the desired impression. In general, however, it is better to under-punctuate than to over-punctuate.

The following are the chief stops or marks of punctuation:

1. *Full Stop or Period* (.). It is used:

(*a*) At the end of every complete sentence (unless a question or an exclamation).

Thank you for your letter of the 7th May.

(*b*) After initials and abbreviations.

J. C. Jones, Esq., M.A., LL.B.
Co. Messrs. Mr. Ltd.[2]
9.30 a.m. MSS. e.g. i.e.

NOTE. When the abbreviation ends with the last two letters of the word abbreviated it is customary to omit the full stop; e.g.:

1st, 2nd, 4to (quarto), 8vo (octavo)

2. *Comma* (,). The comma denotes the shortest pause in punctuation. It is used:

(*a*) To separate words or phrases forming a series.

She is an efficient, hard-working, dependable person.

The box contained a large sum of money, a few pieces of jewellery, and a number of old deeds.

[1] Adopted by *Chambers's Dictionary* as the alternative pronunciation.

[2] Many people omit the point when the last letter of the word is included in the abbreviation; but it should be noted that it is still standard typewriting practice to insert the full stop after most abbreviations.

NOTE. A comma is inserted before *and* when the words or phrases are separate in meaning from each other. *But:* I ordered tea, toast, egg and bacon.

(*b*) To separate introductory words or phrases from the rest of the sentence.

In conclusion, may I remind you that . . .
Unfortunately, we cannot accept your offer.

(*c*) To mark off 'thrown-in' words or phrases that do not affect the meaning of the sentence.

I shall not, however, be present.
There is, I am convinced, some perfectly good explanation for his behaviour.

(*d*) To mark off the nominative of address.

We appeal to you, sir, to help us.
Mr. Smith, will you sign this letter, please?

(*e*) To introduce speech.

He said, "Please take a letter, Miss Jones."
She asked, "Will that be all?"

(*f*) To separate words or phrases in apposition.

Sir John West, the Chairman of the company, presided.
Robert Burns, Scotland's greatest poet, was born in 1759.

(*g*) To separate an absolute phrase from the rest of the sentence.

The lecturer having arrived, the chairman opened the meeting.
This being your decision, there is nothing more I can say.

(*h*) In complex sentences, to separate subordinate clauses from the main clause; but if the subordinate clause is short the comma may be omitted.

The prices quoted, as we have already explained, are for prompt cash.
When their officer entered the room the soldiers stood smartly to attention.

(*i*) In compound sentences, to separate the co-ordinate clauses from each other.

The comma is frequently over-used, and sometimes it is misused.
He hurried to the station, but the train had already left.

(*j*) When, in order to avoid repetition, a verb is omitted, its place is taken by a comma.

> Reading maketh a full man; conference, a ready man; and writing, an exact man. (Bacon.)
> To err is human; to forgive, divine.

(*k*) Words or clauses denoting contrast, or an opposite meaning, may be separated by commas.

> Will you deliver the goods today, or tomorrow?
> Do you consider his work satisfactory, or unsatisfactory?

(*l*) In writing or typing the date a comma is usually inserted between the month and the year.

> 8th April, 19–

(*m*) A comma is required between a name and any title, honours, or degrees that may follow it.

> J. B. Brown, Esq., M.B.E., M.A.

(*n*) To separate figures, where large, into groups of three counting from the right.

> 19,321 500,000 8,000,000

3. *Semicolon* (;). The semicolon marks a longer pause than that indicated by a comma. It is used:

(*a*) To separate the two parts of a compound sentence when the conjunction is omitted.

> The comma is frequently over-used; sometimes, indeed, it is misused. (Cf. *Comma*: 2(*i*).)
> The comparative degree is used when we compare two objects; the superlative, when more than two objects are compared.

(*b*) To separate the two parts of a compound sentence, even when the conjunction is inserted, if a longer pause is required than would be indicated by a comma.

> The secretary must be able to relieve her employer of routine tasks such as the answering of correspondence and the arranging of engagements; and, in addition, she must be capable of taking his place, if required to do so at any time, with efficiency and tact.

(*c*) To separate statements which, though independent grammatically, are closely connected in thought.

> The secretary must know how to meet people and put them at their ease; she should have a good memory, and be able to plan for the job ahead; she must be able to take responsibility; and, above all, she must possess a genuine enthusiasm for work.

(*d*) To show antithesis or contrast.

> I do not want to possess a faith; I want a faith which possesses me.

NOTE. In strong antithesis the semicolon is sometimes replaced by a colon.

(*e*) To separate a number of items or phrases, to which it is desired to give emphasis.

> The case, when opened, was found to contain a quantity of jewellery, some of it extremely valuable; a few furs; half a dozen exquisite ornaments; and a bundle of old letters, now quite faded.

4. *Colon* (:). The colon marks a slightly longer pause than the semicolon. It is used:

(*a*) To separate the two parts of a compound sentence when the second part explains or amplifies the first.

> My labour is not yet at an end: man's labour never ceases.
>
> Go to bed early tonight: you have a busy day ahead of you.

(*b*) To introduce a quotation or a speech.

> Shakespeare said: "There is nothing either good or bad, but thinking makes it so."
>
> The Chairman, who presided, said: "Ladies and Gentlemen, . . ."

(*c*) To introduce a list of items (usually after such expressions as 'as follows,' 'the following,' 'thus,' etc., or when 'namely' or 'viz.' is understood).

> Some of the qualities essential in a good secretary are: discretion, loyalty, tact, common sense, orderliness, and punctuality.
>
> Kindly supply the following order:
>
> 2 reams of Y.D. Bank Paper (A4);
> 3 reams of Y.D. Bank Paper (A5).

NOTE: In typewriting practice the colon is usually followed by a dash when introducing a list that begins on a new line.

5. *Interrogation or Question Mark* (?). The interrogation or question mark is used instead of the period at the end of every sentence that contains a *direct* question.

What shall we do now?

Should we hand the cheque to your representative, or would you prefer us to post it to you direct?

NOTE. The question mark is *not* used after an indirect question.

He asked whether she would accept the post.

6. *Exclamation Mark* (!). The exclamation mark is used instead of the period after words, phrases, and sentences that are exclamatory in tone.

Hello! Good gracious! How could you be so stupid!

7. *Dash* (–). The dash is used as follows:

(*a*) The double dash has exactly the same effect as the parenthesis.

The result of the election – so I am given to understand – will be announced tomorrow.

(*b*) A single dash is used to indicate a sudden change of thought.

I am certain it was he – who else could it have been?

(*c*) In dialogue, to show hesitancy of speech.

I–er–would rather–not say.

NOTE. In typewriting the dash is represented by a hyphen sign, preceded and followed by a space. When the sign is used as a hyphen, no space is required either before or after it.

8. *Hyphen* (-). The hyphen is used:

(*a*) Between two or more words to show that they form a compound word.

book-keeping mother-in-law
night-watchman subject-heading

(In permanent compounds, however, the hyphen is omitted; e.g., notebook, bookcase, housekeeping, homesickness, etc.)

(*b*) To indicate that two vowels are to be pronounced separately.

co-operate re-enter pre-eminent

(*c*) Between the tens and units in numbers written in word-form.

twenty-five ninety-three sixty-two

(*d*) To divide words at the end of a line, the part cut off being carried to the following line.

con-duct atten-tion writ-ing

(See *Line-end Division of Words*, pp. 71–73.)

9. *Parentheses* (). Parentheses are used to separate explanatory or supplementary words or phrases from the rest of the sentence more effectively than would be the case with commas.

> I enclose my cheque for ten pounds fifty pence (£10·50) in payment of your account.

10. *Quotation Marks* or *Inverted Commas* (" ").

(*a*) Quotation marks are used to indicate quotations or *direct* speech – i.e., the exact words of the speaker.

> As she was about to leave, Mr. Brown hurried in and said, "Please take a letter, Miss Smith."
>
> "Certainly, Mr. Brown," she replied.

(*b*) Quotation marks are also used to indicate *thoughts*.

> As she removed her coat, she thought, "Oh, dear, late again tonight!"

NOTE. Indirect or reported speech does not require inverted commas.

> When she had finished the letter she told him that it was ready for signature.

(*c*) In the case of lengthy quotations extending over several paragraphs (e.g., a company report) the quotation marks are placed at the beginning and end of the quotation and also at the beginning of *each new paragraph*.

(*d*) A quotation within a quotation is indicated by single quotation marks (‘ ’).

> She told the policeman: “I heard him speak to the old man. He said, ‘May I carry your bag?’ ”

(*e*) Inverted commas are also used to indicate names of books, plays, ships, newspapers, trade names, etc.

> The article appeared in yesterday’s “Daily Mail.”
> Goldsmith wrote “She Stoops to Conquer.”

NOTE. In printed matter italics usually take the place of inverted commas, except in the case of trade names. (Italics can be indicated in a typescript by underscoring.)

(*f*) Colloquialisms, slang, and dubious expressions are usually placed within inverted commas.

> He was in “a bit of a jam,” he explained.
> The boy was told to “beat it.”

NOTE. In typewritten matter the period and the comma (both tiny signs) are usually placed *inside* the closing inverted commas – for appearance’ sake. Other punctuation marks, used in conjunction with inverted commas, are placed according to their correct grammatical position. (In printed matter the period and the comma also are usually placed in their correct grammatical position.)

> She replied, “Yes, you may go.”
> May I have a copy of Pitman’s “Business Typewriting”?

11. *The Apostrophe* (’). (1) The apostrophe is used to indicate the genitive (possessive) case.

(*a*) The possessive singular is formed by adding ’*s* to the nominative, as:

the child’s toys
the boy’s book
a week’s wages

(*b*) The possessive plural is formed by adding an apostrophe *only* to the nominative plural when it ends in -*s*, as:

the boys’ books
two weeks’ holiday

(*c*) If the nominative plural does *not* end in *-s* the possessive is formed by adding *'s*, as:

children's toys
men's work

NOTE. (i) For the sake of euphony, the *'s* in the possessive singular is omitted in phrases like the following, the apostrophe only being retained:

for conscience' sake
for appearance' sake
for goodness' sake

But: St. James's Square
H. G. Wells's novels
Jones's house (possessive singuiar)
the Joneses' house (possessive plural)

(ii) The possessive form of a firm-name is indicated as follows:

Marks & Spencer's branches
Lawrie & Smith's sale

(2) The apostrophe is also used:

(*a*) To indicate the omission of a letter in a word.

It's (it is) a lovely day.
Don't (do not) do that!

(*b*) To indicatc the plural of figures and single letters.

Your 5's and 3's are not clearly formed.
Mind your p's and q's.

But: M.P.s, M.A.s, N.C.O.s, etc.

(*c*) To indicate a quotation within a quotation.

She said, "Thank you for lending me your copy of 'Modern English Usage.' "

(*d*) In such names as: *O'Connor*, *M'Gregor*, etc.

12. *Capital Letters.* Capital letters should be used:

(*a*) At the beginning of a sentence.

Thank you for your letter.

(*b*) At the beginning of direct speech.

The butler announced, "Dinner is served."

But: "Don't be alarmed," he said, "if I am a little late."

(The words "he said" interrupt the quotation in the middle of a sentence, and "if" does not therefore require a capital letter.)

(*c*) For all proper nouns and adjectives derived therefrom.

Great Britain	Lord John Hooper
The Spanish Armada	Good Friday

(*d*) At the beginning of every line of classical poetry (though not always in modern verse).

The quality of mercy is not strained,
It droppeth as the gentle rain from heaven
Upon the place beneath: it is twice blest;
It blesseth him that gives and him that takes:

(*e*) For titles of books, plays, newspapers, etc.

"Pride and Prejudice"
"The School for Scandal"
"The Guardian"

(*f*) In business correspondence, for subject-headings, trade names and brands, etc.

Freehold Property: 1 West Street, Leeds

"Bear" Brand "Quink" Ink

(*g*) For the *first* word of the complimentary close of a letter.

Yours faithfully,
Yours sincerely,
Very truly yours,

(*h*) For abbreviations indicating civil, academical, and professional qualifications, and all titles.

Sir James McNab, K.B.E., D.S.O., J.P.
John Hutton, Esq., M.A., F.C.I.S.

(*i*) For the personal pronoun "I" and all interjections.

(*j*) In personification.

> O Death, where is thy sting? O Grave, where is thy victory?

The Paragraph

(*a*) A new paragraph indicates a change of subject-matter.

(*b*) In dialogue a new paragraph indicates a change of speaker.

3

English (2)

Vocabulary – Correct Use of Words – Errors of Style – Common Grammatical Errors.

Vocabulary

IN secretarial work a good active vocabulary is as important as a sound knowledge of grammar or correct spelling and punctuation. By 'active' vocabulary is meant the words that you can use correctly both in speech and in writing.

The most effective way to increase your active vocabulary is to read as widely as possible, and always to keep a notebook handy in which to jot down new words and their meanings. This necessitates your being strict with yourself and allowing no word that is new to you to pass before you have thoroughly understood its meaning. Jot it down at once, and look up its meaning in a dictionary as soon as an opportunity presents itself.

It goes without saying that your notebook should be studied regularly and the new words introduced into your writing or conversation sufficiently often to permit them to become part of your active vocabulary.

If the shorthand outline of the word is written down at the same time, you will be taking effective steps to improve your shorthand vocabulary also.

Correct Use of Words

The following list contains pairs of words that are often confused. Make sure that you thoroughly understand the difference between the words in each pair by referring to a good dictionary and noting the exact meanings given.

accede	exceed	erratic	erroneous
adverse	averse	fictitious	spurious
affect	effect	forceful	forcible
alternate	alternative	historic	historical
appreciable	appreciative	illegible	ineligible
artificial	artistic	imaginary	imaginative
authentic	genuine	imply	infer
beneficent	beneficial	impracticable	unpractical
canvas	canvass	impressionable	impressive
carat	caret	incredible	incredulous
complexity	complicity	ingenious	ingenuous
compliment	complement	incite	instigate
compose	comprise	insuperable	invincible
comprehensive	comprehensible	intense	intensive
concise	precise	lay	lie
contemptible	contemptuous	licence	license
continual	continuous	lightening	lightning
continuance	continuation	literate	literal
contrast	compare	luxuriant	luxurious
council	counsel	mendacity	mendicity
cynic	sceptic	mystic	mysterious
deceased	diseased	nationalism	nationalization
defective	deficient	notable	notorious
defer	differ	obsolescent	obsolete
delusion	illusion	palate	palette
dependant	dependent	partake	participate
deprecate	depreciate	possible	probable
discover	invent	practice	practise
dissatisfied	unsatisfied	precedence	precedent
divert	diverge	presumptive	presumptuous
economic	economical	principal	principle
efficient	efficacious	prophecy	prophesy
elicit	illicit	raise	rise
emigrate	immigrate	respectfully	respectively
eminent	imminent	salubrious	salutary

sentiment	sentimentality	temporal	temporary
specie	species	tolerable	tolerant
stationary	stationery	uninterested	disinterested
stimulant	stimulus	veracious	voracious
straight	strait	virtual	virtuous

Errors of Style

Some of the more common errors of style are: long and involved sentences, misplaced words or phrases, careless use of pronouns, incorrect punctuation, etc. These faults frequently give rise to *ambiguity*, which must be avoided at all costs. It should be remembered that the first essential in any piece of writing is that it shall be *clear*.

Other equally common errors are as follows:

Colloquialisms. Words or phrases used in ordinary conversation, but not in formal speech or writing; e.g.:

don't, I'll, I'd, etc.   quite all right
'aggravate' in the sense 'annoy' or 'exasperate'
get even   couldn't care less

Avoid also the colloquial misuse of 'nice,' 'awful,' 'frightful,' 'ghastly,' etc., as in:

a nice girl   simply awful weather
a frightful hat   a ghastly mistake

Clichés (sometimes called 'stereotypes'). Expressions which, by reason of constant use, have become hackneyed or stale; e.g.:

conspicuous by its absence; at the parting of the ways; last but not least; it stands to reason; between you and me; be that as it may.

Tautology (from the Greek *tauto*, the same, and *logia*, speech). The repetition of the same thing in different words; e.g.:

The inevitable crash is bound to come.
They arrived one after the other in succession.
need not necessarily; final conclusion, etc.

Verbosity – or the use of more words than are necessary.

Journalese. Chambers's Dictionary defines journalese as

"the jargon of bad journalism." In journalese, a building would be called an *edifice*, and the edifice might be destroyed, not by a fire, but by a *conflagration*. The competitor in a race who tried hard to win would be described as having made *strenuous* (or *herculean*) *efforts to achieve victory*. At a presentation, Mr. Smith would be made *the recipient of* a gold watch, whereupon he would *reply in suitable terms.* A report on the proceedings of a meeting might state: "*At this juncture* the motion was put to the meeting," instead of the simpler and preferable form, "The motion was then put to the meeting."

Commercial Jargon (*'Commercialese'*). Examples of *commercialese* are: *inst.* (the present month); *ult.* (last month); *prox.* (next month). Other examples are:

We are in receipt of your favour of the 10th inst.
("We have received your letter of the 10th April.")

Enclosed please find . . . ("We have enclosed . . .")

Yours of the 10th inst. to hand. ("Your letter of the 10th April has been received" *or* "Thank you for your letter of the 10th April.")

At your earliest convenience ("as soon as possible")

We shall use every endeavour ("We shall try")

We beg to remain, etc. ("We are," etc.)

Writers of business letters in the past were guilty of this kind of jargon, but such expressions are today regarded as being in the worst possible taste and should be avoided at all costs. Let your aim be always to express yourself clearly and concisely in good plain English.

Common Grammatical Errors

Incorrect Sequence of Tenses

When the main verb of a sentence is in the *past* tense the subordinate verb(s) must also be in the *past* tense.

He *said* that he *would* (not 'will') come.

NOTE. A main verb in the present tense may be followed by any tense.

Shall and Will

(1) The simple future tense is expressed as follows:

First person: I (we) *shall.*
Second and third persons: You *will*; he (they) *will.*

I *shall* be glad if you *will* call soon.

(2) Determination, promise, or intention is expressed as follows:

First person: I (we) *will.*
Second and third persons: You *shall*; he (they) *shall.*

I *will* not do such a thing.
You *shall* do as I say.

Should and Would

The same rules apply to these words as to *shall* and *will.*

NOTE. *Shall* and *will*, *should* and *would*, must not be mixed in the same sentence.

I *shall* be glad if you *will* (not 'would') advise me.
I *should* be glad if you *would* (not 'will') advise me.

Between and Among

Between is used when only *two* persons or things are involved.

Divide the money *between* John and David.

Among must be used when there are more than two persons or things.

Divide the money *among* John, David, and Michael.

NOTE. (1) *Between* must be followed by *and* (not 'or').

She was compelled to choose *between* the post she had been offered *and* the prospect of a holiday abroad.

(2) We say "*between* you and *me*" (not "*between* you and *I*"), because *between* is a preposition and must be followed by the objective case.

That and Which

The relative pronoun *that* defines or restricts the meaning of its antecedent.

> The typewriters *that* have attractive colours sell rapidly.

The meaning brought out here is that only *some* of the typewriters have attractive colours – the ones that sell rapidly.

> The typewriters, *which* have attractive colours, sell rapidly.

Here the use of *which* (with the insertion of commas) entirely changes the meaning of this sentence, the implication now being that *all* the typewriters have attractive colours.

Who and Whom

Who is used when it is the subject of a sentence or clause; *whom* is used when it is the object, or when governed by a preposition.

> He spoke to the man, *who* had just alighted from the train.
> The man *whom* I interviewed is the new salesman.
> The man to *whom* I spoke yesterday will be calling tomorrow.

Similar to and Different from

The correct preposition to use after *similar* is *to.*

> She wore a coat *similar to* mine.

It is now the accepted practice to use *from* after *different*, although the use of 'different *to*' is defended by H. W. Fowler in his *Dictionary of Modern English Usage.*

NOTE. *Different than* is also better avoided; e.g., This report was intended for a *different* purpose *than* that stated. (Say, instead, ". . . a *different* purpose *from* that stated"; or ". . . for another purpose than that of . . .")

Due to and Owing to

It is a common error to use *due to* instead of *owing to*, as:

> The match was cancelled *due to* the bad weather.

(Substitute for *due* the compound preposition *owing to* to govern *weather.*)

Due is an adjective and should therefore qualify a noun, as:

> The rent is now *due.*
> The *due* date.
> The accident was *due* to carelessness.
> The cancellation was *due* to bad weather.

Kind and Sort

Errors like the following should be avoided:

> These *kind* of things . . .

(Say, instead, "This kind of thing . . ." *or* "Things of this kind . . .")

> Those *sort* of people . . .

(Say, instead, "That sort of person . . ." *or* "People of that sort . . .")

It should be remembered that *kind* and *sort*, being singular, require the adjective to be singular – i.e., *this* and *that.*

Above

Above may be used as an adverb or preposition, but preferably *not* as an adjective.

> The *above* information is misleading.

(For *above* substitute *foregoing* or *above-mentioned.*)

After

After may be used as a preposition or conjunction, but *not* as an adverb.

> I have an appointment now, but will see you *after.*

(For *after* substitute *afterwards.*)

Either

Either is used to denote one of two alternatives, as: I do not care for *either* of the books. (There are only two books.)

But: I do not care for *any* of the books (if there are more than two).

NOTE. *Either* is singular and must always be followed by a singular verb.

Either Tom or Harry *is* likely to be chosen.

Neither

The word *neither* is singular and must always be followed by a singular verb.

Neither of the books *is* for sale.

NOTE. *Neither*, like *either*, is used only when referring to one of two persons or things.

Either . . . or – Neither . . . nor

Two singular subjects connected by *either . . . or*, *neither . . nor*, require a singular verb.

Neither Mr. Jones *nor* Mr. Brown *was* (not 'were') available.

NOTE. When two subjects of different person are connected by *either . . . or*, *neither . . . nor*, the verb must agree with the *nearer.*

I do not consider that either you or he *is* a suitable candidate.
I do not consider that either he or you *are* a suitable candidate.
Neither you nor I *am* able to go.

Each, Every, Everybody, Everyone

These words also require a singular verb.

Each of the girls *was* awarded a prize.
Every student *has* agreed to attend the lecture.
Everyone (*everybody*) *is* required to do his (*not* 'their') share.

None

None may be singular or plural, according to the sense. When it means *not a single one* it must be followed by a singular verb.

None of the girls *has* completed her work.

But when it means *not any* it may be followed by a *plural* verb.

None of those present *seem* to be in favour of the proposal.

Ours, Yours, Its, Theirs

These possessives are used without an apostrophe.

This is one of *ours.*
Is this *yours*?
No, it is *theirs.*
The train arrived at *its* destination.

NOTE. When *its* means *it is*, the apostrophe must be used, as: *It's* a long story.

Like

A common error is to use *like* as a conjunction, as: Nothing succeeds *like* success does. This should be: "*as* success does" or "*like* success."

Same

It is utterly incorrect to use *same* as a noun; e.g.:

> We have received your order for six typewriters, and shall be dispatching *same* by rail tomorrow.

(Instead of *same*, use *them* or some other suitable construction.)

Unique

A thing is unique when it is *the only one of its kind.* It is therefore incorrect to speak of something as being 'quite' unique, 'rather' unique, or 'very' unique.

(Other absolute terms, which do not admit of degrees of comparison, are: *universal*, *essential*, and *perfect*.)

Reason why . . . Because

The following sentence contains a very common error due to redundancy of expression:

> *The reason why* he left was *because* he found the work uncongenial.

Because merely repeats the idea already expressed in *the reason why.*

The sentence may be corrected by substituting *that* for *because*, or by altering it to read as follows:

> He left *because* he found the work uncongenial.

Providing that

Providing that is often incorrectly used for *provided that*; e.g., *Providing that* you can assure us of early delivery, we shall be pleased to place an order with you. (For *providing*, substitute *provided.*)

The Split Infinitive

The use of the split infinitive (i.e., inserting another word or words between *to* and the verb) sometimes results in clumsy constructions and should then be avoided; e.g.:

> *To* absolutely and entirely *abstain.*

Pairs of Conjunctions

Pairs of conjunctions, such as *both—and*; *not only—but also*; *either—or*, etc., are often misplaced in a sentence. It should be remembered that the second conjunction must be followed by the *same* part of speech as the first.

Both—and:

> Let this *both* be a lesson *and* a warning. (*Both* should follow *be.*)

Not only—but also:

> She has *not only* proved herself to be hard-working *but also* efficient. (*Not only* should follow *be.*)

Either—or:

> The news may *either* come today *or* tomorrow. (*Either* should follow *come.*)

Collective Nouns

A collective noun is the name of a group of persons or

things – e.g., *committee*, *staff*, *crew*, etc. Compare the following two sentences:

> The committee *is* to meet tomorrow.
> The committee *were* unanimous in *their* decision.

In the first sentence the committee is regarded as a single body, taking a singular verb. In the second, the individual members of the committee are regarded separately.

NOTE. It is incorrect to mix these two ideas, as:

> The committee *is* to meet tomorrow, when *they* will be considering the new proposal.

For *they* substitute *it.*

Degrees of Comparison

(1) *Positive* (the simple form); e.g., bright, good, beautiful.
(2) *Comparative* (used when comparing *two* persons or things); e.g., brighter, better, more beautiful.
(3) *Superlative* (used when comparing more than two persons or things); e.g., brightest, best, most beautiful.

A fairly common error is to use the superlative degree when only two things are being compared.

Double comparatives or double superlatives should be avoided in modern writing, as: "This was the *most* unkind*est* cut of all" (Shakespeare).

Unrelated Participles

This is a very common error, as will be seen from the following examples:

> *Driving* homewards, it began to rain.

The participle *driving* is unrelated (there is no relation between *driving* and *it*), and the sentence would be more grammatical as follows:

> As I drove homewards it began to rain.

> *Speaking* as an observer, it must be agreed that the prospects are exceptionally bright.

Speaking is unrelated. Write instead:

> Speaking as an observer, I must agree that the prospects are exceptionally bright.

Unrelated Relative Pronouns

A relative pronoun must have an antecedent. In the following sentence this rule is violated:

> The fire spread rapidly, which caused considerable panic.

The relative pronoun *which* has no antecendent. The sentence should therefore be altered to read:

> Considerable panic was caused when the fire spread rapidly. *Or:* The fire spread rapidly, causing considerable panic.

Relative Pronoun and Antecedent

An important grammatical rule is that a relative pronoun must agree with its antecedent in number and person. This rule is violated in the following sentences:

> She is one of those who never *makes* the same mistake twice.

The antecedent of the relative pronoun *who* is *those*, not *one*. *Who* is therefore plural and requires the plural verb *make.*

> The earthquake at Skopje is one of the most tragic disasters that *has* occurred in modern times.

The antecedent of the relative pronoun *that* is *disasters*, not *one*. *That* therefore takes the plural verb *have.*

4

Shorthand and Typewriting Hints

The Secretary's Notebook – Taking Dictation – Transcription of Notes – Estimating Length of Letters – Typing Correspondence (Personal, Business, Official) – Legal Documents – Commercial and Technical Work – Deciphering Manuscript – Literary Work – Poetry – Dramatic Work – Line-end Division of Words – Numerals – International Paper Sizes.

The Secretary's Notebook

Your shorthand notebook should be a complete record of correspondence dictated, and should therefore be carefully kept.

Start each day's dictation on a fresh page, and write the date boldly (in longhand) at the top of the page. Rule a margin of about an inch in width on the left-hand side of each page, and use it to record any special instructions you may be given; e.g., "Take an extra copy," "Register this letter," "Mark this one 'Confidential'," and so on. Additions or alterations in the course of dictation should also be noted in the margin. If, however, the alteration is a lengthy one, put a mark in the margin against the line to be altered. Then take down the alteration on a later page, and put a similar mark in the margin alongside this for cross-reference. Draw a line across the page before and after this additional matter, so that it will not be confused with the rest of the dictation.

Write the name of your correspondent (and, if time permits, his address also) in longhand at the top of each letter, or in the left-hand margin.

Number your letters and draw a line after each one. Before beginning a fresh session of dictation, slip a wide rubber band around the used pages, so that you will always have the following page ready for the next 'take.'

As each letter is typed score it neatly through in the notebook. Any letter that is not typed, or that for some reason is not sent out, must be indicated by writing "Cancelled" across the notes.

When your notebook is full, write the starting and finishing dates clearly on the front cover. Old notebooks should be carefully stored in consecutive order and kept for about a year. Carbon copies of letters have been known to go astray, and in such cases the secretary's notebook is the only record of what was said.

Taking Dictation

As you may be called upon to take dictation at any moment during the day, always be prepared and keep pen or pencils and notebook ready for use. If you are nearing the end of your notebook, take in an extra one with you, so that you do not need to interrupt the dictation by having to fetch a new book.

See that you are comfortably seated during dictation – facing the speaker and, if possible, resting your notebook on a table or desk. A helpful tip for turning over pages quickly is to turn the bottom left-hand corners of the pages up slightly, so that as you approach the end of a page your first finger and thumb will close easily over the turned-up corner.

During dictation be quiet and composed in manner. Concentrate on the subject-matter and make an effort to follow the sense of the dictation. Should your chief dictate an unfamiliar word or technical term, put a mark in the margin and, as soon as he reaches the end of that particular letter, query the elusive word or phrase. (Avoid interrupting him in the middle of a letter, however, unless as the result of a sudden burst of speed you find yourself being left behind.)

When, as often happens, the dictation session is interrupted by the ringing of the telephone, take the opportunity to read through your notes, correcting faulty outlines and inserting punctuation marks where necessary. (Full stops should, of course, be inserted during the course of dictation.) Be alert and ready to take down any information or instruction your employer may give you during the telephone conversation.

Transcription of Notes

The following hints will help you to transcribe your shorthand notes with accuracy and intelligence.

1. Read over the notes of each letter carefully before beginning to type.
2. Insert punctuation marks as you read, and indicate paragraphs by means of the paragraph sign (*or* //).
3. Refer to your shorthand dictionary in order to correct faulty outlines and verify the spelling of any doubtful word.
4. Do not 'edit' your employer's letters unless asked to do so. But it is usually safe to correct (tactfully) obvious errors such as grammatical slips or the repetition of some word too frequently in the same sentence or paragraph.
5. After transcribing each letter draw a line neatly through the notes, so that there will be no danger of typing the same letter twice.
6. Before submitting a letter for signature read it over very carefully – checking your spelling, punctuation, and the general 'sense' of the letter.

NOTE. Type letters in strict rotation, unless a particular letter is 'urgent,' when it should be typed first.

Estimating Length of Letters

By knowing the average number of outlines you can fit into a line of your shorthand notebook, and multiplying that number by the number of lines of shorthand, you will be able to estimate the length of any letter. This, in turn, will enable you to judge the appropriate size of paper. (See *International Paper Sizes*, pp. 75 and 76.)

TYPING CORRESPONDENCE

Letters may be divided into three general classes:

(*a*) Personal
(*b*) Business
(*c*) Official

(*a*) **Personal Correspondence**

For short letters A5 paper (148 mm × 210 mm) is usual, while A4 paper (210 mm × 297 mm) would be more appropriate for longer letters. A well-centred letter has a most pleasing effect, the width of the margins being adjusted according to the length of the letter. Either single- or double-line spacing may be used, but this again depends upon size of paper and length of letter.

The date should begin two or three lines below the printed address. If the address is printed on the right-hand side of the paper the date must not extend into the right-hand margin. Where the address has been centred, the date too could be centred. As with business letters, the usual method of typing the date is in the logical order of day, month, year; e.g., 20th March, 19–.

The correspondent's name and address are usually placed at the *foot* of the letter, instead of at the beginning. In the case of very personal letters – for example, a letter beginning "Dear John" – the inside address is frequently omitted from the letter itself, although it is advisable to add it to the carbon copy.

A closing phrase, such as "With kind regards," or "With best wishes," should be suitably indented from the left-hand margin, and typed two line-spaces above the subscription or complimentary close. (Note the use of the comma after these phrases.)

Enclosures. These are not usually indicated in personal correspondence unless the letter is definitely business-like in character.

(*b*) Business Letters

The diagram opposite illustrates the layout of a business letter (*Indented Form*).[1]

Key to Diagram

(1) Reference.
(2) Date.
(3) Addressee's name and address.
(4) Salutation.
(5) Subject-heading.
(6) Body of letter (arranged in paragraphs).
(7) Complimentary close (subscription) and name of firm.
(8) Signature and designation.
(9) Enclosures.

The various parts of the letter are briefly dealt with as follows:

(1) *Reference*

The reference is usually placed at the left-hand margin, in line with the date, and two or three line-spaces below the printed letter-heading. The reference may consist merely of the initials of the dictator and the typist (JBB/MS), or refer to a departmental file number (ADV/563). The purpose of the reference is to identify the person or department sending the letter.

When a reference number is given in the letter to which you are replying, both references should be included – your correspondent's and your own.

(2) *Date*

The date is typed two or three line-spaces below the printed letter-heading, and must not extend beyond the right-hand margin. The date should be typed in full, usually in the order: day, month, year, as:

23rd January, 19–.

[1] The alternative form is the '*blocked*' style, in which *every* line of the letter begins at the left-hand margin.

DIAGRAM SHOWING THE ARRANGEMENT OF A BUSINESS LETTER
(Indented Form)

J. B. BROWN & COMPANY

Telephone:
041 221 1234

Central Street,
GLASGOW G1 7AP

(1)——— (2)———

(3)———

(4)———

(5)———

(6)———

(6)———

(6)———

(7)———

(8)———

(9)———

(3) *Addressee's Name and Address (Inside Address)*

The inside address is typed (in single spacing) two or three lines below the reference and date line, at the left-hand side of the paper. It may be in *blocked* form, as:

```
Messrs. R. Jones & Son,
100 Axminster Street,
Halifax, Yorkshire HX9 1AN
```

or *indented* form, as:

```
J. C. Barclay, Esq.,
      3 Rosemead Drive,
            London SW3 5AZ
```

The address should, wherever possible, be confined to three or four lines. If necessary, two items may occupy a single line; e.g., the name of a house and the street, or the name of the town and the county. (On the *envelope*, however, each item of the name and address should be placed on a separate line, as this is helpful to the Post Office.)

NOTE. It is important to remember that *Messrs.* should be used only when addressing a *partnership*, except when the name of the firm is preceded by the word "The" or when a title is included; e.g.:

Messrs. Jones & Brown
Messrs. A. Mortimer & Company
The Hubert Lane Publishing Company
Sir Robert Smith & Company

Messrs. must not, however, be used before the name of a *limited* company. (See chapter on Titles and Forms of Address, page 156). When writing to a limited company it is usual to address the letter to the *Secretary*, or to some other official of the company – e.g., the *General Manager*, the *Sales Manager*, the *Accountant*, etc.

Examples:

The Secretary,
Johnson & Jones Ltd.

The Sales Manager,
J. B. Brown & Co. Ltd.

Confidential Letters. When it is necessary to indicate that a particular letter is of a confidential nature, the word

"CONFIDENTIAL" should be typed a double space *above* the address – both in the letter and on the envelope, thus:

CONFIDENTIAL
The Contracts Manager,
John Smith & Co. Ltd.,
55 Main Street,
MANCHESTER M1 5DN

'Attention' Line. The words "For the attention of –" should be typed a double space *after* the inside address, and two or three spaces before the salutation, thus:

```
The Royal Printing Company,
151 Crown Street,
Glasgow G51 7PQ

For the attention of Mr. A. Black.

Dear Sirs,*
```

NOTE. When typing the *envelope*, however, the 'Attention' line should be placed two spaces *above* the address. (See specimen envelope on p. 61.)

(4) *The Salutation*

The salutation (e.g., *Dear Sir* or *Dear Madam*) is typed at the left-hand margin, two or three spaces below the inside address; it should be followed by a comma.

(5) *Subject-heading*

The subject-heading is centred over the writing line, two line-spaces below the salutation, and is followed by two line-spaces. It may be typed in small or capital letters and should be underlined, thus:

* The salutation "Dear Sirs" is used because the firm is being addressed – *not* Mr. Black.

Dear Madam,

Secretarial Examinations*

Thank you for your letter of the 12th January, in which you draw our attention to ...

NOTE. When using the *blocked* style the subject-heading would, of course, appear at the left-hand margin.

(6) *Body (or Message) of the Letter*

This may be typed in single- or double-line spacing, with double spacing between the paragraphs. Single spacing is, however, smarter, and a short letter is more effectively displayed in single spacing on A5 paper than in double spacing on A4 paper. In the *indented* form of letter an indentation of five (or six) spaces at the beginning of each new paragraph is usual, the tabulator stop being set for this purpose.

The subject-matter of the letter must be expressed in clear and concise English, correctly spelt, and properly punctuated and paragraphed.

A letter should never be written in one paragraph, unless it is a very short letter. On the other hand, too many paragraphs can easily spoil the appearance of an otherwise well-typed letter.

In general, the use of abbreviations, unless recognized ones (e.g., *Esq.*, *etc.*) should be avoided. The ampersand (&) should not be used for "and" in the body of the letter except when referring to the name of a firm (e.g., Smith & Company) or when quoting numbers (e.g., pages 51 & 52).

Continuation Sheets. In the case of lengthy letters a continuation sheet may be necessary. At the head of each continuation sheet (about an inch from the top) the name of the

* A centred heading must *not* be typed with a full stop, unless it ends with an abbreviated word, e.g., *Ltd., Co.,* etc.

addressee is typed, together with the number of the page and the date, as shown below:

J. Smith, Esq. - 2 - 5th May, 19--

or, if the name of the addressee is lengthy, the page number is centred a double space above the heading.

NOTE. In the *blocked* form of letter, the page number, date, and name of addressee are *all* typed at the left-hand margin, one below the other.

(7) *Complimentary Close (Subscription)*

The most common forms in business correspondence are *Yours faithfully* and *Yours truly*, although *Yours sincerely* is used where a more personal relationship exists. It is important that the subscription should agree in wording with the salutation; e.g.:

Dear Sir(s), – Yours faithfully,
Dear Mr. Smith, – Yours truly *or*
Yours very truly,
Dear Mr. Smith,
Dear Smith, Dear John, – Yours sincerely,

The complimentary close should be typed *two* line-spaces below the last line of the final paragraph, only the first word being capitalized. It should be followed by a comma.

(8) *Signature and Designation*

In the *indented* form of letter, the name of the firm is usually centred in capitals immediately below the complimentary close, about six line-spaces being left between the name of the firm and the designation to allow room for the signature. The designation should also be centred (see diagram on p. 56), and it is helpful to your correspondent to type your chief's name just *above* the designation.

(9) *Enclosures*

Enclosures are usually indicated by the abbreviation *Enc.* (*or Encs.* (2), *Encs.* (3), etc.) typed at the bottom left-hand margin, two or three spaces below the designation.

Addressing of Envelopes

In order to comply with Post Office regulations the address must be placed parallel with the long side of the envelope and sufficient space left above it for postage stamps and postmarks. The address should therefore begin approximately half-way down the envelope, and should be centrally placed.

As stated on p. 57, each item of the address should occupy a separate line, and the name of the town should be typed in *capitals*. If there is any doubt about the correct postal address reference should be made to the *Telephone Directory* or to *Post Offices in the United Kingdom.*

When it is necessary to add "Personal," "Confidential," or "For the attention of—" to the address, the word(s) in question should be typed a double space *above* the address, as:

For the attention of Mr. A. Black.

The Royal Printing Company,
151 Crown Street,
GLASGOW G51 78Q

NOTE. It is important to remember that a well-displayed, neatly typed, and carefully punctuated letter will not only create a favourable impression on the recipient but will also do much to keep the reputation of your firm at a high level.

Open Punctuation

It is becoming increasingly common (in the *blocked* form of letter) to *omit* punctuation in the date, inside address, salutation, and complimentary close of the letter, as well as in the envelope address, thus:

9th October 19–

The Secretary
John Smith & Co Ltd
101 Main Street
London WC1P 30L

Dear Sir
. . . .
Yours faithfully

(*c*) Official Letters

The chief points of difference between business letters and official correspondence (i.e., letters from Government Departments) concern: margins, inside address, salutation, complimentary close, catchword, and enclosures.

Margins

A wide margin (at least one inch for A4 paper and half an inch for A5) is allowed on the left-hand side of the paper, and on the right-hand side a minimum of two or three spaces. When typing on the back of the sheet (which is quite usual in official correspondence) this procedure is reversed – the wide margin being on the right-hand side and the narrow margin on the left-hand side.

Inside Address

As distinct from business letters, in *official* correspondence, the inside address is typed at the foot of the *first* page, the indented form of address being used. On A4 paper the first line begins at 5 on the scale (pica type) or 6 (elite type), each subsequent line being indented five spaces. On A5 paper the first line begins at 3 on the scale (pica *or* elite), and each subsequent line is also indented three spaces.

Salutation

The usual salutation is: *Sir*, *Madam*, *Gentlemen*. When writing to Secretaries of Government Departments the salutation is: *Sir*.

Complimentary Close

For official letters the usual form adopted is:

I am, Sir,
Yours faithfully,

When writing to Secretaries and Under-Secretaries of State the form is:

I have the honour to be, Sir,
Yours faithfully,

Catchword

In official correspondence pages are not numbered, a 'catchword' being used instead. This means that the first word appearing on the second page would also be typed at the foot of the first page, thus:

/business

Enclosures

An enclosure in an official letter would be indicated by means of three hyphens typed in the margin opposite the place where reference is made to it. When an enclosure is referred to on the first page the hyphens are typed inside the left-hand margin, and inside the right-hand margin when mentioned on the second page.

Legal Documents

Because legal documents are usually subjected to extensive revision before being finally approved, they are typed in three stages.

1. *Draft* – which is the first rough copy of a document. It is typed in treble-line spacing with a wide left-hand margin to permit of additions and alterations being made.
2. *Fair copy* – which is a copy of the corrected draft for perusal by the solicitor or client.
3. *Engrossment* – which is the final or completed copy prepared for signature.

An engrossment is typed in double-line spacing on *both* sides of the paper (special double sheets are used for this purpose), the pages being numbered in the middle at the *foot* of the page. A black record ribbon, which has the advantage of being absolutely permanent, is generally used for legal documents.

In typing the engrossment accuracy is of paramount importance, as erasures are not permitted in legal documents such as agreements, deeds, and wills. Abbreviations must be avoided, and also division of words at line-ends. The right-hand margin should be kept as even as possible, if necessary, by inserting hyphens up to the margin level, thus: --------------------------------

Punctuation

Punctuation is usually omitted in legal documents, with the possible exception of the period at the end of each clause or recital. The reason for this is that the law requires the meaning of legal documents to be clearly conveyed without the aid of punctuation marks. This is easy to understand when it is realized that the meaning of a clause or sentence can be entirely altered by the addition or omission of punctuation marks.

Dated 15th January, 19--

JOHN SMITH, Esq.

and

JAMES BROWN, Esq.

A G R E E M E N T

for

T E N A N C Y

McKinnon & Watt,
10 Barclay Street,
Glasgow G2 5LX

Capitalization is made use of to draw attention to the following: the names of the parties, when first mentioned; the title of the document; the first word in each clause; and certain other prominent words – e.g., "As Witness," "Signed," etc.

Endorsement

All legal documents need to be endorsed. A specimen endorsement is given on page 64. It contains the date, the names of the parties to the Agreement, a brief description of the document, and the name of the firm of solicitors – all these particulars being typed on the *outside* of the document.

Commercial and Technical Work

In addition to general correspondence, the typing of invoices and accounts is a very common task that falls to the lot of the typist in a commercial office. These documents are generally typed on the firm's specially printed forms.

Technical documents, including *Specifications* and *Bills of Quantities*, form part of the work of the secretary or typist employed in an architect's or engineer's office.

Specifications are usually typed on A4 paper with a record ribbon, double-line spacing being used for short specifications and single-line spacing for long ones. A specification is divided into three parts:

1. *The Heading*, which is always typed in double spacing.
2. *The Body*, which is typed with a wide margin (usually 2½ in.).
3. *Side-headings*, which are typed in capitals in single-line spacing with a one-inch margin.

Technical documents are endorsed in the same manner as legal documents.

Deciphering Manuscript

The transcription of manuscript calls for intelligence and common sense, and necessitates a sound knowledge of English. Always have at hand a good dictionary in order to check the spelling of unfamiliar words. It is also helpful to make yourself familiar with the list of longhand abbreviations given in *The Dictionary of Typewriting* (Pitman). There is a similar list of legal abbreviations in *The Dictionary of Typewriting* which will be found useful by typists and secretaries in law offices.

In addition to these longhand abbreviations, it is necessary to know the meaning of the various proof-correction signs, as these are frequently used in making alterations in a manuscript.

The following advice will be found helpful in deciphering manuscript. The whole of the manuscript should be read through, if possible, before proceeding to type. This will enable you to arrive at the 'sense' of the passage more readily and, at the same time, to become familiar with the writer's style of handwriting.

Spelling and obvious grammatical errors should be corrected, and abbreviations written in full. If a word is completely indecipherable, encircle it and leave a blank in the typescript. Don't be tempted to guess! Read carefully through your typescript (before removing it from the machine) to ensure that it is free from error.

Literary Work

The secretary to an author or journalist may be called upon to type novels, short stories, articles, essays, or lectures. Literary matter is typed on A4 paper with wide margins (about 1½ in.). Double-line spacing should be used, as this permits of corrections and additions being made if necessary. (In the final typed copy, however, corrections should be kept to a minimum.) Quotations, footnotes, or synopses should always be typed in single-line spacing so that they stand out clearly from the body of the work. Type on one side of the paper only, and use a black record ribbon.

There is no hard-and-fast rule about *pagination*, but it is usual to number pages in the middle about an inch from the top of the page. Arabic figures should be used, and the pages should be numbered consecutively. (It is not necessary to number the first page, however.) Chapter numbers are usually typed in large roman numerals (e.g., Chapter 16). A preface or introduction may be numbered in small roman numerals.

Each new chapter must begin on a fresh page, the chapter

number and title being centred and placed at a lower level on the page than the first line of subsequent pages. Headings displayed in this manner are called *dropped headings.*

NOTE. Try to ensure that each page contains the same number of lines, but avoid finishing a paragraph with one line at the top of a new page.

Footnotes

In printed matter footnotes appear at the *foot* of the page, as their name implies; but when a typescript is being prepared for the printer the footnote should be typed (in single-line spacing) immediately below the line to which it refers. To separate the footnote from the text, two lines should be ruled across the page (from margin to margin) by means of the underscore – one before the insertion of the footnote and the other immediately after it.

When two reference numbers occur at a short interval from each other *both* footnotes may be typed within one pair of lines.

The reference number or sign (e.g., an asterisk) should be raised slightly above the line of typing and placed immediately after the word or passage to which the footnote refers, and a corresponding number or sign placed immediately in front of the relevant footnote.

Example:

Once a book or other matter has been set up in type, it is most important that alterations, other than the correction of printing errors,(1) should

---

(1) Broken and inverted letters, letters of the wrong fount (i.e., size and style), misprints, etc.

---

be kept to a minimum. Alterations made on the proofs that represent a change from the original copy can prove most expensive, as the cost of correcting type is very much greater than the cost of setting it up.

Book Manuscripts

When typing book manuscripts a *title page* containing the following particulars must be prepared:

(*a*) The title of the book and the author's name beneath it.
(*b*) The author's name and address in the bottom left-hand corner.
(*c*) Approximate number of words in the bottom right-hand corner.

In addition to the title-page, a page containing the list of contents should also be prepared.

In typing a lengthy piece of work it is important to be consistent in regard to spelling and capitalization, use of words and figures, numbering of pages and sections, display, etc. It should also be noted that the quality of the paper or of the typewriter ribbon should not be changed in the middle of the work. Remember to return the original manuscript with the completed typescript.

NOTE. It is necessary for the literary typist or secretary to have a thorough knowledge of printers' proof-correction signs. These are explained in Chapter 14.

Estimating Quantity

In order to estimate the number of words contained in a page of typescript, you should first count the words in a few lines of type (say, five or six) to find the average number of words per line, and then multiply this by the number of lines in the page. This will give the average number per page.

To estimate the approximate number of words in a lengthy manuscript, proceed as follows: Find the average of five or six pages, and multiply this number by the total number of pages in the manuscript, after making allowance for half-pages, etc., at the ends of chapters.

Literary work is charged for at so much a thousand words. Other typewritten work is charged for at so much a folio – a folio in Britain consisting of seventy-two words, while in the United States it is one hundred words.

NOTE. *Pica* type measures ten letters or spaces to the inch; and *Elite* type measures twelve to the inch.

Poetry

Poetry should be typed on A4 paper in single-line spacing with two or three line-spaces between the verses, and in classical verse (though not always in modern) each line must begin with a capital letter. It should be so arranged on the page that the effect of equal margins is secured. The following general rules apply to indentations:

1. When alternate lines rhyme, begin the first, third, fifth, etc., lines at the margin, and indent the second, fourth, sixth, etc., three spaces to the right, thus:

```
"The time has come," the Walrus said,
   "To talk of many things:
Of shoes - and ships - and sealing-wax -
   Of cabbages - and kings -
And why the sea is boiling hot -
   And whether pigs have wings."

                          Lewis Carroll
```

2. When successive lines rhyme or in blank verse (where the lines do not rhyme) no indentation is required, thus:

```
Best and brightest, come away,
Fairer far than this fair Day,
Which, like thee to those in sorrow,
```

```
Comes to bid a sweet good-morrow
To the rough Year just awake
In its cradle on the brake.

                        - P. B. Shelley
```

3. When the last line is comparatively short it should begin about the middle of the preceding lines, as:

```
Is there a bard of rustic song,
Who, noteless, steals the crowds among,
That weekly this area throng,
               O, pass not by!
But, with a frater-feeling strong,
               Here heave a sigh!

                          - Robert Burns
```

NOTE. The title of a poem is usually centred in capitals, and the name of the author should appear at the end, as illustrated in the foregoing examples.

Dramatic Work

Dramatic work involves the typing of plays – both the general copy containing the complete play and the actors' parts with cues.

A *complete* play consists of the Title Page (typed on page one), the Synopsis of Acts and Scenery (on page two), the List of Characters and Cast (on page three), and the play itself (commencing on page four).

The play itself should be typed in double spacing, with single spacing for stage directions, etc. A wide left-hand margin (about 2 in.), in which the names of the characters are typed in capitals, must be allowed. A4 paper and a black record ribbon should be used.

Actors' parts (or *single* parts) are typed in double spacing on A5 paper, and contain the words spoken by one character only – the name of the character being centred in capitals beneath the title of the play on the first page.

Cues, which are the last few words spoken by the previous speaker, should be preceded by a series of full stops.

In both the general copy of the play and the actors' parts it is important to underline in red, or rule in red ink, all stage directions, etc., so that these portions will not be confused with the spoken words.

Line-end Division of Words

In order to avoid an irregular right-hand margin – which would, of course, detract from the appearance of an otherwise well-displayed typescript – it is the accepted practice to divide words at the end of lines. (The experienced typist will, however, find that by careful arrangement of her work undue line-end division can be avoided.)

It should be noted that pronunciation is the typist's chief guide, as will be seen from the following general rules for the correct division of words:

(1) Divide after a prefix of *more* than two letters, as:

con-duct	pro-gramme	trans-port
com-plete	intro-duction	tran-scend
over-whelm	mis-direct	tra-verse

(2) Divide before a suffix of *more* than two letters, as:

bring-ing	friend-ship	possib-ility
separ-ate	tempor-ary	min-ority
absol-ute	observ-ant	permis-sion
arrog-ance	manage-ment	notice-able
atten-tion	physi-cian	import-ance

(3) Divide before *-tial* or *-cial*, as:

residen-tial	provin-cial
influen-tial	finan-cial

(4) When the final consonant of a root word is doubled for the addition of a suffix, divide between the two consonants, as:

regret-ting	begin-ning	occur-ring
appal-ling	excel-lent	concur-rence

(*But:* address-ing harass-ing spell-ing)

(5) In words containing a doubled consonant medially, divide between the two consonants, as:

gazet-teer	recom-mend	accom-modate
com-munal	syl-lable	coquet-tish

(6) In words containing *two* different consonants medially, divide between the two consonants, if separately sounded, as:

resig-nation	main-tain	splen-dour
oppor-tunity	legis-late	cam-paign

(7) In words containing *three* consecutive consonants medially, divide after the first consonant, as:

frus-trate	infil-trate	magis-trate
chil-dren	hun-dred	dis-creet

(8) Divide between two vowel sounds, or after the first vowel when followed by a diphthong, as:

continu-ous	continu-ally	circu-itous
conveni-ence	retali-ation	invidi-ous

(9) Compound words should be divided into their original parts, as:

school-master mantel-piece house-keeper

(10) Words containing a hyphen should be divided only at the point of the hyphen, as:

co-operate book-keeping pre-eminent

NOTE. Where derivation and pronunciation do not agree it is better to divide a word according to its pronunciation, as:

attrac-tive	(*not* attract-ive)
sen-tence	(*not* sent-ence)
prop-erty	(*not* pro-perty)

prod-uct	(*not* pro-duct)
chil-dren	(*not* child-ren)
acknowl-edge	(*not* acknow-ledge)

The following set of rules is intended to indicate when words should *not* be divided:

Do not divide:

(*a*) proper nouns – e.g., Newcastle, Sutherland, etc.
(*b*) words of one syllable or the plural forms of one-syllable words, as:

strength packed cases noises

(*c*) short words of two syllables, as:

into until duly enrol

(*d*) words that would leave a syllable of one or two letters at the beginning or end of the word, as:

quickly	expense	above
receive	between	equipped

(*e*) the last word in a paragraph or the last word on a page;
(*f*) an abbreviation or between initials of names;
(*g*) in the middle of figures or sums of money;
(*h*) at the end of more than two consecutive lines;
(*i*) words in legal documents; and finally –
(*j*) do not divide a word if there is any doubt about the correct division.

Numerals

The following are some general rules indicating when to use words and when figures.

Words should be used:

(*a*) when a number begins a sentence, as:

Two hundred and thirty-seven entries were received.

(*b*) when the number is expressed in an indefinite manner, as:

There were two or three urgent calls.

(*c*) for the time of day when 'o'clock' is used, as:

ten o'clock

(*But:* 10 00 hrs.; 16 15 hrs.)

(*d*) for ages, when expressed as *ordinal* numbers, as:

She is in her twenty-second year.

(*But:* 22 years of age)

(*e*) when used with the words 'per cent,' as:

five per cent; fifty per cent, etc.

(*But:* 2½%, 10%, etc.)

(*f*) in *legal* documents, for figures, sums of money, and dates;

(NOTE. Numbers of houses and postal districts are, however, written in *figures*; e.g., 16 West Street, London W1M 7HG

(*g*) in *literary* work, for numbers up to *one hundred* and *round* numbers over one hundred, as:

five hundred; two million

(NOTE. *General* numbers over one hundred are written in *figures*; e.g., 101, 367,576.)

Figures should be used:

in *business letters:* for dates, measurements, quantities, and sums of money; e.g.:

15th January, 19–
25·40 mm.
20 kg.
£5·52½

and, in general, for reference numbers and statistics.

Roman numerals

In typing roman figures the capital letter I should be used for the figure one – e.g., III, IX, XI; whereas in arabic figures the small 'el' is used, as in 116,321, if there is no figure one on the typewriter keyboard.

The following simple table should be memorized:

I	equals	1	C	„	100
V	„	5	D	„	500
X	„	10	M	„	1000
L	„	50	$\overline{\mathrm{M}}$	„	1,000,000

Examples: IV (4); VII (7); XIII (13); XIX (19); LVIII (58); LXIX (69); XC (90); CXC (190); CCC (300); CD (400); CM (900); $\overline{\mathrm{IX}}$ (9000); $\overline{\mathrm{LX}}$ (60,000); MLXVI (1066); MCMLXXII (1972).

NOTE. No full stop should follow these numerals.

Roman numerals may be used as follows:

(*a*) In numbers attached to the names of monarchs, and in classes and form numbers, as:

Elizabeth II
Form V

(*b*) In expressing the number of the year, as:

MCMLXV

(*c*) In numbering chapters or paragraphs, as:

Chapter XV

(*d*) Small roman numerals are used:

(*i*) in numbering the introductory pages of books and for subsections, etc., as:

Part II, Section (3), Subsection iv;

(*ii*) in quoting Biblical references, as:

2 Kings v. 6
1 John iii. 18

NOTE. Arabic numerals are used to indicate the number of the Book and of the verse.

International Paper Sizes

The traditional sizes of typewriting paper (quarto, octavo, foolscap, etc.) are rapidly being superseded in business offices throughout the country by *International* paper sizes, the most common of which are:

	mm	in. (approx.)
A4	210 x 297	$8\frac{1}{4}$ x $11\frac{3}{4}$
A5	148 x 210	$5\frac{7}{8}$ x $8\frac{1}{4}$
A3	297 x 420	$11\frac{3}{4}$ x $16\frac{1}{2}$

The following are the main uses of International paper:

A4 – Letters (business and official); legal and technical work; reports, minutes, and agendas; literary work.

A5 – Letters (short business and official); inter-departmental correspondence (memorandums); actors' parts (plays).

A3 – Legal documents.

It should be noted that paper is supplied in either *quires* or *reams*, the quantities being as follows:

24 sheets = 1 quire
20 quires = 1 ream*

* Stationers' reams consist of 480 sheets, while printers' reams usually have 500 or 516 sheets.

5

Book-keeping and Accounts

Object of Book-keeping – Neatness and Accuracy – Double-entry System – Ledger and Subsidiary Books – Classification of Ledger Accounts – Trial Balance – Classes of Error Not Disclosed by a Trial Balance – Purchase and Sale of Assets on Credit – Columnar or Tabular Book-keeping – Card Index Ledger System – Petty Cash Book – 'Imprest' System – Advantages of the Imprest System – Accounts of Non-trading Concerns – Receipts and Payments Account – Income and Expenditure Account – Preparation of Final Accounts of a Non-trading Concern – Commercial Documents.

Object of Book-keeping

The object of book-keeping is to record business transactions in a systematic manner, so that at any time the books will give accurate and detailed information concerning

(1) the debtors and creditors – i.e., what is owing to the business by customers, and what is owing by the business to suppliers;
(2) the property or assets of the business;
(3) the profit made or loss incurred by the business during any particular period; and
(4) the expenses of the business – e.g., wages, rates, etc.

Neatness and Accuracy

Accuracy in book-keeping is, to a great extent, dependent upon neatness and legibility of words and figures. In entering figures in the money columns care should be taken to place units under units, tens under tens, etc., as this will greatly facilitate accurate addition. Entries should be made in ink, and lines should be ruled and not drawn freehand.

The folio column should be completed as each entry is made, and the date should always be recorded in the appropriate column, thus: Mar. 2; Apr. 25. The year should be indicated at the top of the date column.

When a statement of any sort is being prepared the heading must show clearly the period covered by the statement; e.g., "Bank Reconciliation Statement as at 31st August, 19–"; "Income and Expenditure Account for the year ended 30th April, 19–."

Double-entry System

The fundamental principle of double-entry book-keeping is that for every debit entry there must be a corresponding credit entry, and vice versa. It should be clearly understood that every business transaction involves both a receiver (or debtor) and a giver (or creditor), and must therefore be recorded in *two* ledger accounts – on the *debit* side of one and on the *credit* side of the other.

NOTE. All debit entries are preceded by the word 'To,' which means that the receiving account is debtor *to* the giving account. All credit entries are preceded by the word 'By,' which means that the giving account is creditor *by* the receiving account.

Ledger and Subsidiary Books

The *Ledger* is the most important book of account, as it contains in summarized form a record of every transaction entered in the subsidiary books. Each transaction, after being entered into its appropriate subsidiary book, is posted to the Ledger, the entries affecting personal accounts being posted separately, while the *totals* of the various subsidiary books are posted to the appropriate Ledger accounts; e.g., total sales to Sales Account, total purchases to Purchases Account, etc.

The Ledger is thus relieved of much unnecessary and cumbersome detail.

The *Purchases* and *Sales* books, the *Returns Inward* and *Outward* books, as well as the *Journal*, are subsidiary to the Ledger and are referred to as 'subsidiary books' (or 'books of original entry'). The *Cash Book*, though also a book of original entry, is really part of the Ledger – i.e., the *Cash Account* of the Ledger.

Classification of Ledger Accounts

Ledger accounts may be divided into *three* classes:

(*a*) *Personal Accounts*, those recording transactions with persons or firms. They may be either debtors or creditors.

(*b*) *Real Accounts*, which relate to property or other assets; e.g., buildings, furniture, cash, machinery, etc.

(*c*) *Nominal Accounts*, those recording losses or gains; e.g., wages, trade expenses, bad debts, discount allowed or received, interest received, etc.

('Real' Accounts and 'Nominal' Accounts are also referred to as 'Impersonal' Accounts.)

Trial Balance

A *Trial Balance* is a classified list of the balances appearing, at any given date, in the Ledger. The object of preparing a trial balance is to test the accuracy of the posting. If the total of the debit balances equals the total of the credit balances, this may be regarded as proof (though not necessarily *conclusive* proof) of the accuracy of the book-keeping.

NOTE. In practice, a trial balance is usually extracted at the end of each month and, in all cases, before closing the books at the end of the financial period – usually a year.

Should the trial balance *not* agree, the following procedure must be adopted:

(*a*) Check the casting (addition) of the trial balance.
(*b*) Check the items from ledger account to trial balance, and ensure that all balances have been included. (Do not overlook *Cash* balances.)

(*c*) Check total purchases, sales, returns, and discounts, and also check the posting of each to the ledger.
(*d*) Finally, check the castings and balances of all accounts.

Classes of Error Not Disclosed by a Trial Balance

It should be remembered that the trial balance affords proof only of the arithmetical accuracy of the postings. There are certain classes of error that a trial balance fails to disclose, these being as follows:

(1) *Errors of Omission*, where a transaction has been omitted entirely from the books. As both debit and credit entries have been omitted, the trial balance will not, of course, reveal the error.

(2) *Errors of Commission*, where the wrong account has been debited or credited. If, for example, £10 has been posted to the credit of J. Smith, instead of to the credit of A. J. Smith, the error will not affect the agreement of the trial balance.

(3) *Errors of Principle.* This type of error occurs when an expense item (e.g., Repairs) has been posted to the debit of an asset account (e.g., Machinery) instead of to Repairs Account.

(4) *Compensating Errors*, where a mistake on the debit side of the ledger is equalled by another (unconnected) mistake of identical amount on the credit side.

Purchase and Sale of Assets on Credit

While the *Purchases Book* is used to record particulars of goods *bought on credit*, and the *Sales Book* particulars of goods *sold on credit*, it is important to note that the credit purchase or credit sale of an *asset* – i.e., property possessed by the business and intended for use in the business (e.g., furniture, equipment, etc.) – must be recorded in the *Journal.*

(*a*) *Purchase of Asset on Credit*

		Dr.	Cr.
Office Equipment Account	Dr.	£90	
To Smith & Jones Ltd.			£90
Being purchase of "Resolute" typewriter (No. K64788)			

(*b*) *Sale of Asset on Credit*

		Dr.	Cr.
Smith & Jones Ltd.	Dr.	£20	
To Office Equipment A/c			£20
Being sale of second-hand typewriter.			

Columnar or Tabular Book-keeping

This term is used to denote books of account that have been ruled with a number of analysis columns in order to adapt them to the special requirements of a particular business. Where, for example, a business is divided into departments, it is desirable that the trading results of each department should be ascertained in addition to the results of the business as a whole. The method of using columnar books is very much simpler than that of keeping a separate set of books for each department.

The following is the ruling for a *Columnar Sales* (*Purchases*) *Book*:

DATE	PARTICULARS	FO.	TOTAL	CHINA	FURNITURE	CARPETS

In the ledger a "Columnar Sales (Purchases) Account" would be found more convenient than a separate sales or purchases account for each type of commodity. See specimen below:

SALES ACCOUNT

Cr.

DATE	PARTICULARS	FO.	TOTAL	CHINA	FURNITURE	CARPETS
19–			£ p	£ p	£ p	£ p
Jan. 31	By Sundries	S.1	270 –	15 –	175 –	80 –

For purposes of comparison, Trading and Profit and Loss Accounts can also be prepared in tabular form.

Columnar Cash Book

In this form of Cash Book the analysis columns are used for the purpose of collecting items of expenditure or receipts in a classified form. Each item of expenditure or income is extended into its appropriate column in addition to being entered in the usual manner in the Cash or Bank column. At the end of the trading period the totals of the various expenditure accounts are posted to the debit of the appropriate ledger accounts; and on the debit side of the Cash Book the totals of the various receipts are posted to the credit side of the appropriate accounts.

The analysed Cash Book not only obviates the tedious posting of details, but also makes it possible to see at a glance the exact amount spent on the various items of expenditure such as Wages and Salaries, Lighting and Heating, Rent, Rates and Taxes, etc.; and (on the debit or receipts side) the amount received from the various sources of income – e.g., Sales, Rents Received, Dividends, etc.

Card Index Ledger System

As will be seen in Chapter 9, the *Card Index* provides an excellent substitute for the bound ledger. Cards are widely used by doctors and dentists, hospitals, schools and colleges, and for accounts work – especially where payment is made on the instalment system.

The cards are ruled in the form of an ordinary ledger account (representing the accounts of individual patients, students, etc.), in which amounts due (e.g., fees) are debited to the account, and cash paid is credited to the account.

Petty Cash Book

Petty cash payments for small items of expenditure are usually recorded in a special book called the *Petty Cash Book*. This book is subsidiary to the principal Cash Book, upon which it depends for its funds, and its purpose is to prevent that book becoming overloaded with numerous small payments. The Petty Cash Book is ruled with suitable analysis columns for recording different kinds of expenditure (e.g., Postage, Stationery, Office Cleaning, Sundry Expenses, etc.), the totals being posted periodically to the debit of the appropriate accounts in the Ledger.

'Imprest' System

Perhaps the most popular, and certainly the most reliable, method of keeping petty cash is the *Imprest System*, which operates as follows:

The Petty Cash Book is started with a sum sufficient to meet probable requirements for a definite period of time (e.g., a week or a month). As the money is expended entries are made in the Petty Cash Book giving details of expenditure, which should always be supported by receipts or vouchers. (These vouchers should be numbered consecutively and later filed.) At the end of the period the Petty Cash Book should be balanced and the vouchers for the disbursements submitted to the principal cashier, who, after checking them, will draw a cheque for *the amount expended*, thus bringing the balance in hand back to the original sum – the 'imprest' amount.

If, for example, the imprest amount (or 'float,' as it is sometimes called) is £5 at the beginning of the period (say, a week), and the disbursements total £3·77½, the amount of £3·77½ (being the exact amount expended during the week) will be refunded to the petty cashier. This will bring the balance in hand back to £5 with which to start the new period. The entries would be recorded in the Petty Cash Book as shown on p. 84.

NOTE. Small payments by cash or by postal order may be conveniently recorded in the Petty Cash Book (under the heading "Ledger Accounts"), the postings being made direct to the Ledger in the usual way.

Advantages of the Imprest System

1. The possibility of fraud is greatly reduced, because
   (*a*) the amount of cash handled by the Petty Cashier never exceeds the original sum, or 'imprest'; and

Dr. PETTY CASH BOOK Cr.

CASH RECD.	DATE	DETAILS	VCHR. NO.	TOTAL	POSTAGE	STATIONERY	CLEANING	CARRIAGE	SUNDRY EXPENSES
£ p	19–			£ p	£ p	£ p	£ p	£ p	£ p
5 –	Oct. 1	To Cash							
	2	By Stamps	1	1 –	1 –				
		,, Ink	2	47½		47½			
	3	,, Carriage	3	25				25	
	4	,, Tea and Biscuits	4	32½					32½
	5	,, Office Cleaning	5	1 50			1 50		
		,, Envelopes	6	22½		22½			
				3 77½	1 –	70	1 50	25	32½
3 77½	6	To Cash							
		By Balance c/d		5 –					
8 77½				8 77½					
5 –	8	To Balance b/d							

(*b*) further sums are issued to the Petty Cashier only against *receipts* for actual expenditure ('vouchers' – see p. 303).

2. It provides a check on expenditure, because the Petty Cashier is required to furnish an analysis of payments with supporting vouchers before he is issued with a further cheque.

3. The system requires the Petty Cash Book to be written up regularly and kept up to date.

Accounts of Non-Trading Concerns

There are clubs and associations (social, political, etc.) whose aims are not the making of profits but rather the provision of recreational or other facilities and services for their members.

In the case of a very small club or association, whose transactions are all on a cash basis, a Receipts and Payments Account will usually be considered sufficient.

Receipts and Payments Account

The *Receipts and Payments Account* of a non-trading concern is a classified summary of the Cash Book and operates in the same manner as an ordinary Cash Book, in which receipts are debited and payments are credited.

It should be noted that *all* cash received or paid out during the period covered by the accounts must be recorded in the Receipts and Payments Account, whether it refers to that particular period or not – e.g., subscriptions paid in advance or in arrears.

The Receipts and Payments Account is usually ruled with analysis columns as in the following example:

RECEIPTS AND PAYMENTS ACCOUNT OF THE CLIFTON BADMINTON CLUB FOR THE YEAR ENDED 30th APRIL, 19–

Dr.

DATE	NAME	TOTAL	ENTRANCE FEES	SUBSCRIPTIONS	LOCKER RENTS

CONTRA Cr.

DATE	PARTICU-LARS	TOTAL	WAGES	EQUIP-MENT	PRINTING AND STATIONERY

In the larger clubs and associations it will be found that, in addition to the Receipts and Payments Account, it is usual to prepare an Income and Expenditure Account and a Balance Sheet, these being the final accounts of a non-trading concern.

Income and Expenditure Account

This is the equivalent of the Profit and Loss Account of a trading concern, expenses being debited and gains credited in the usual way; and, as in the case of a Profit and Loss Account, the Income and Expenditure Account must contain only those items of income or expenditure which relate to the period under review, so that amounts paid in advance are excluded, while those outstanding (i.e., still unpaid) must be included.

A credit balance in the Income and Expenditure Account represents *excess of income over expenditure* – and is referred to as such (*not* as 'net profit'), and a debit balance represents *excess of expenditure over income* – the equivalent of a *net loss* in a Profit and Loss Account. An excess of income would be *added* to the *Accumulated Fund* (like the Capital Account of a trading concern), and an excess of expenditure would be *deducted* from that fund.

The Accumulated Fund (as in the case of the Capital Account in a trading concern) is shown on the liabilities side of the Balance Sheet, because it represents the liability of the club or association to its members.

Preparation of Final Accounts of a Non-Trading Concern

The specimen set of accounts shown below is intended to illustrate the method of preparing an Income and Expenditure Account from a given Receipts and Payments Account followed by the Balance Sheet.

CLIFTON BADMINTON CLUB
Receipts and Payments Account for
Season ended 30th April, 19–

Dr.	£	p	Cr.	£	p
To Balance b/d. . . .	11	20	By Wages	100	–
Entrance Fees . . .	2	10	Stationery	4	50
Subscriptions . . .	160	–	Printing and Duplicating	5	75
Locker Rents . . .	5	–	New Equipment . .	10	–
			Loss on Refreshments.	2	25
			Balance c/d	55	80
	£178	30		£178	30
To Balance b/d	£55	80			

You are required to prepare an Income and Expenditure Account and a Balance Sheet after taking into account the following additional information.

Subscriptions paid in advance for 19– amount to £10. Locker rents (£1) are due but unpaid. £20 is owing in respect of wages. Club equipment is worth £110. The club owns its premises, which are valued at £1,500.

Before preparing the final accounts of this club, the following points should be noted:

1. The balance of cash (£55·80), being an asset, must appear in the Balance Sheet and not, of course, in the Income and Expenditure Account.

2. The expenditure on new equipment (£10), which represents capital expenditure, must also be shown on the Assets side of the Balance Sheet.

3. The locker rents outstanding and wages owing must be brought into the Income and Expenditure Account, and the

CLIFTON BADMINTON CLUB
Income and Expenditure Account for
Season ended 30th April, 19–

Dr.	£	£	p	Cr.	£	£	p
To Wages	100			By Subscriptions	160		
Add amount owing .	20			Less amount prepaid	10		
		120	–			150	–
Stationery		4	50	Entrance Fees		2	10
Printing and Duplicating		5	75	Locker Rents	5		
Loss on Refreshments,		2	25	Add amount owing	1	6	–
Excess of Income over Expenditure . .		25	60				
		£158	10			£158	10

CLIFTON BADMINTON CLUB
Balance Sheet as at 30th April, 19–

Liabilities	£ p	£ p	Assets	£	£ p
Accumulated Fund:			Club Premises		1500 –
Balance at 1st September, 19–.	1621 20		Equipment	110	
			Additions	10	120 –
Add Excess of Income over Expenditure	25 60				
		1646 80	Sundry Debtors		1 –
			Cash in Hand		55 80
Sundry Creditors:					
Wages	20 –				
Subscriptions prepaid	10 –				
		30 –			
		£1676 80			£1676 80

subscriptions prepaid (which do not, of course, belong to this period) must be excluded.

4. The amount of capital (i.e., Accumulated Fund) at the beginning of the season is found by adding together Cash in Hand (£11·20), Equipment (£110), and Club Premises (£1,500).

Commercial Documents

The more important commercial documents are illustrated below.

Orders

The following is the usual procedure when goods are ordered:

(1) An *inquiry* from the prospective buyer as to prices, terms of payment, rates of discount, payment of carriage, etc.

(2) A reply from the supplier enclosing a *price-list* or *quotation* and stating terms of payment and delivery.

(3) The placing of the *order* – if the prices and terms are considered satisfactory.

An *order* may be sent in the form of a letter stating requirements, or it may take the following form:

ORDER

Telephone: 041 221 1234

No. 163
10th March, 19–

From:

J. B. BROWN & COMPANY,
14 North Street,
Glasgow G1 5PQ

To:

Messrs. McBain & Thomas,
160 Central Street,
Glasgow G1 3ML

Please supply the following goods and charge to our account:

50 pcs. Wallpaper, Design No. B.13 @ 75p
50 ,, ,, ,, ,, C.10 @ 62½p
40 ,, ,, ,, ,, J.11 @ 52½p

J. B. BROWN & COMPANY

Terms: Net monthly account.
Delivery: As early as possible.

Invoices

An *invoice* is a document sent to the customer by the supplier, giving full details of the goods dispatched, including quantities, prices, amount charged, and terms of payment. In addition, a statement is usually made regarding method of delivery, and whether 'carriage paid' or 'carriage forward.'

Returns Outward

Sometimes goods that have been purchased are returned (in whole or in part) for various reasons – e.g., inferior quality, wrong size, damaged condition, etc. It is necessary to keep a record of any such returns, the book used for this purpose being the *Returns Outward Book* or *Purchases Returns Book.* It is ruled in a similar manner to the Purchases Book.

The Returns Outward Book is also used for recording empties returned (e.g., packing cases), overcharges, and allowances – so that it could be called, perhaps more aptly, a 'returns and allowances book.'

INVOICE

Telephone: 041 221 9807
Telegrams: "McThomas, Glasgow."

160 Central Street,
GLASGOW G1 3ML

12th March, 19–

Messrs. J. B. Brown & Company,
14 North Street,
Glasgow G1 5PQ

Bought of McBAIN & THOMAS

Order No. 163	Per Delivery Van			Carriage Paid	
		£	p	£	p
50 pcs. Wallpaper, No. B.13 @ 75p		37	50		
50 „ „ „ C.10 @ 62½p		31	25		
40 „ „ „ J.11 @ 52½p		21	–		
				89	75
Less 10% Trade Discount				8	97½
				£80	77½

Terms: Net monthly account.
E. & O.E.

Debit Notes. The first book-keeping step when making returns is for the purchaser to prepare a *debit note*, which is sent to the supplier together with the goods being returned. The debit note is made out in duplicate, the original being forwarded with the goods and the carbon copy remaining in the book to provide the details for the entry which is then made in the Returns Outward Book.

An ordinary invoice form may be used instead of a debit note, or it may be printed as shown on p. 91:

Returns Inward

When the goods that have been returned by the customer are received by the supplier, he should send the customer an acknowledgment in the form of a *credit note.* This, like the debit note, is made out in duplicate, the original being sent to

DEBIT NOTE

Telephone: 041 221 1234

14 North Street,
GLASGOW G1 5PQ

15th March, 19–

Messrs. McBain & Thomas,
160 Central Street,
Glasgow G1 3ML

Dr. to J. B. BROWN & COMPANY

	£ p	£ p
20 pcs. Wallpaper, No. B.13 @ 75p (Damaged)	15 –	
Less 10% Trade Discount	1 50	
		£13 50

the customer and the carbon copy being retained in the book to provide the details for the appropriate entry in the *Returns Inward Book* (sometimes known as the 'Sales Returns Book'). This book, which is ruled in a similar manner to the Returns Outward Book, is also used for recording empties returned inward and allowances granted to the customer.

CREDIT NOTE

Telephone: 041 221 9807
Telegrams: "McThomas, Glasgow."

160 Central Street,
GLASGOW G1 3ML

17th March, 19–

Messrs. J. B. Brown & Company,
14 North Street,
Glasgow G1 5PQ

Cr. by McBAIN & THOMAS

	£ p	£ p
20 pcs. Wallpaper returned @ 75p	15 –	
Less 10% Trade Discount	1 50	
		£13 50

(Invoiced on 12th March, 19–)

Credit Notes. As explained in the previous paragraph, the supplier should send his customer a *credit note* advising him that his account has been credited with the amount stated in the credit note. Credit notes are usually printed in red ink to distinguish them from invoices.

Statements of Account

At the end of the month McBain & Thomas will send a reminder to J. B. Brown & Company that the amount of £67·27½ is due. This reminder takes the form of a *statement of account* (usually referred to as a 'statement'), particulars of which are obtained from J. B. Brown & Company's ledger account in the books of McBain & Thomas. The statement is made out as follows:

STATEMENT OF ACCOUNT

Telephone: 041 221 9870
Telegrams: "McThomas, Glasgow."

160 Central Street,
GLASGOW G1 3ML

31st March, 19–

Messrs. J. B. Brown & Company,
14 North Street,
Glasgow G1 5PQ

In Account with McBAIN & THOMAS

Terms: Net monthly account.

19–		£ p	£ p
Mar. 12	To Goods	80 77½	
17	By Returns	13 50	
			£67 27½

J. B. Brown & Company will probably send a cheque to McBain & Thomas in payment of this account, the usual practice being to return the statement with the cheque.

CHEQUE

No. A 10612	No. A 10612 — 7th April, 19–
7th April, 19–	THE BRITISH LINEN BANK
McBain & Thomas	Pay Messrs. McBain & Thomas or Order Sixty-seven Pounds 27
Payment of March A/c	£67–27
£67–27	J. B. Brown & Company

McBain & Thomas will then acknowledge receipt of this amount, the following being a typical form of receipt:

RECEIPT

No. 156

160 Central Street,
GLASGOW G1 3ML

9th April, 19–

McBAIN & THOMAS

Received from Messrs. J. B. Brown & Company *the sum of* Sixty-seven Pounds twenty-seven pence *in payment of account rendered.*

£67–27

McBain & Thomas

6

Planning the Day's Work

The Daily Routine – Diaries and Memory Aids.

THE secretary's day is one of constant interruption – from callers, the telephone, her employer. . . . A methodical and orderly approach is therefore of vital importance. She must, as far as possible, plan her day in advance; try to shape it to a definite routine pattern, in order to ensure its smooth running; and, throughout the day, attend to every item of work *in order of urgency.*

In planning the day's work the importance of punctuality should not be overlooked. The efficient secretary recognizes the wisdom of a punctual start, knowing how much it can contribute not only to a calm, unflurried manner, but also to the success of a well-ordered day.

The Daily Routine

As a secretary, you will find the following routine helpful:

1. On arrival at the office (which should be at least five minutes before the starting-hour) get ready the equipment you will need – notebook, pen, pencils, letter-sorting trays, date-stamp, etc.
2. Prepare your notebook for dictation as explained on pp. 51 & 52. Fill your pen, or sharpen pencils.
3. See that your chief's desk and your own are tidy. Remove any dead flowers; renew blotting-paper, if necessary; change date on calendar.

4. Uncover and clean your typewriter. Pay particular attention to the type, which must be spotlessly clean.

5. Refer to your diary (or reminder cards) to see what appointments there are for the day and what matters are urgent. (Remember to prepare any material needed in this connection.)

6. *Opening the Mail*

(*a*) If you are responsible for attending to the incoming mail, open and sort letters (except those marked 'Personal' or 'Private'), following the procedure outlined in Chapter VII. Stamp each with a date-stamp and enter in Letters Received Book, if this is normal practice in your office.

(*b*) Letters containing remittances should have a pencilled note made in the top left-hand corner, giving brief details of the remittance – e.g., "Chq. £5." Cross any uncrossed cheques or postal orders, and lock up immediately all money enclosed in letters.

7. Read through letters, and enter in your diary (and in your chief's diary) any engagements referred to in the correspondence. (Afterwards, enter any other engagements quoted in the replies.)

(NOTE. Always be ready to take dictation at any time during the day.)

The foregoing routine deals with those matters that require attention at the beginning of the day's work. The daily routine then proceeds as follows:

8. Type any *urgent* letters requiring signature before lunch.

9. Prepare paying-in slips and money to be banked.

10. Type the remainder of the letters and leave ready for early signature.

11. Attend to filing. (It is most important that filing should be done daily, so that files are always up to date.)

12. In addition to these duties, books of account or ledger cards must be entered up regularly each day; the Petty Cash Book and Postage Book entered up daily and balanced; and stationery supplies checked regularly each week.

(NOTE. It is important to exercise economy in the use of stationery.)

Diaries and Memory Aids

A good memory is an important secretarial qualification, and the young secretary should strive to develop this quality from the beginning of her career. Why, then, should the need for memory aids arise? There are two important reasons.

1. If the mind is cluttered up with a host of small details it is unable to concentrate on more important matters.
2. If the secretary should happen to be absent for any reason, the written records provide a check on work to be done or appointments to be kept.

It is therefore essential that a written note be made in the diary of every appointment or interview arranged, and (in the diary or on reminder cards) of every matter requiring attention at a later date.

Diaries

The most suitable form of diary for the private secretary is the 'page-a-day' desk diary. This may be obtained with times of the day printed on the top half of the page, the lower half of the page being reserved for the secretary's own notes or reminders. The secretary to a doctor or dentist, for example, would find this type of diary especially useful.

The following is a typical page from a secretary's diary:

MONDAY, APRIL 12

09 30 Prepare material for Board Meeting.
10 00 Mr. Wilson calling to demonstrate ABC duplicator.
11 00 Interview with Mr. Watson re new sales territories.
11 30 Mr. Smith calling re proposed canteen facilities.
12 45 Lunch with Sir John Dale (Carlton Hotel).
14 30 Board Meeting.

Renew Fire Insurance policy.
Remind Mr. Brown to prepare his speech for Rotary lunch on Friday.
Ring dentist and arrange Mr. Brown's appointment – next week, if possible.
Order typewriter ribbons and carbons.
Renew subscription to *Business Management* magazine.
Correct proofs of Staff Magazine.

NOTE. The entries that actually concern "Mr. Brown" will also appear in his diary, while those relating to the secretary will appear only in hers.

In addition to a diary, you will also find it useful to have at hand a jotting pad, in which to take down telephone messages or scribble notes that are not worth recording in your diary.

Appointments Cards

If your employer's appointments are likely to take him away from the office for a whole day (or even part of a day) he would find it helpful if you were to list his engagements in the form of an *appointments card*, which should be of a convenient size for him to carry around. (You should also prepare for him any material needed in this connection, or see that he has any relevant papers or files of correspondence.)

Card Index Reminder

A simple but effective type of memory aid is the small Card Index, in which cards (measuring approximately five inches by three inches) are arranged vertically in a box or drawer, these cards being divided by twelve projecting guide cards bearing the names of the months. (See pp. 116 & 117.) Any matter requiring attention at a later date is indicated briefly on a card, which is slipped behind the appropriate guide card *in order of date.*

For example, the firm's fire insurance policy expires on the 31st August. Type on a card the note "31st August: renew Fire Insurance policy," and place it behind the *August* guide card, after all the other cards for that month.

NOTE. These cards *must* be referred to daily if the system is to prove effective.

Memoranda Pages of the Secretary's Diary

Where, however, no specific date is mentioned, the memoranda pages of your diary could be used to draw attention to a particular matter. For instance, if instructed to report on the quality and durability of a certain make of typewriter ribbon or brand of carbon paper, you would make the appropriate note in the memoranda pages – remembering to refer to these pages daily to ensure that nothing is overlooked.

Reminder 'Flag' (or Signal) System

This is of great value to the secretary of a doctor or dentist (or, in fact, any employer with many appointments), and may be adapted to either the *Vertical* Card Index or the *Visible* Card Index. (See Chapter 9, p. 118.)

NOTE. The best memory aid is that which is the simplest and quickest.

7

Handling the Mail

Incoming Mail – Outgoing Mail – Correspondence Records – Dispatch of Mail – Certificate of Posting – Recorded Delivery – Urgent Letters – Dispatch of Money – Post Office Guide.

IN a large organization the mail – both incoming and outgoing – is handled in a centralized (and usually highly mechanized) mailing room, the mailing clerks being responsible to a supervisor.

Here the incoming mail is received and distributed to the departments concerned. Where the volume of mail justifies such a device, a mechanical letter-opener (which will cut the edge off each envelope without damage to the contents) is used, the electric models handling approximately five hundred letters a minute. The letters are then date-stamped (a time-stamp being frequently incorporated in the date-stamp) and stamped with a departmental distribution stamp. After being stamped the letters are sorted by means of a device known as a 'document sorter' and then delivered to the departments concerned.

When the outgoing mail has been received in the mailing room it is usually entered in a postage book; and once again its dispatch is considerably expedited by means of a variety of mechanical aids. There are folding machines, sealing and stamping machines, franking machines, etc. There is also a machine that will gather as many as eight enclosures of different sizes, feed them into envelopes, seal the envelopes, count them, and stack them ready for dispatch – at the rate of sixty envelopes a minute!

Incoming Mail

In a small firm or professional office, however, the chief will either open the mail himself or authorize his secretary to do so. If so authorized, she will first carefully put aside all letters marked 'Personal' or 'Private,' as well as those in the recognized handwriting of her employer's friends or relatives. (To open such letters would be a breach of good taste on the part of the secretary.) She will then proceed as follows:

1. *Opening Letters*

(*a*) Open envelopes carefully, in order to prevent damage to the contents.

(*b*) Stamp letters with date-stamp (or date-and-time stamp).

(*c*) Check enclosures and clip or pin neatly to the accompanying letter. (If any enclosure has been omitted a note to this effect should be pencilled on the letter and initialled, and the envelope attached.)

(*d*) Enter in Letters Received Book, if this is normal practice.

NOTE. Before envelopes are placed in the waste-paper basket, they should be held up to strong light to check that all enclosures have been removed.

2. *Sorting Letters*

(*a*) Read through the letters.

(*b*) Sort into appropriately labelled trays – e.g., for Dictation, for Attention by Secretary, for Filing, etc.

3. *Letters containing Remittances*

(*a*) When remittances are received with letters the secretary should make a brief pencilled note at the top of the letter, giving appropriate details – e.g., Chq. £5, P.O. 80p, M.O. £9·50.

(*b*) Uncrossed cheques and postal orders must be crossed.

(*c*) Money should be checked to ensure that it corresponds with the amount stated in the covering letter or accompanying statement.

(*d*) Cheques should be carefully scrutinized to ensure that they are correctly drawn. (If not, the cheque must be returned to the sender at once with a courteous covering letter, pointing out the discrepancy and tactfully requesting that the cheque be altered and the alteration initialled or a fresh cheque drawn.)

NOTE. Letters should be dealt with in order of urgency.

Outgoing Mail

1. *Letters that can be dealt with by the Secretary:*

(*a*) Those that she will write and sign as "Secretary." Considerable tact is called for here and the avoidance of any suggestion of self-importance.

(*b*) Those that she will write on behalf of her employer (usually in his absence), writing her initials after his name, e.g.:

J. B. Brown *or* J. B. Brown
M.S. per M.S.

NOTE. Such letters should *not* be signed "*p.p.* J. B. Brown" unless the secretary has her employer's legal authority to act on his behalf. Such authority is granted by a *power of attorney*, which is a very powerful authority not normally given by a principal to his secretary.

(*c*) Those that she will compose for her employer to sign personally.

It is important that such letters should be clearly and concisely expressed in the chief's customary style and phraseology, and that they should as far as possible be indistinguishable from those normally dictated by him.

2. *Letters that will be dealt with by the Chief:*

Such letters will be dictated to the secretary. In this connection, when taking in letters to her employer for dictation, she should also take in any previous correspondence or relevant papers that are likely to be required.

Should her employer not be available to sign such letters she would then sign "for J. B. Brown," *or* "Dictated by J. B. Brown and signed in his absence."

NOTE. In the chief's absence urgent letters of importance are sometimes received requiring his personal attention. Such letters must be formally acknowledged by the secretary, explaining her employer's absence and indicating that the matter will be dealt with upon his return. She should sign such letters personally, adding her designation, "Private Secretary", e.g.:

Moira Smith

Private Secretary to Mr. J. B. Brown

Correspondence Records

1. *Letters Received Book*

This is used by many firms for recording incoming letters. Each letter, as it is received, is numbered consecutively and recorded in tabular form. The following is a typical form of heading:

Date	No. of Letter	Name of Correspondent	Town	Enclo-sures	Remarks

2. *Postage Book* (or *Stamp Book*)

This important book serves a dual purpose. As its name implies, it records postal expenses incurred by a firm and, at the same time, provides a record of outgoing letters and parcels. The Postage Book, which must be totalled and balanced each week, is usually kept by the *Imprest* system, which operates as follows:

The book is started with, say, £2 in stamps, the stamp value of each outgoing letter or parcel being entered. At the end of the week these amounts are totalled, and stamps to this value (i.e., the value of the *used* stamps) are purchased. This amount, together with the value of the unused stamps in hand, brings the total value at the beginning of each week back to £2 – the amount of 'imprest,' or 'standing float.'

For example, on 1st January, the value of stamps received might be £2. At the end of the week, on 6th January, the total value of stamps used might be £1·48½. The value of stamps purchased on this date would therefore be £1·48½, and this amount together with the value of the unused stamps in hand (51½p) brings the total value, on the 8th January, back to £2 – the amount of imprest.

This information would be recorded as follows:

Dr. Cr.

STAMPS RECEIVED	DATE	NAME	ADDRESS	NATURE OF PACKET	TIME POSTED	POSTAGE
£ p	19–					£ p
2 –	Jan. 1	Smith & Green	Manchester	pcl.	4 p.m.	17½
		Morley Bros.	Liverpool	ltr.	5 p.m.	3
		Smith & Green	Manchester	ltr.	5 p.m.	3
	2	R. S. Malcolm	New York	A/ltr.	5 p.m.	7½
		A. McNab & Co.	Glasgow	ltr.	5 p.m.	3
	3	Galt & Co. Ltd.	Bristol	pcl.	4 p.m.	14
		Galt & Co. Ltd.	Bristol	ltr.	5 p.m.	3
	4	Stuttaford Ltd.	Cape Town	pcl.	4 p.m.	77
		Wade & North	Leeds	R/ltr.	4 p.m.	10
	6	J. McQueen	Glasgow	ltr.	1 p.m.	3
		T. A. Deane	New York	A/ltr.	1 p.m.	7½
						£1 48½
1 48½	6	Cash				
		Balance c/d				2 –
£3 48½						£3 48½
2 –	8	Balance b/d				

It will be realized that where these correspondence records are kept it is possible at any time to trace the receipt or dispatch of a particular letter or parcel.

Dispatch of Mail

If the secretary is responsible for the dispatch of letters she should pay attention to the following points:

(*a*) Check the address on the envelope.

(*b*) Check enclosures, and see that the envelope is large enough and strong enough to hold all the enclosures.

(*c*) Weigh letters of more than average bulk and all foreign letters. Make a pencilled note of the postage in the stamp corner.

(*d*) Ensure that printed matter for abroad is sent by the cheapest method available.

(*e*) Enter every letter in the Postage Book.

(*f*) Register (and obtain receipt for) any letter or parcel that is of especial importance or value.

Certificate of Posting

If proof is required that an *unregistered* letter or postal packet (other than a parcel) has been posted to a particular person, it must be handed in at a Post Office and a 'Certificate of Posting' requested. This involves a small extra charge, payable by means of a postage stamp which must be affixed by the sender to the certificate.

It should be noted, however, that in the event of loss or damage no compensation is available (as in the case of registration or recorded delivery); nor does the certificate furnish proof of the nature of the contents.

A similar certificate may be obtained, free of charge, from the Post Office for an unregistered parcel.

Recorded Delivery

This Post Office service (which is especially suitable for documents) provides proof of posting, a record of delivery, and compensation up to £2 in the event of loss or damage in the post. Any kind of inland postal packet (except a parcel or a railway or air-mail letter) can be sent by the Recorded Delivery service, for which a charge is made additional to postage. (For method of posting see *Post Office Guide*.)

NOTE. Recorded Delivery packets travel in the ordinary unregistered post and are given no special treatment, except that a receipt is taken on delivery and kept at the delivery office. The Post Office does not undertake to deliver a Recorded Delivery packet to the addressee in person.

Advice of Delivery. The sender of a Recorded Delivery packet may arrange, either at the time of posting or subsequently, for an Advice of Delivery to be sent to him. The fee involved will not be refunded if the packet proves to be undeliverable.

NOTE. Recorded Delivery is not suitable for articles that are valuable in themselves. In particular, Recorded Delivery mail must *not* contain money or jewellery, or any other contents with a total cash value in excess of £2.

Urgent Letters

The *Post Office Guide* gives full details of the special Post Office facilities that are available for the dispatch of urgent letters. These are *Special Delivery*, *Express*, and *Railex* Services; and, for letters abroad, *Air Mail* Services. (*Note*. Up-to-date information about the services available by air will be found in the *Air Mail Leaflet*, which is issued monthly by the Post Office.)

Dispatch of Money

The usual method of dispatching money by post is by means of:

(*a*) Cheque;
(*b*) Postal Order;
(*c*) Money Order.

Note that cheques and postal orders should always be crossed.

If coin or bank-notes are dispatched by post they must be enclosed in the special (registration) envelopes provided by the Post Office, and registered.

In addition to Registration, the Post Office also offers an Insurance service, details of which will be found in the *Post Office Guide.*

Post Office Guide

The secretary should familiarize herself with this extremely useful reference book, and should note in particular the regulations relating to inland and overseas post, which will be found under the following headings: Letters and Postcards, Printed Papers, Samples, Newspapers, Parcels, Business Reply Service, Method of Address, Poste Restante, Redirection, Non-delivery, Late Posted Packets, Express Services, Special Delivery, Railway Letters and Parcels, Cash on Delivery, Registration, Recorded Delivery, Air Mail and Surface Mail Services, etc.

8

Filing

Object of Filing – Vertical Method of Filing – Suspension Filing – Coloured 'Signals' – Methods of Classification – Horizontal Method of Filing – Lateral Filing – Micro-filming – Box Files – Pending Files – Fire-proof Filing Cabinets – Transfer of Correspondence – Absent Cards or Out-guides – Centralized Filing – Selection of the most Suitable System – Practical Hints on Filing.

Object of Filing

A *filing system* has been described as "a device whereby documents can be safely preserved in a methodical manner so that they can be referred to quickly and easily."

A good filing system is an essential part of the organization of any firm, and – although in most large firms the bulk of the filing is *centralized* (i.e., carried out in a central filing office) – the private secretary will usually be responsible for the filing of her employer's correspondence.

Vertical Method of Filing

By this method the papers of each correspondent are placed in a manilla folder, all the folders being arranged *vertically* (i.e., in an upright position) in a cabinet of drawers or on shelves.

Suspension Filing

In the most up-to-date filing systems the folders are placed inside 'pockets' which are suspended from the side rails of a light metal frame fitted into the filing drawer. The flat metal top from which each pocket hangs carries the *index title strip* for its particular pocket – i.e., the name, number, or subject of the folder, which has been typed on a strip of paper and slipped beneath a transparent shield attached to the metal top of each pocket. The system is thus completely 'visible,' in that one can see at a glance the title of every folder in the drawer.

Coloured 'Signals'

Where *suspension* filing is in use, a variety of information can be 'signalled' by means of coloured metal or plastic tabs which are affixed to the visible surface of the filing system. A Sales Manager, for instance, might use them for the 'follow-up' of prospective customers. A Production Manager, on the other hand, might find them more useful for indicating which jobs were urgent; while the Accountant of a firm that specialized in credit sales would certainly find them of use as a means of indicating the accounts of customers whose instalments were in arrears.

Methods of Classification

The chief methods of classification of these vertically arranged file-folders are:

(*a*) Alphabetical;
(*b*) Numerical;
(*c*) Alphabetical-numerical;
(*d*) Geographical;
(*e*) Subject.

(*a*) *Alphabetical Method*

This is probably the most common method in use. A folder is made out for each correspondent, the folders being arranged in strict alphabetical order in accordance with the telephone directory system. The following is an example of this system:

Smith, John.
Smith, Jones, Robertson & Co.
Smith, Martin J.

Smith-Parkinson, C. K.
Smith, Sir Robert.
Smythe, Arnold & Co.

NOTE. Under the directory system, names beginning with 'Mac,' 'Mc,' 'M',' etc., regardless of spelling, are all filed under 'Mac.'

Coloured projecting guide cards are used to divide up the letters of the alphabet, A from B and so on, the individual letters being further subdivided (e.g., Aa-Ah; Ai-Am; An-Ar; As-Az) to facilitate reference to the files.

Miscellaneous Folders. A 'miscellaneous' folder is provided at the back of each section for less-frequent correspondence, where the number of letters is not sufficient to justify the use of individual folders. In the event of an increase in correspondence such letters will be transferred from the *Miscellaneous* file to individual files.

Advantages of Alphabetical Classification:

(1) It is simple to understand – since everyone knows the alphabet.

(2) It is *direct* filing – i.e., no separate index is required.

(3) It is capable of expansion – by means of adequate subdivision of the index.

(4) It is convenient to have all the papers referring to the same person, company, etc., in one file.

Disadvantages:

(1) The larger the filing system, the longer it takes to locate a particular file.

(2) It is difficult to estimate how much space will be required for each section.

(3) Letters are often replaced in the wrong file (e.g., A. J. Smith's instead of J. A. Smith's).

(*b*) *Numerical Method*

Under this system each correspondent is allocated a numbered folder, the files being arranged in strict numerical order in the cabinet. Guide cards may be used here to divide up the folders into groups of ten or twenty. Alternatively, distinctive colours may be used to indicate every tenth (or twentieth) file.

This system is widely used in very large firms, as well as in hospitals for filing patients' 'case' sheets.

It will be apparent that, in order to locate a particular file, it is necessary first of all to refer to an alphabetical index, thus linking up names and numbers.

Card Index. This alphabetical index is usually in the form of a card index, the cards being arranged in strict alphabetical order and bearing the name and address of each correspondent, together with his file number.

Advantages of Numerical Classification:

(1) It is simple to operate because numbered files are easily found and are less likely to be replaced incorrectly.

(2) The file number provides a reference number for correspondence.

(3) It is not necessary (as in the alphabetical system) to estimate how much space will be required for each section.

(4) The system is capable of indefinite expansion, as new file numbers are simply added as required to existing ones.

(5) The card index, in addition to providing an index for numerical files, serves many other useful purposes. (See *Office Records and Visual Aids*, pp. 116–117.)

Disadvantage:

It is not *direct* filing, as it requires an alphabetical card index in order to trace a particular file number. It therefore takes a little longer to file correspondence, since reference has first to be made to a card index.

(*c*) *Alphabetical-numerical Method*

This method of classification is a combination of the alphabetical and numerical methods without the use of a separate card index.

Under each letter of the alphabet – and here too the letters may be subdivided – the files are given numbers, and a guide index card in front of each letter contains an index of the numbered files in that letter-group. Each new name added to the system is given the next serial number, which is entered on the appropriate guide card.

Strict alphabetical order within each division is not necessarily followed; e.g., in the subdivision *An-Ar*, Archibald might come before Andrews, which in turn might be followed by Anderson.

(*d*) *Geographical Method*

Geographical (or regional) filing is widely used by firms that employ sales representatives, agents or travellers, and where it is necessary to divide the country into a number of sales territories. All correspondence and relevant reports are filed under such geographical areas – usually in alphabetical order; e.g., Ayrshire would follow Argyllshire, Devon would come before Dorset, and so on.

(*e*) *Subject Filing*

Under this system correspondence is filed according to its subject-matter, and not according to the names of the correspondents. For example, there might be folders for *Advertising*, *Rates*, *Staff Welfare*, etc., the various subjects being filed in alphabetical order.

Should a letter deal with two or more subjects, it will be necessary to make out a 'cross-reference' card or sheet, indicating where the original letter has been filed, and to place a copy of it on each file to which it refers.

Horizontal Method of Filing

This method – which involves the storing of files in a flat, horizontal position in special cabinet drawers or on shelves – is *not* recommended for the filing of general correspondence for the reason that access to files is more difficult and cumbersome. It is, however, suitable for filing stencils, maps, photographs, drawings and plans, etc.

Lateral Filing

An important feature of the *lateral* method of filing is the saving effected in floor space. This is achieved by making use of *height*, which is not possible with the orthodox filing cabinet. Five or six shelves can be accommodated in one lateral filing 'unit,' all the files being easily accessible from floor level without the use of steps, etc. The files are suspended from rails *side by side*, and are fitted with adjustable title-holders which enable the titles to be read at, above, or below eye-level.

NOTE. An ordinary vertical cabinet drawer (when open) takes up approximately 1¼ metres of space, whereas a lateral filing unit takes up only half a metre.

Microfilming

This method of photographing and reducing in size original documents, such as financial records, sales invoices, etc., is very popular with many large firms and organizations, largely because of the tremendous saving of storage space. Microfilming would not, of course, be used for current correspondence, which requires frequent reference.

Box Files

Where correspondence is infrequent and limited in scope, or where an auxiliary file is required for correspondence of a specialized or temporary nature, box files may be used to advantage. These boxes, which are usually made of cardboard, are obtainable in the standard sizes. The papers are filed under alphabetical index sheets and are held in place by a spring clip, or the file may be of the lever-arch type.

Pending Files

Pending files are used to file letters that cannot be answered immediately. The contents of the file may be arranged alphabetically, numerically, etc. – or in date order. It will be obvious that such files must be checked frequently to ensure that nothing is overlooked.

Fire-proof Filing Cabinets

Ordinary steel cabinets do not, as a rule, safeguard their contents from the risk of fire. Really important documents, such as credit-sale ledger accounts, should be stored each night in special fire-proof cabinets, as the financial loss to the firm would be considerable if such records were to be lost in a fire.

Transfer of Correspondence

In order to prevent a filing system from becoming cluttered up with 'dead' material – i.e., old records that are scarcely ever referred to – such records should be periodically transferred (say, every twelve to eighteen months) to transfer storage cases or boxes.

When dealing with correspondence it is desirable to remove the entire contents of the files at the end of each calendar year and to place them in transfer files, leaving the folders free for use the following year.

These transfer cases or files should be consecutively numbered, the transfer being recorded on the current file or on transfer record cards, so that reference can be made to the papers at any time.

Absent Cards or Out-guides

A frequent cause of delay and inconvenience is to find that a file has been removed from its place in the cabinet, necessitating a lengthy and annoying search from one department to another in an attempt to trace it. This can be avoided by the use of 'absent cards,' 'out-guides,' or 'tracers' as they are sometimes called, which are inserted in the cabinet in place of the missing files.

Such a card records: (*a*) the name or number of the file; (*b*) the name or signature of the person to whom issued; and (*c*) the date. It remains in the cabinet until the file is returned and the entry on the card cancelled.

Centralized Filing

Centralized filing, as its name implies, is carried out in a central filing office.

Advantages. The chief advantages of such a system are:

(1) Since all the files are kept in one room, greater control can be exercised over the filing system.
(2) The filing is carried out by a special filing staff, thereby resulting in greater efficiency.
(3) Departmental code letters (e.g., 'C' for Claims Department, 'S' for Staff Department, 'PT' for Publicity and Travel Department) may be used to provide a reference number for correspondence.
(4) Accommodation is more economically used.

Disadvantages:

(1) Files are not as readily accessible as those kept in the department.
(2) The system of filing in use in the central filing department is not always suited to the requirements of the individual department.
(3) The larger the filing system, the more difficult it is to handle.

Selection of the most Suitable System

In any business the filing system adopted should be that which

(*a*) gives the quickest reference;
(*b*) is easy to understand and to operate;
(*c*) is suited to the requirements of the business; and
(*d*) bears relation to the accommodation available.

Practical Hints on Filing

(1) *Sort and classify all letters before starting to file.* If this is not done, considerably more time will be wasted in moving from one filing cabinet to another, and in opening and

shutting drawers, than in the actual filing. Alphabetical document sorters are in use in many firms, and they simplify the task of sorting and classifying.

(2) *Strict date order must be followed in filing*, the most recent letter always being on top.

(3) *The files and their contents must be kept tidy.* Do not allow papers to stick out untidily. Renew the folders as soon as they begin to show signs of wear, and write or type the index labels neatly and clearly. Stencil lettering is very effective, and stencils suitable for use on files (e.g., "Econasign") can be obtained very cheaply. (NOTE. The stencils will also be found useful for office notices that might be required from time to time.)

(4) *Do not allow folders or filing drawers to become overcrowded.* Transfer out-of-date material to a 'dead' file, and make a note on the current file of the 'dead' file number, so that it may be referred to at any time. (See Transfer of Correspondence, p. 112.) When current files relating to important customers or clients become too full the material can be divided into two or more separate files.

(5) *Do not remove individual letters or documents from a file.* If any letter is required the entire file (not just the letter itself) should be removed from the cabinet, and an 'Absent' marker or card inserted in its place. (See Absent Cards or Out-guides, p. 112.)

(6) *Use 'Miscellaneous' folders for less-frequent correspondence*. (See p. 108.)

(7) Where a letter can be filed under more than one heading or file title, choose the most appropriate heading and *insert a cross-reference card or sheet* indicating the file in which it will be found *under the alternative headings.* (See Subject Filing, p. 110.)

(8) *File daily*, so that the last letter is always available for reference.

9

Office Records and Visual Aids

Card Indexing – Vertical Card Index – Visible Card Index – Advantages of the Card Index System – Purposes for which a Card Index is used – Loose-leaf System – Reminder Signals, or 'Flags' – Press Cuttings – Follow-up (Bring-forward) Systems – Strip Indexing – Visual Control Boards – Graphs – Tabulation – Pictorial Display.

Card Indexing

IN addition to a filing system, certain records are kept by every firm. These records may take many forms, one of the most useful being the *card index system.*

Object of Card Indexing

The object of the card index system is to provide a quick, accurate, and easy means of reference to desired information.

There are two main types:

(*a*) Vertical System.
(*b*) Visible System.

Vertical Card Index

A separate card is made out for each customer, client, or patient, as the case may be – the cards being arranged in strict alphabetical order and placed in an upright position in cabinet drawers or boxes.

Stiff, projecting guide cards are used to divide up the letters of the alphabet, A from B and so on, the individual letters being further subdivided if necessary.

Visible Card Index

This is the modern alternative to the vertical card index. Under this system approximately 60–70 cards are held flat in transparent plastic covers in a shallow 'tray' or drawer, each card overlapping its neighbour by a quarter of an inch, so that only the name or subject, together with any other essential particulars, can be seen. These tray-drawers are usually contained in cabinets, and when any tray is pulled out all the cards in that tray are seen simultaneously.

The chief advantage that this system has over the *vertical* is that of *quick visibility* – all the cards being seen at a glance. It is also very suitable for the employment of reminder signals, or 'flags.' (See p. 188.)

Advantages of the Card Index System

1. Because of the strict alphabetical arrangement of the cards, the desired information can be found very quickly.
2. The cards are easily handled, removed, or replaced.
3. They may be typewritten – resulting in a much neater record.
4. Obsolete cards can be withdrawn and new cards inserted without interfering with the continuity of the record.
5. A great deal of information can be contained on each card.
6. Reminder signals, or 'flags,' may be affixed to the cards to draw attention to essential information.
7. The use of different-coloured cards for classified information enables one set of cards to provide a variety of information.

Purposes for which a Card Index is used

1. As an *index to numerical files* (see p. 109), thus linking up names and numbers and at the same time providing a useful record of names, addresses, and telephone numbers of clients or patients.

2. As a *memory aid or card index reminder*, in which the cards are divided by twelve projecting guide cards bearing the names of the months. Any matter requiring attention at a later date is indicated briefly on a card, which is slipped behind the appropriate guide card in order of date. (see p. 97.)

3. As a *substitute for bound book records* – e.g., Ledger accounts.

Advantages:

(*a*) Closed or 'dead' accounts can be withdrawn.

(*b*) It is not necessary to estimate, as in a book, the amount of space an account is likely to require.

(*c*) Cards can be typed neatly and quickly.

(*d*) Classification is easier.

4. For *Medical and Dental Work.* Such cards are ruled in tabular form and, in addition to the patient's name, address, and file number, indicate briefly details of treatment and attention given, date and time of appointment, and (in the case of private patients) account for services rendered.

5. For *Schools, Colleges, or Institutions.* Particulars included on the card are: student's or inmate's name and address; file number; date admitted; date left; and (in the case of schools or colleges) brief particulars of examinations passed. The back of the card is often ruled as a Ledger account in which fees due and paid are recorded.

6. As a *Subscriber's Record*, indicating name and address, subscriber's number, date on which subscription is due, and an account showing amounts paid and dates on which paid.

7. As a *Library Catalogue*, which operates as follows: a card is made out for each book in the library, indicating the name of the author, the contents of the book, and where it is to be found. To facilitate reference, there are usually *two* such catalogues – one in which the cards are arranged according to the name of the author, and the other according to the subject-matter of the book. (Thus, if a reader desired the book of an author known to him he would refer to the first catalogue; if he desired a book upon a certain subject he would refer to the second catalogue.)

Loose-leaf System

The loose-leaf system is another substitute for the bound book record, and has many uses such as bank statements, minutes, accounts, etc.

It should be noted that in the case of a *visible* loose-leaf book coloured signals, or 'flags,' may be employed to advantage (see below).

Advantages of the Loose-leaf System

(1) The loose leaves are easily handled, removed, or replaced without interfering with the continuity of the record.

(2) Obsolete or 'dead' accounts or records can be withdrawn, and new leaves inserted as required, so that the book is 'perpetual.'

(3) It is not necessary, as in a bound book, to estimate the amount of space an account or other record is likely to require.

(4) The pages can be typewritten.

Disadvantage

Pages may be lost or misplaced, or even tampered with.

NOTE. In the case of private accounts or confidential work, such as minutes, the following special precautions should be taken: the loose-leaf binder must be locked, the key being held by the person responsible, who alone should unlock it, issue the blank pages required (which must be consecutively numbered), and insert new matter.

Reminder Signals, or 'Flags'

The card index system provides an easy means of drawing attention to important dates or other information by the use of reminder signals, or 'flags.' These are movable coloured tabs, which are attached to the top of the card (in a *vertical* card index) or to the lower edge of the card (in a *visible* card index).

Signalling devices can be used for a variety of purposes, e.g.:

(*a*) to indicate the financial standing of customers;
(*b*) to record quantities of stock items;
(*c*) to draw attention to dates when 'follow-up' action is required;
(*d*) to draw attention to dates and times of appointments.

Medical or Dental Work

It should be noted that cards for medical or dental work may be obtained ready printed with the day of the month and the hour of the day – the name and address of the patient being typed on the visible edge of the card. When an appointment is made for a patient a coloured signal is placed against the appropriate date and time.

Every morning the secretary ascertains the appointments for the day by running her eye down the index and noting the signals placed against that date. She then withdraws those cards and places them on the doctor's (or dentist's) desk in order of appointment. After the patient's visit the signals are moved on to the next appointment.

Different-coloured signals can be used, if necessary, to record various types of information. For example, one colour might indicate the appointments for the day, and a second colour reminders of quarterly or half-yearly visits.

Press Cuttings

The Press Cuttings Book is another record that appears in many offices. It may take the form of a subject file, the cuttings being pasted on A4 paper and filed and indexed under subjects; or, where the number of cuttings is very limited, they may be pasted in an indexed scrap-book. Another method is to paste the cuttings in the Press Cuttings Book in date order, and to index them separately.

NOTE. All cuttings should indicate the date and name of newspaper from which taken.

Follow-up (Bring-forward) Systems

A *follow-up* (or *bring-forward*) system is simply a type of memory aid. Its purpose is to ensure that matters requiring attention at a later date are not overlooked.

If, for example, the Sales Manager has been instructed to submit a fortnightly report to the General Manager, it would be your responsibility as his secretary to bring this matter to his notice at the appropriate time.

There are several methods that would be found equally effective, and three of them are mentioned here.

(1) *Card Index Reminder System.* This system, which is particularly quick and easy to operate, is described in the section on Diaries and Memory Aids (p. 97). Briefly, a note is made on a 'tickler' card as follows:

Sales Report due 5.3.19–

and the card placed in the correct position behind the March guide card.

Similar cards (dated 19.3.19–, 2.4.19–, 16.4.19–, and so on, at fortnightly intervals) are placed in date order behind the appropriate card, these cards being referred to daily, of course, to ensure that nothing is overlooked.

(2) *Follow-up Filing System.* Instead of using a card index, divided by twelve guide cards bearing the names of the months, the 'follow-up' filing drawer contains twelve pockets titled January to December – the pocket for the current month containing a file which is subdivided by thirty-one insert sheets representing the days of the month. 'Tickler' cards or memos are filed in the appropriate monthly pocket of the 'follow-up' cabinet – those for the current month being inserted behind the appropriate daily insert. At the end of the current month these memos are removed and the file containing the daily inserts is transferred to the pocket for the following month.

As with the reminder card system, the 'follow-up' files must be referred to *daily.*

NOTE. The actual correspondence to which the 'tickler' memo refers is filed away in its proper file, where it can be found when required.

(3) *Visible Card Index.* The 'follow-up' record may, however, be in the form of a 'visible' card index, which is ruled and printed as required. A great deal of useful information may be contained on both sides of the card – the name of the customer or 'prospect' appearing on the visible edge of the card, which is printed with a year scale indicating months and (if necessary) weeks.

In addition to indicating the appropriate date – for instance, the month or week of the last or next intended call – the coloured signals convey a variety of additional information; e.g., 'hot' prospects are picked out by red signals, while a proposed 'trade-in' transaction might be shown by a blue signal.

Strip Indexing

Where information needs to be recorded for quick and frequent reference – such as names, addresses, and telephone numbers – the *strip-indexing system* will be found both useful and efficient.

The various items of information are recorded on separate strips, which are arranged one above the other in alphabetical, numerical, or other desired order, so that all the information contained in them is clearly visible. These strips may be attached to wall panels, desk stands, revolving units, or cabinets.

OFFICE VISUAL AIDS

Visual Control Boards

Visual control boards are intended to provide the busy executive with a summary of the essential facts contained in his detailed records. They can be used in the control of production and sales, to indicate progress of contracts and the movement of stores; they can show trends in expenditure and the allocation of personnel, etc.

There are various types of control board. One of the more common consists of a framework on which are built up a series of adjustable channels, each providing one main line of information. Within these channels, coloured markers or signals can be moved freely, showing progress of the separate factors which each represents.

Graphs

The use of graphs for comparative purposes is of considerable value in business. Instead of being obliged to wade through a mass of facts and figures, the business man can see at a glance the essential information he requires presented simply and clearly in the form of a graph. There are two types of graph:

(*a*) Line Graph.
(*b*) Bar Graph.

Line Graphs

Shown below is an example of a simple line graph used for the purpose of recording shop takings, which are as follows:

Monday	£130
Tuesday	£140
Wednesday (early-closing day) . .	£115
Thursday	£135
Friday	£150
Saturday	£165

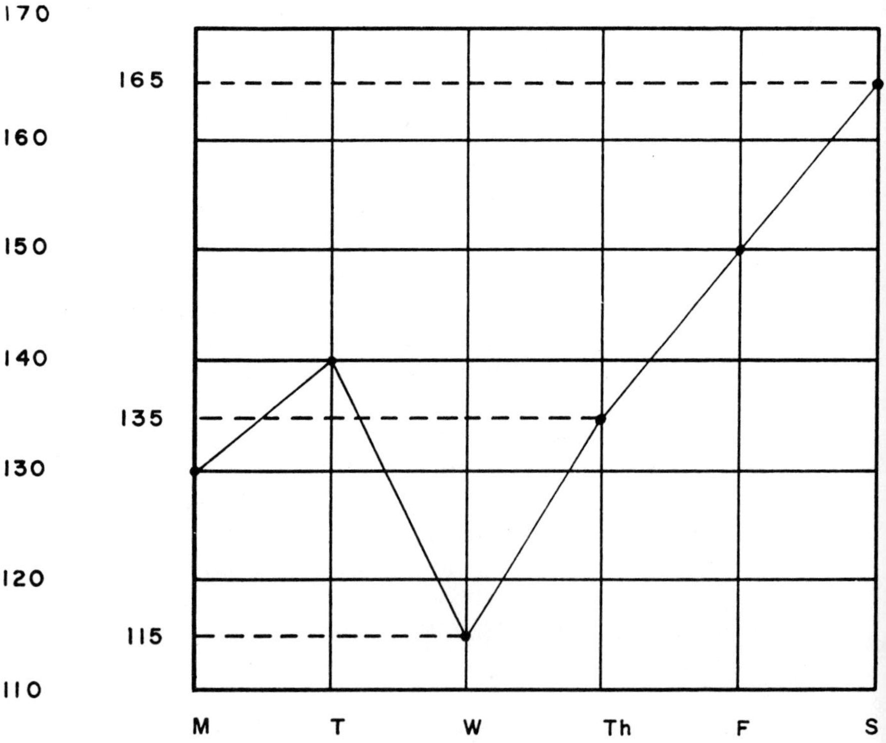

Fig. 1. Line graph recording shop takings

It will be seen that the base line accommodates the days of the week, while the amounts or takings are shown on the left-hand vertical line. When the positions of the different figures

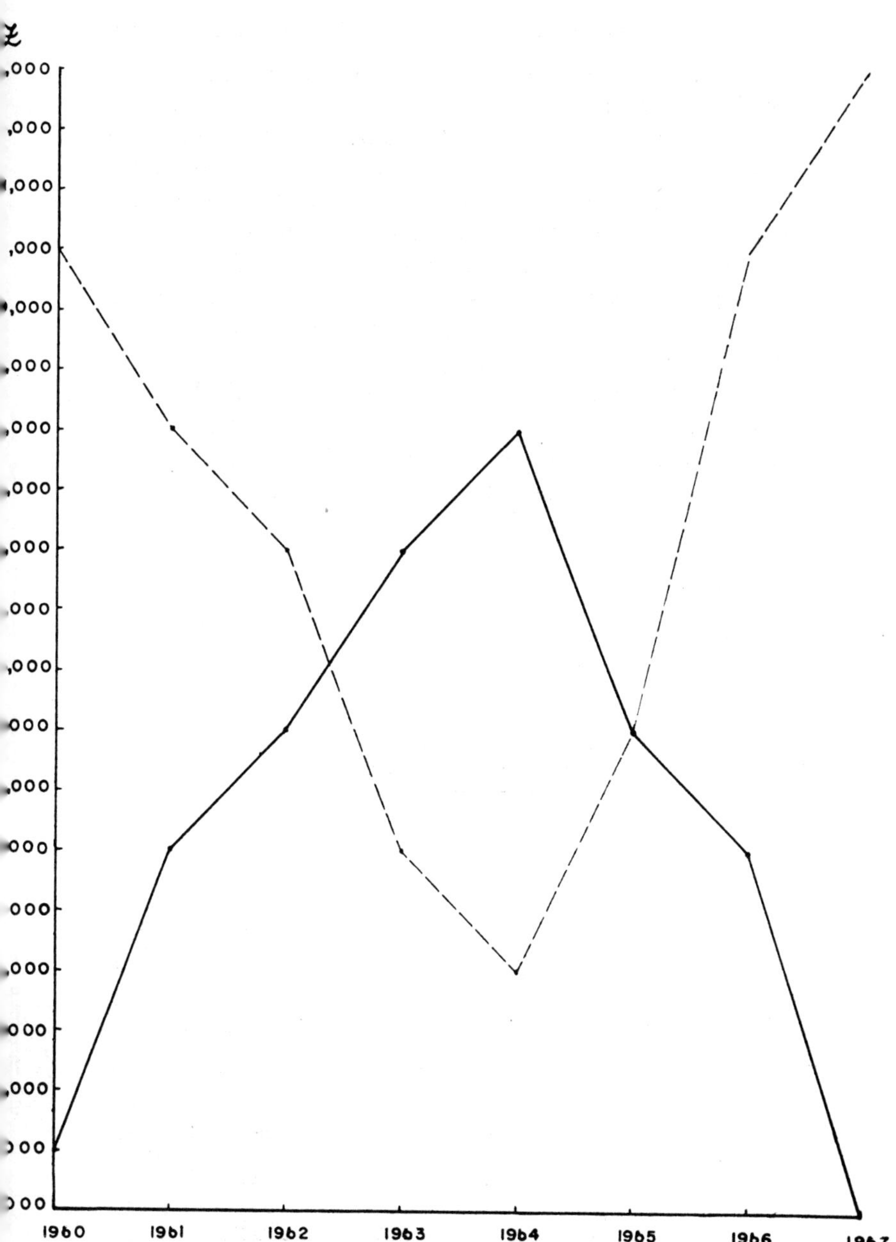

— LONDON BRANCH – – – PROVINCIAL BRANCH

Fig. 2. Line graph showing comparative sales

have been plotted they are joined by a continuous line – thus making a graph.

If desired the graph could be extended, for instance, to show the takings for the remainder of the month; or a comparison might be made with the corresponding figures for the previous week (or the same week in the previous year) by drawing distinctive lines to represent this information.

Figure 2 on p. 123 illustrates the use of line graphs for comparative purposes. A further example of a simple line graph is given on p. 126 (Fig. 5).

Line graphs can be used to display a great deal of statistical information – e.g., the ratio of expenses to sales; the ratio of profit to capital invested; imports and exports; cost of living; birth, death, and marriage rates; temperatures, etc.

Bar Graphs

The following examples illustrate the use of bar graphs:

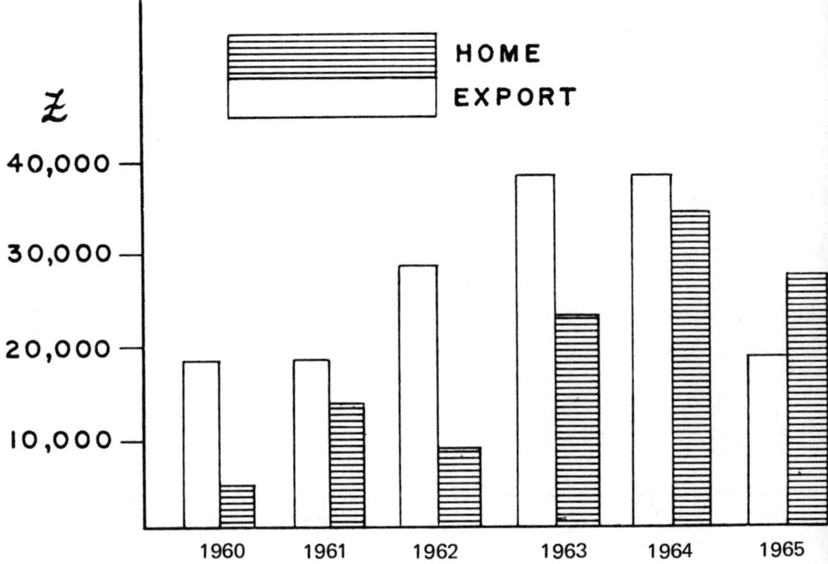

Fig. 3. Bar graph showing comparative sales

Bar graphs are used to display similar information to that shown in line graphs, but are generally more effective for showing and contrasting figures for short periods. In a bar graph individual bars are used instead of continuous lines to represent each week or month, etc.

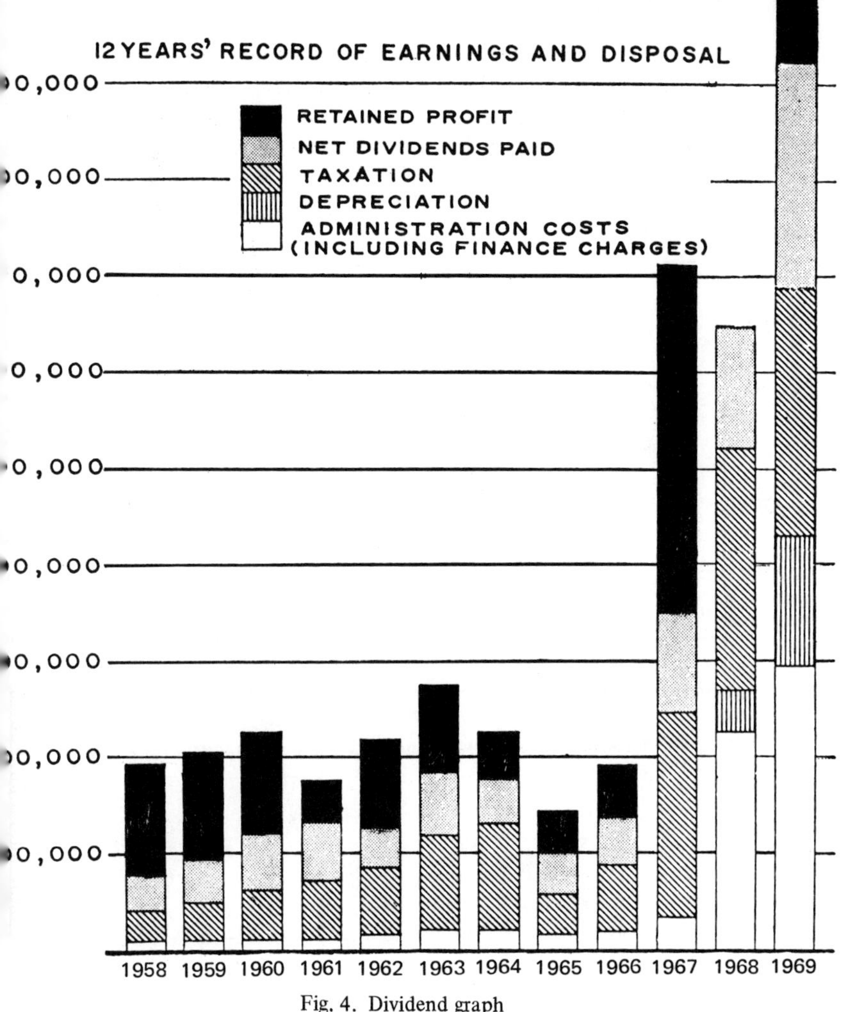

Fig. 4. Dividend graph

Tabulation

In addition to graphs, typewritten tabulation statements are very widely used in business offices as a means of displaying and comparing information. Tabulation is particularly suitable where several departments or products involving large amounts are concerned.

Pictorial Display

Yet another method of displaying information is by means of simple pictures. Pictorial methods of display are especially useful for drawing attention to important facts and figures in newspapers, magazines and booklets, posters, etc.

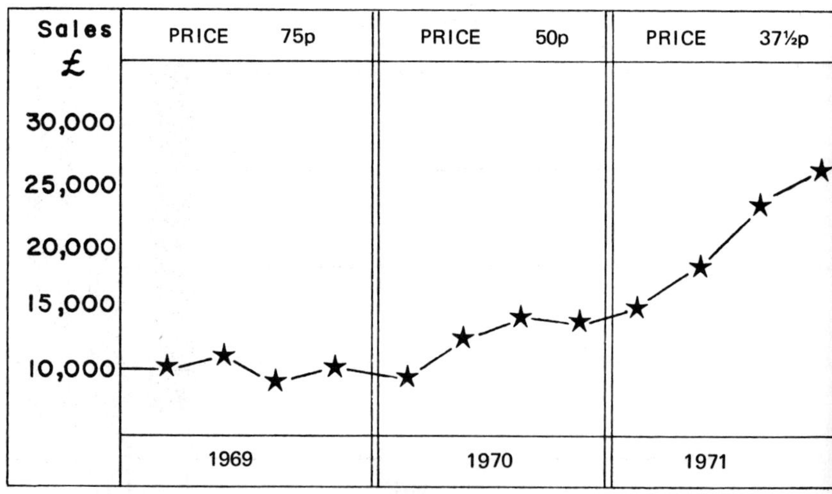

Fig. 5. Graph showing changes in sales and prices of a commodity over a period of three years.

10

Sources of Information

Reference Libraries – Commercial Libraries – Dewey Decimal Classification – General Reference Books – Special Reference Books: People, Places and Travel, Financial, Political, Literary, Legal, Medical, Engineering, Education, The Church, The Services, Trade Directories – Other Sources of Information – Travel Arrangements.

Reference Libraries

IT is an important secretarial qualification to know just where to find any information that may be required – and to find it quickly. Most of this information will be found in reference books, and it is essential for the secretary to know how to use the principal books of reference.

That excellent book *English Exercises for Secretaries*, by R. A. Kelly, in a section entitled "Reference and Practical Work," gives the following helpful rules for fact-finding:

1. *Refer to the general reference book first.* If the detail given there is insufficient, the reader will be guided to a more specialized work.
2. Make sure you know the difference between *Contents* and *Index*.
3. Learn how to use an index properly. Do not 'flip' desperately through the reference book, but find out how the material is arranged. Use that arrangement to save time and labour, and be prepared for centre indexes, special sections, etc.
4. Practice the quick method of referring to an alphabetically arranged book. It is surprising how many people waste time thumbing slowly and meticulously over the early sections of a dictionary when the word they want is much further on. Open the book approximately at the middle pages, and flick the pages through at speed with your

thumb, moving in the appropriate direction and watching the sample words or roots given as guides at the top of each page.

5. Learn to search for alternative classifications in an index. If you are looking for information about Filing, you may not find it in the index under that heading – it may be entered as a sub-section under Secretarial Duties.

Commercial Libraries

Commercial libraries are to be found in all big cities and are maintained for the benefit of the business community. A commercial library may be a department of a public library, and is simply a huge collection of directories – trade directories, professional directories, telephone directories, cable codes (e.g., *A.B.C.* and *Bentley's*), newspapers and trade periodicals, the most important of which are filed away after current use.

Dewey Decimal Classification

This is a system of arranging books in libraries in subject order. The majority of the libraries in Great Britain are classified under this system. It is also used extensively in the United States of America and on the Continent.

A numerical notation is used to indicate both the subject of the book and its place on the shelf. There are ten main classes, viz.:

000–General Works
100–Philosophy
200–Religion
300–Social Sciences
400–Language
500–Natural Science
600–Applied Science or Useful Arts
700–Fine Arts and Recreations
800–Literature
900–History, Biography, and Travel

Each of these main classes is divided into ten sections; for example, 600 (Applied Science) is divided into:

610–Medical Sciences
620–Engineering
630–Agriculture

640—Domestic Economy
650—Commerce
660—Chemical Technology
670—Manufactures
680—Mechanic Trades
690—Building Construction

Each section may be further divided as follows:

650 (*Commerce*)—
651—Office Economy
652—Typewriting, etc.
653—Shorthand
654—Telegraph, Cables, etc.
655—Printing and Publishing
656—Transport
657—Book-keeping and Accounts
658—Business Methods, Industrial Management, etc.
659—Advertising, etc.

Each sub-section may, by decimals, be further divided into still smaller sections – e.g., 655.1, 655.2, 655.3, etc.

The great advantage of the Dewey Decimal Classification is that even in a strange town it is a simple matter to locate a particular book merely by knowing its classification or by referring to the Subject Index. A further advantage is that books on related subjects are arranged close together on the library shelves.

General Reference Books

There are several *general* reference books that should prove useful to most secretaries. They include the following:

(1) *English Dictionary.* A good English dictionary (e.g., *The Concise Oxford Dictionary*) is indispensable and should always be referred to when in doubt about the meaning or spelling of a word.

(2) *Shorthand Dictionary.* This should also be part of the equipment of both the secretary and the shorthand-typist. *Pitman's English and Shorthand Dictionary* is a most useful book in that it combines (1) and (2).

(3) *The Dictionary of Typewriting* (Pitman). An excellent reference book, which is alphabetically arranged and deals with all matters relating to typewriting and typewriters.

(4) *A Dictionary of Correct English* (Pitman) contains much helpful information and advice on points of grammar, idiom, style, use of words, punctuation, spelling, correct pronunciation, etc.

(5) *A Dictionary of Modern English Usage* (Oxford University Press). An extremely useful reference book dealing with points of grammar, idiom, and style that arise every day.

(6) *Whitaker's Almanack.* (Published annually.) This is probably the most useful of general reference books, as it contains a vast amount of information likely to be of interest to the private secretary. The list of contents will give some idea of the variety of information to be found in *Whitaker.*

(7) *Post Office Guide.* Another very useful reference book, which gives details of all the services provided by the Post Office – postal, telephone, telegraphic, remittance, etc. It is issued annually (usually in July) by the Post Office, and is kept up to date by monthly supplements.

(8) *Telephone Directories.* In addition to providing an index to telephone subscribers – names, addresses, and telephone numbers – the front pages of the directory furnish a great deal of useful information regarding telephone services. *Classified* Telephone Directories contain names of professional men and commercial firms, arranged according to *occupation*; e.g., under 'A' would be found Accountants, under 'B' – Butchers, under 'S' – Solicitors, etc.

(9) *Post Offices in the United Kingdom* (published by the Post Office). Most helpful to the secretary in enabling her to verify postal addresses and place-names.

(10) *Local Street Directory and Map.*

(11) *Kelly's Directories.* Published for the principal cities and towns, and divided into four main sections:

(*a*) General Directory – list of residents and firms, arranged in alphabetical order.
(*b*) Street Directory – alphabetically arranged.
(*c*) Professions and Trades Directory – alphabetically arranged.
(*d*) Official Directory – containing details of Parliamentary, county, municipal, and postal information, etc.

(12) *Railway Time-tables*

(*a*) *A.B.C. Railway Guide*. (Issued monthly.) This is alphabetically arranged, and gives times of departure and arrival of trains between the town of issue and the station of destination (but does not include details of stations or changes en route). It also gives details of fares, as well as brief but useful information about each town – population, early-closing day, etc.

(*b*) *Regional Time-tables* (issued by British Rail).

(13) *Titles and Forms of Address* (published by A. and C. Black). Contains very full information on the use of titles and the correct way to address persons of title and rank. It also includes a list of abbreviations and gives the pronunciation of a large number of surnames.

(14) *Ready Reckoner.* Useful for the more complicated calculations of both quantities and money.

(15) *The Annual Register.* A summarized record of important world events. There are four main sections: Great Britain, the Commonwealth, Foreign, and a section covering Art, Law, Finance, Trade, etc. (Published continuously since 1758.)

(16) *Keesing's Contemporary Archives* (published continuously since 1931). A weekly diary of world events. It is issued each week in the form of loose-leaf news pages, which are sent to subscribers by post for filing in a special binding case. Because of its cumulative index, Keesing's is invaluable as an up-to-date work of reference.

The information contained in the diary is selected from the world's leading newspapers, as well as from the official Government Information Departments and the recognized International News Agencies.

A useful feature of the service is the 'cut-back' index. At the end of each report reference is made to the page number of the previous entry dealing with the same or related subjects. This makes it possible to trace back the development of every item from the most recent event to its very earliest mention without having to refer again to the alphabetical index.

(17) *The World Almanack.* The American equivalent of *Whitaker*, but with greater emphasis on the U.S.A.

(18) *Encyclopaedias:*

(*a*) *Encyclopaedia Britannica.*
(*b*) *Chambers's Encyclopaedia* (Pergamon).
(*c*) *Everyman's Encyclopaedia* (Dent).

The three most important general encyclopaedias in the English language, containing information on all subjects, and arranged in alphabetical order of subject.

(*d*) *Pears Cyclopaedia* (Pelham Books). This is a compact and useful single-volume work, divided into twenty-one sections including: Important Events, Prominent People, Gazetteer and Atlases, General Information, etc.

Special Reference Books

Other reference books of a more specialized nature, which will be found useful by many private secretaries, are:

People

Who's Who. (Published annually.) Gives brief biographical details of prominent contemporaries in this country, and includes a few well-known names of other nationalities. (Also *Who Was Who*, which gives information about distinguished people who have died.) Specialist versions include: *Who's Who in the Theatre*, *Who's Who in Science*, *Who's Who in Literature*, etc., as well as those relating to prominent people in other countries – *Who's Who in America*, *in Canada*, *in New Zealand*, etc.

International Who's Who. (Also published annually.) Gives information about world-famous people of all nationalities.

Debrett's Peerage, Baronetage, Knightage, and Companionage (usually referred to as "Peerage and Titles of Courtesy").

Burke's Peerage, Baronetage, and Knightage.

Burke's Genealogical and Heraldic History of the Landed Gentry ("Landed Gentry").

Kelly's Handbook to the Titled, Landed, and Official Classes.

These four books give biographical notes regarding persons of title or rank, or those occupying official positions. They are useful reference books, especially in professional offices, in that they enable the secretary to check the names, titles, or qualifications of correspondents.

The Dictionary of National Biography, which may be consulted at any public library. The original *D.N.B.* comprised sixty-three volumes, but was later reissued on thinner paper by the Oxford University Press as twenty-two volumes. There are a further five volumes for the twentieth century. It is the most important reference work for English biography, covering the British Isles and the Commonwealth, and includes notable Americans of the Colonial period. There is now a *Concise D.N.B.*, which is an epitome of the main work. It consists of two parts: (1) covering those living from the earliest times until 1900, and (2) from 1901 to 1950.

Places and Travel

The Oxford Atlas (Oxford University Press). This is an inexpensively priced atlas, the detail and colouring of which are remarkably good.

Gazetteers (Geographical dictionaries):

Columbia Lippincott Gazetteer of the World (Columbia University Press). Very comprehensive.

Chambers's World Gazetteer and Geographical Dictionary. A useful desk book.

The Survey Gazetteer of the British Isles (Bartholomew). Gives in alphabetical order brief accounts of all towns, villages, and hamlets, also country seats, forests, lakes, streams, grouse moors, etc.

The Statesman's Year-book (Macmillan). "Statistical and historical annual of the states of the world." Gives concise and reliable information about the Governments of the world. Arranged in four sections: (1) International Organizations; (2) the British Commonwealth; (3) the United States of America; (4) other countries (in alphabetical order). Information is given concerning the constitution and government of each country, area and population, religion, education, justice and crime, finance, production and industry, social services, etc. A useful list of reference books (both statistical and general) is included for each country.

Ward Lock's Guide to the British Isles. Illustrated guide books for all parts of Britain – Lake District, Yorkshire Dales, Norfolk Broads, etc., though most of the volumes of this series are centred on particular resorts.

Fodor's Modern Guides to the Continent (Hodder) – Austria, France, Germany, Spain and Portugal, Switzerland, Scandinavia, etc.

Hotels and Restaurants in Britain (the Official Guide of the British Travel Association). Lists, under their respective towns, the principal hotels and restaurants in this country. In addition to a useful index to Places of Interest, there are also Touring Notes and Sectional Maps of Great Britain and Northern Ireland.

The Good Food Guide (Hodder and The Consumers' Association). (Published annually.) Contains unbiased reports on recommended restaurants and hotels in Great Britain "where you can rely on a good meal at a reasonable price."

The Automobile Association Handbook. (Issued to members of A.A.) In addition to other useful information, there is a comprehensive list of approved hotels classified according to type.

The Royal Automobile Club Handbook. (Issued to members of R.A.C.) Contains similar information.

Railway, Air, and Shipping Guides:

A.B.C. Railway Guide. (See p. 131.)
British Rail Regional and Continental Time-tables.
A.B.C. World Airways Guide.
Airport Times. (International and Regional Services.)
Bradshaw's International Air Guide.
A.B.C. Shipping Guide.
Journal of Commerce (daily) for movements of ships.

(For *Travel Arrangements*, see pp. 140–143.)

Financial

Stock Exchange Official Year Book. (Published annually.) Contains summarized information about companies whose shares are quoted on the Stock Exchange, including particulars of securities, investments, subsidiary companies, directors and officials, etc.

Directory of Directors. (Published annually.) An alphabetical list of the directors of all the principal companies in the United Kingdom, together with the names of the companies with which they are associated.

The Financial Times. (Published daily.) A financial newspaper quoting prices of stocks and shares, also rates of exchange.

The Investors' Chronicle and Money Market Review. (Published weekly.) Also quotes prices of stocks and shares, and contains news about companies and investments, financial reports, etc.

Bankers' Almanac and Year Book. A directory of the principal banks of the world, and the banker's guide to the principal insurance offices. This is the standard international banking reference book.

Insurance Blue Book and Guide. Gives an alphabetical list of insurance companies with particulars of directors, branches, class of business, etc.

Building Societies Year Book. The official handbook of the Building Societies Association.

Political

Municipal Year Book. (Published annually.) Contains information and statistics relating to local authorities in Great Britain and Northern Ireland; also details of members of local councils and their officers.

The Parliamentary Debates (known as "Hansard"). Issued daily by H.M. Stationery Office for both Houses of Parliament; also in a weekly abbreviated version with an index. These official reports of Parliamentary Debates constitute a full (verbatim) record of each day's proceedings.

Dod's Parliamentary Companion. (Published annually.) This is a useful little volume containing a great deal of Parliamentary information – e.g., an alphabetical list giving biographical details of Members of the House of Commons, together with their constituencies; the constitution of the House of Lords with biographies of the peers; Parliamentary terms and proceedings in both Houses of Parliament; details of the Ministry, Government Offices, etc.

Vacher's Parliamentary Companion. (Published quarterly.) Contains a considerable amount of up-to-date Parliamentary information, including details of Members of the House of Commons and of the House of Lords, Cabinet and other

Ministers, and the personnel of Government and Public Offices.

Sir T. Erskine May's Parliamentary Practice (Butterworth). The standard work of reference on Parliamentary procedure for both Houses of Parliament.

Whitaker's Almanack. Although previously referred to as a *general* reference book, the considerable amount of Parliamentary as well as general information contained in *Whitaker* makes it almost indispensable to the secretary of a Member of Parliament. It includes an alphabetical list of Members of the House of Commons, and another of Parliamentary constituencies; a list of Cabinet Members and other Ministers; notes on Parliamentary procedure; an extensive section dealing with Government and Public Offices (the Civil Service); Acts of Parliament passed during the preceding year; and, in addition, a summary of the events of the preceding year in both Houses of Parliament.

Acts of Parliament. It should be noted that copies of all Acts of Parliament are obtainable from H.M. Stationery Office; and annual compilations of the *Public General Acts* are to be found in most reference libraries.

Literary

The secretary to an *author* would find the following reference books useful:

Writers' and Artists' Year Book. (Published by A. and C. Black.) A directory for writers, artists, photographers, and composers. Contains lists of British, Commonwealth, and American journals and magazines, with information as to the kind of material accepted by each and rate of payment; also lists of publishers, literary and art agents, a classified index of papers and magazines, a comprehensive markets section, and other information useful to writers and artists, etc.

Newspaper Press Directory (Benn Brothers Ltd.). An alphabetical list of the newspapers and periodicals published in Great Britain, together with a list of the more important Commonwealth and foreign publications; also a classified list of publications under subject-headings, an alphabetical list of publishers, and a list of news agencies, etc. (Also *Willing's Press Guide*.)

The Bookseller (issued weekly) contains lists of current British publications. These weekly lists are cumulated in *Whitaker's Cumulative Book List* in quarterly and annual volumes. Each issue consists of a classified list of recent publications, with an index to authors and titles.

The Authors' and Writers' Who's Who. Published annually.

Who's Who in the Theatre. Who's Who in Literature.

The Oxford Companion to English Literature. A dictionary of authors, literary works, characters in fiction, drama, poetry, etc.

The Oxford Companion to the Theatre. A comprehensive one-volume encyclopaedia of the theatre in all countries and all periods.

Granger's Index to Poetry (Columbia University Press). Indexes poems by titles, authors, and first lines.

Stevenson's Book of Quotations. Arranged alphabetically according to *subject*, and contains a good index. Most useful for providing the apt quotation to illustrate points in a speech or lecture.

The Oxford Dictionary of Quotations. A list of well-known quotations arranged alphabetically according to *authors' names*, and indexed.

Chambers's Book of Days. "A miscellany of popular antiquities, in connection with the calendar." Useful for journalistic articles.

Roget's Thesaurus of English Words and Phrases (Longman; Penguin). A collection of synonyms and antonyms, classified according to the ideas they express. There is a good index. Most useful in literary composition.

Legal

The Law List. (Issued annually.) A legal directory, giving details of solicitors, barristers, judges, magistrates, etc. There is a separate list for Scotland – the *Scottish Law List.* (Note that the Scottish equivalent of a *barrister* is an *advocate*.)

Stone's Justice's Manual.

The Scottish Justices' Manual. The Scottish Law Directory.

The Councillor's Manual. Acts of Parliament in force, relating to Scotland only.

Osborn's Concise Law Dictionary.
Traynor's Latin Maxims. Definitions of Latin legal terms.
The Parliament House Book.
Valuation Roll. (Also useful as a local directory.)
Whitaker's Almanack.
The various indexes to Acts, Statutes, etc.

Medical

Black's Medical Dictionary.

Medical Directory. (Published annually.) Contains brief biographical details of qualified medical practitioners in Great Britain, arranged alphabetically under surnames.

Medical Register. List of names and addresses of registered medical practitioners.

The Dentists' Register. A similar list of registered dentists.

Medical Who's Who.

Engineering

Kempe's Engineer's Year Book. This covers all branches of engineering – civil, mechanical, aeronautical, etc.

Molesworth's Handbook of Engineering Formulae and Data.

Jones's Engineering Encyclopaedia.

Chambers's Technical Dictionary.

Pitman's Technical Dictionary in Seven Languages.

Education

University calendars, handbooks, and regulations are issued annually for Oxford, Cambridge, and other universities.

Yearbook of the Universities of the Commonwealth.

The World of Learning. (Europa Publications.) Gives details of universities, colleges, scientific institutions, museums, libraries, etc., in all parts of the world.

Scholarships Guide. (Daily Mail.)

Public and Preparatory Schools Year Book. Lists boys' schools.

Girls' School Year Book. Public schools for girls.

Schools. A directory of the schools in Great Britain and Northern Ireland, arranged under counties and towns.

Independent Schools Association Year Book.
Education Authorities Directory and Annual.

The Church

Crockford's Clerical Directory. (Issued annually.) Gives brief biographical details of the clergy of the Church of England, with a great deal of other information about the Anglican communion. Also *The Church of England Year Book.*

The Church of Scotland Year Book. Directory of churches, clergy, and officers of the Church of Scotland.

The Catholic Who's Who and Year Book. (Issued annually.) Gives a great deal of current information about the Roman Catholic Church.

Other Church publications are *The Congregational Year Book*, *The Methodist Year Book*, *The Baptist Handbook*, *The Zionist Year Book*, etc.

The Services

The Navy List.
The Army List.
The Air Force List.

These three official volumes (published by H.M. Stationery Office) are revised periodically, and give the complete officer establishment for each service, arranged under the various branches or regiments; there is also an alphabetical index of serving officers, and another of officers on the retired list.

Trade Directories

U.K. Kompass (in association with the Confederation of British Industry) – two volumes. (Vol. 1) Products and Services (with Classification Index). (Vol. 2) Company Information (with Alphabetical Index of Companies).

Kelly's Manufacturers and Merchants Directory.

Stubbs' Directory. Manufacturers, merchant shippers, business and professional firms (British and Foreign).

Scottish National Register of Classified Trades.

Each branch of trade and industry has its own trade directory, such as the *Building Trades Directory*, *Timber Trades Directory*, *Cotton Trade Directory*, etc.

Other Sources of Information

Information	*Source*
(1) Banking and Foreign Currency.	Bank.
(2) Driving and Road Licences.	Local Motor Taxation Office.
(3) Income Tax and P.A.Y.E.	Local Offices of Inland Revenue.
(4) Insurance of any kind.	Insurance Company or Insurance Broker.
(5) Local Government Matters.	Offices of the County, City, Town, or District Council.
(6) National Insurance.	Local Office of the Department of Health and Social Security.
(7) Passports.	Any Passport or Department of Employment Office, or Travel Agency.
(8) Postal and Telephone Services, etc.	Post Office.
(9) Stocks and Shares.	Stockbroker.
(10) Trade and Technical Journals, Newspapers, Magazines, etc.	Local Reference Library.
(11) Trade and Industry generally.	Local Offices of the Chamber of Commerce.
(12) Travel.	Travel Agency; British Rail; Steamship Company; Airport; A.A. or R.A.C. Offices.

Travel Arrangements

As a secretary you must be able to make your employer's travel arrangements – whether it be a journey by road, rail, sea, or air. Complete arrangements for any such journey can, of course, be made through a travel agency; but you must be able to check that all the travel documents and tickets are in order, and to plan the details of the journey so carefully that no last-minute hitch is likely to disorganize the entire trip.

The secret of planning a successful journey for your principal is to know where to go for information. In addition to having available for your guidance the appropriate books of reference, time-tables, etc., you will find it helpful to make a note of the places where reservations can be made, tickets bought, and the relevant information obtained – e.g., a travel agency, railway or airline office, etc.

A list of *Railway, Air, and Shipping Guides* is given on p. 134, and suitable accommodation may be found by consulting the handbooks of the Automobile Association and the Royal Automobile Club, or that useful reference book issued annually by the British Travel Association – *Hotels and Restaurants in Britain.*

Should your employer be planning a business trip abroad, be sure to keep in touch with the travel agency, airline office, or shipping company handling the arrangements, and seek their advice on matters of currency, health and insurance regulations, passports and visas, baggage allowance, etc. See also *Hints to Business Men Going Abroad*, issued free of charge by the Department of Trade and Industry (there is a separate booklet for each country) and containing a wealth of general information indispensable to the businessman travelling abroad.

NOTE. In regard to the issue or renewal of your employer's passport, the necessary form of application may be obtained from any Passport or Department of Employment Office, or a travel agency.

Preparations for the Journey

(1) Confirm the booking of hotels.

(2) Obtain the tickets for the journey (including those for a reserved seat and sleeping berth, if required).

(3) Check carefully all the travel documents – tickets and reservations, passport, visa, entry and exit permits, etc. – and put them in a strong envelope.

(4) Obtain foreign currency and travellers' cheques (or letters of credit) from the bank. (See *Banking*, pp. 198–199.)

(5) Collect (and place in a folder) all the correspondence and documents your employer will require on his trip, and check these papers with him to ensure that nothing has been omitted.

(6) Prepare a supply of office stationery to enable him to write letters or reports on his trip.

(7) Make arrangements for him to be met at his destination, if necessary.

(8) Prepare and type an itinerary of your employer's journey, giving the departure and arrival times of trains, flights, etc.; the hotels at which he will be staying; and a list of appointments, meetings, etc., together with names and addresses and telephone numbers. (Also keep a copy of the itinerary in your office, so that at any time you will know where he may be contacted, if necessary.)

(9) Discuss with him any outstanding matters and the action (if any) you should take.

SPECIMEN HOTEL BOOKING (Letter of Confirmation)

3rd May, 19–

The Manager,
Claremont Hotel,
London SW7 2AB

Dear Sir,

As requested by telephone this morning, will you please reserve a single room, with private bathroom, for Mr. J. B. Brown for the night of Tuesday, 9th May?

Mr. Brown will be travelling by the night train from Glasgow on Monday, and will require breakfast on his arrival.

Yours faithfully,

EXCELSIOR COMPANY LIMITED

(Moira Smith)
Private Secretary to
District Manager

SPECIMEN ITINERARY

ITINERARY

Monday, 8th May	Depart Glasgow (Central)	22 25
Tuesday, 9th May	Arrive London (Euston)	07 45
	Breakfast at Claremont Hotel	08 30
	District Managers' Conference (at Head Office)	10 00
	Dinner at Claremont Hotel (with Mr. Walker-Douglas)	19 00
Wednesday, 10th May	D.M. Conference – 2nd Day	10 00
	Depart London (Euston)	21 35
Thursday, 11th May	Arrive Glasgow (Central)	06 40

NOTE. "Sleeper" accommodation reserved.

11

Titles and Forms of Address

Appropriate Reference Books – Orders, Decorations, and Degrees – The Peerage – General Rules regarding Titles – Orders of Chivalry – General Rules regarding Orders of Chivalry – Forms of Address: Some General Rules – Foreign Forms of Address (in Correspondence).

IN dealing with correspondence the utmost care must be taken to ensure that the correct form of address is used, the 'address' in this context being the manner in which the writer of the letter addresses the person to whom he is writing.

Appropriate Reference Books

In addressing persons of rank or title there are certain rules that should be observed. These rules are explained very fully in *Titles and Forms of Address* (Black); while *Whitaker's Almanack* has an extensive section devoted to the Peerage and Titles of Courtesy, Orders of Chivalry, and the principal Decorations in order of precedence. *Debrett's Correct Form* (Kelly's Directories Ltd.), in addition to the foregoing information, deals also with the correct procedure to be adopted when organizing and attending functions, precedence of guests, table seating plans, proposing toasts, etc.

When any doubt exists as to the rank of a correspondent reference should be made to one of the following books:

Burke's Peerage, Baronetage, and Knightage;
Debrett's Peerage and Titles of Courtesy;
Kelly's Handbook to the Titled, Landed, and Official Classes;
Burke's Landed Gentry; or *Who's Who.*

A secretary who had a great deal of social work would require an up-to-date edition of some standard book on etiquette; e.g., *Manual of Modern Manners*, by Judith, Countess of Listowel (Odhams).

Orders, Decorations, and Degrees

In addition to verifying the rank of a correspondent, care should be taken to verify the spelling of his name and the correct initials, and also any orders, decorations, or degrees he may possess.

It is customary, in professional or business correspondence, to give correspondents their full complement of orders and degrees; but in private correspondence letters indicating university degrees or membership of professional associations are usually omitted. Note, however, that a *doctorate* must always be indicated; e.g., The Rev. Ernest Jones, D.D.; Robert McLeod, Esq., D.Litt.; Peter Hutchison, Esq., M.D. (*or* Dr. Peter Hutchison – but *not* both 'Dr.' and 'M.D.').

The only decorations for Valour that must be indicated in *all* correspondence (social and professional) are *V.C.* and *G.C.* They must come even before the Orders of Chivalry.

Correct Sequence

Care should also be taken to place orders and degrees, etc., in their correct sequence. Where any doubt exists the appropriate reference book should be consulted.

As a general rule, Orders of Chivalry or Knighthood come first (unless preceded by V.C. or G.C.); then decorations, followed by university degrees; and, finally, professional or non-university qualifications.

Example: Sir John Mortimer, K.C.M.G., D.S.O., D.Sc., F.R.S.

When addressing the holder of several university degrees the lowest is indicated first, leading up to the highest. Note, however, that a higher degree includes a lower degree in the same faculty.

The Peerage

The British Peerage has *five* ranks – Duke, Marquess, Earl, Viscount, Baron.

NOTE. The spelling of the second rank of the Peerage may be either 'Marquess' or 'Marquis.' It is necessary, therefore, to ascertain which form your correspondent uses by referring to *Debrett*, *Burke*, or *Who's Who*.

All Dukes and most Marquesses and Earls take territorial titles (i.e., from the name of a place); e.g., The Duke of Argyll, The Marquess of Milford Haven, The Earl of Essex.

All Viscounts and Barons (and a few Marquesses and Earls) omit the 'of'; e.g., Viscount Falkland, Lord Boothby, Earl Avon.

There are *two* forms of address for any member of the Peerage. One is used socially, and the other formally for official or business purposes.

The title of 'Duke' (or 'Duchess') is the *only* rank of the Peerage that is used in social speech. In the other ranks, from Marquess down to Baron, the prefix 'Lord' (or 'Lady') is used in conjunction with the name. For example, the Marchioness of Ailsa would be addressed as 'Lady Ailsa,' and Viscount Falkland, as 'Lord Falkland.'

In order to distinguish the widow of a previous holder of a title from the wife of the present holder, the word 'Dowager' is used in the inside address of a letter to her or on the envelope, but *never* in the body of the letter or in social speech; e.g., Her Grace the Dowager Duchess of Dundee; The Right Hon. The Dowager Countess of Clovelly.

The alternative form for 'Dowager' – and perhaps the more usual form today – is to use the Christian name with the title; e.g., Her Grace Dorothy, Duchess of Dundee; The Right Hon. Clare, Countess of Clovelly.

Courtesy Titles. All peers have a family name as well as their titles, although in many cases the two are the same. The family name is used by the sons and daughters of peers, except in the case of an *eldest* son of a Duke, a Marquess, or an Earl, who takes the highest of his father's lesser titles as his courtesy title. For example, the eldest son of the Duke of Buccleuch[1] is known as the Earl of Dalkeith, this being his father's second title, while *his* eldest son, Lord Eskdaill, takes his grandfather's third title. The younger sons and daughters have the courtesy style of 'Lord'/'Lady' *or* 'The Hon.' before Christian name and Surname. (See (2) and (3) below; also (5), pp. 151–152.)

General Rules regarding Titles

(1) The prefix 'The' is used only for Peers and Peeresses,[2] and should never be omitted; e.g., The Rt. Hon. Lady Heaton *or* The Lady Heaton.

(2) The use of the Christian name with the title 'Lady' is permissible only to daughters of Dukes, Marquesses, or Earls; e.g., The[3] Lady Jane Ross.

(3) When addressing a *younger* son of a Duke or Marquess his Christian name must be included in his title; e.g., Lord John Cleveland. (Note, however, that the *eldest* son takes, by courtesy, his father's second title – *without* the use of his Christian name.)

(4) The prefix *The Right Honourable* applies to:

(*a*) Any peer lower than a Marquess (who is termed *The Most Honourable*).

(*b*) The Lord Advocate of Scotland ('The Rt. Hon. The Lord Advocate').

(*c*) The Lord Mayors of London, York, Cardiff, Belfast, Dublin, Adelaide, Brisbane, Melbourne, Sydney, Perth (Western Australia), and Hobart (Tasmania) ('The Rt. Hon. The Lord Mayor of —— ').

NOTE. All other Lord Mayors are addressed: The Right Worshipful the Lord Mayor of——; while *Mayors* are addressed: The Worshipful the Mayor of——*or* The Right Worshipful the Mayor of——(in the case of mayors of cities).

[1] Pronounced: *Bu-cloo'*.

[2] Peers and Peeresses by *courtesy* (see pp. 146 & 147) and former wives of Peers do *not* have the prefix 'The Rt. Hon.', etc.

[3] Although the prefix 'The' is now by general custom used in addressing all daughters of the three highest ranks of the Peerage, it should be noted that the practice exists only *by courtesy*, and is not recognized as correct by, for instance, the College of Arms.

(*d*) The Lord Provosts of Edinburgh and Glasgow ('The Rt. Hon. The Lord Provost of Glasgow,' *but* 'The Rt. Hon. John Smith, Lord Provost of Edinburgh').

NOTE. *Provosts* are addressed: Robert Scott, Esq., Provost of —— .

(*e*) Privy Councillors ('The Rt. Hon. John Smith,' if a commoner; but if a *peer* (who is a 'Right Hon.' in his own right) the letters 'P.C.' are added after his name.

(5) The prefix *Honourable* applies to:

(*a*) The *younger* sons of Earls.
(*b*) *All* sons and daughters of Viscounts and Barons.

NOTE. The *eldest* sons of Scottish Viscounts and Barons are addressed as 'Master'; e.g., The Master of Ballantrae.

(*c*) All Justices of the High Court during office ('The Hon. Mr. Justice —— ').
(*d*) Lords of the Court of Session (Scotland).
(*e*) Officially to present and past Maids of Honour.

NOTE. The title 'Honourable' is *never* used in conversation, on invitations and visiting cards, or in the body of a letter. The address on an envelope, however, should read: The Hon. John Scott *or* The Hon. Jane Scott – *without* the addition of 'Mr.' or 'Miss.' *But* the wife of a son of a Viscount or Baron would be addressed (on the envelope) as: The Hon. Mrs. Scott *or* The Hon. Mrs. John Scott.

(6) The title *Lord*, in addition to being the designation of a *Baron*, is also:

(*a*) a judicial title;
(*b*) given of right or by courtesy to Bishops;
(*c*) the general term for any nobleman from a Baron to a Marquess.

Baronets

Baronets do not rank as peers, but the title is hereditary. The holder has the title 'Sir' used with his Christian name and surname. In correspondence he would be addressed as: Sir Frederick Fanshawe, Bt., and in conversation as 'Sir Frederick.'

His wife has the title 'Lady' used with her husband's surname; e.g., Lady Fanshawe.

Joint invitations would be addressed to: Sir Frederick and Lady Fanshawe.

Knights

A knight also has the title 'Sir' used with his Christian name and surname, but in his case the title is *not* hereditary. His wife has the title 'Lady' used with her husband's surname.

A man may be a Knight Bachelor,[1] which means he has simply been knighted, or he may be a member of some Order of Knighthood.

[1] *No* letters are now usually placed after the name of a Knight Bachelor, but the use of the former 'Kt.' is not incorrect.

FORMS OF ADDRESS (IN CORRESPONDENCE)
THE PEERAGE AND TITLES OF COURTESY

TITLE	ENVELOPE *(Formal)*[1]	SALUTATION		COMPLIMENTARY CLOSE *(Formal)*[2]
		Formal	*Social*	
Duke	His Grace The Duke of Dundee	My Lord Duke	Dear Duke of Dundee (*or* Dear Duke)	I have the honour to be (*or* to remain), my Lord Duke, Your Grace's obedient servant,
Duchess	Her Grace The Duchess of Dundee	Madam	Dear Duchess of Dundee (*or* Dear Duchess	I have the honour to be (*or* to remain), Madam, Your Grace's obedient servant,
Marquess *or* Marquis	The Most Hon. The Marquess of Melrose	My Lord Marquess (*or* My Lord)	Dear Lord Melrose	I have the honour to be, my Lord Marquess (*or* my Lord), Your Lordship's obedient servant,
Marchioness	The Most Hon. The Marchioness of Melrose	Madam	Dear Lady Melrose	I have the honour to remain, Madam, Your Ladyship's obedient servant,

[1] The *social* form of address (on envelope) usually *omits* the distinctive prefix (*Rt. Hon.*,etc.), thus: The Earl of Essex, The Viscount Vale, The Lord Blair, etc.

[2] The *social* form of complimentary close is usually 'Yours sincerely.'

THE PEERAGE AND TITLES OF COURTESY

TITLE	ENVELOPE	SALUTATION		COMPLIMENTARY CLOSE
		Formal	*Social*	(*Formal*)
Earl	The Rt. Hon. The Earl of Essex	My Lord	Dear Lord Essex	I have the honour to be, my Lord, Your obedient servant,
Countess	The Rt. Hon. The Countess of Essex	Madam	Dear Lady Essex	I have the honour to remain, Madam, Your Ladyship's obedient servant,
Viscount	The Rt. Hon. The Viscount Vale	My Lord	Dear Lord Vale	I have the honour to be, my Lord, Your obedient servant,
Viscountess	The Rt. Hon. The Viscountess Vale	Madam	Dear Lady Vale	I have the honour to remain, Madam, Your Ladyship's obedient servant,
Baron	The Rt. Hon. Lord Blair	My Lord	Dear Lord Blair	I have the honour to be, my Lord, Your obedient servant,
Baroness	The Rt. Hon Lady Blair	Madam	Dear Lady Blair	I have the honour to remain, Madam, Your Ladyship's obedient servant,
Baronet	Sir Frederick Fanshawe, Bt.	Sir	Dear Sir Frederick	I have the honour to be, Sir, Your obedient servant,
Baronet's wife	Lady Fanshawe	Madam	Dear Lady Fanshawe	I have the honour to remain, Madam, Your Ladyship's obedient servant,
Knight	Sir John Gilbert	Sir	Dear Sir John	I have the honour to be, Sir, Your obedient servant,
Knight's wife	Lady Gilbert	Madam	Dear Lady Gilbert	I have the honour to remain, Madam, Your Ladyship's obedient servant,

NOTE. Nowadays, the very formal style of *complimentary close* shown above is becoming less frequently used, and is being gradually superseded in business correspondence by the form:

I remain (*or* I am),
Your Grace, My Lord, Sir, Madam, etc.,
Yours faithfully (*or* Yours truly);
or simply by 'Yours faithfully' *or* 'Yours truly.'

THE CHURCH

TITLE	ENEVELOPE	SALUTATION		COMPLIMENTARY CLOSE
		Formal	*Social*	(*Formal*)
The Church of England				
Archibishop	The Most Rev. The Lord Archbishop of –	My Lord Archbishop (*or* Your Grace)	Dear Lord Archbishop (*or* My dear Archbishop)	I have the honour to remain, my Lord Archbishop, Your Grace's devoted and obedient servant,
Bishop	The Right Rev. The Lord Bishop of –[1]	My Lord (*or* My Lord Bishop)	Dear Lord Bishop (*or* Dear Bishop)	I have the honour to remain, Your Lordship's obedient servant,
Dean	The Very Rev. The Dean of –	Very Reverend Sir	Dear Mr Dean (*or* Dear Dean)	I have the honour to remain, Very Rev. Sir, Your obedient servant,
Archdeacon	The Venerable the Archdeacon of ——	Venerable Sir	Dear Mr. Archdeacon (*or* Dear Archdeacon)	I have the honour to remain, Venerable Sir, Your obedient servant,
Canon	The Rev. Canon ——	Reverend Sir	Dear Canon ——	I have the honour to remain, Reverend Sir, Your obedient Servant,
Prebendary	The Rev. Prebendary ——	Reverend Sir	Dear Prebendary	I have the honour to remain, Reverend Sir, Your obedient servant,
Other Clergy	The Rev. John ——	Reverend Sir (*or* Sir)	Dear Mr. ——(*or* Dear Rector *or* Dear Vicar)	I remain, Reverend Sir (*or* Sir), Your obedient servant,

[1] The Bishop of London is, through his office, a Privy Councillor, and must therefore be addressed (on the envelope) as 'The Right Rev. and Right Hon. The Lord Bishop of London.'

TITLE	ENVELOPE	SALUTATION		COMPLIMENTARY CLOSE
		Formal	*Social*	(*Formal*)
The Church of Scotland				
The Lord High Commissioner to the General Assembly	His Grace The Lord High Commissioner	Your Grace	Your Grace	I have the honour to remain, Your Grace's most devoted and obedient servant,
The Moderator	The Right Rev. The Moderator of the General Assembly of the Church of Scotland	Right Rev. Sir	Dear Moderator, *or* Dear Dr. (*or* Mr.) ——	I beg to remain, Right Rev. Sir, Your obedient servant,
Ex-Moderators	The Very Rev. ——(and if a Dr.), D.D.	Very Rev. Sir	Dear Dr. (*or* Mr.) ——	I beg to remain, Very Rev. Sir, Your obedient servant,
Dean of the Thistle and Chapel Royal	The Very Rev. the Dean of ——	Very Rev. Sir	Dear Mr. Dean (*or* Dear Dean ——	I have the honour to remain, Very Rev. Sir, Your obedient servant,
Other Clergy	Rules as for the Church of England apply, with the exception that, instead of the titles of Vicar and Rector, those of 'The Minister' or 'The Parish Minister' are used.			

The Roman Catholic Church

Styles of address, in both speech and writing, for the dignitaries and clergy of the Roman Catholic Church are given in detail in *Titles and Forms of Address.*

The Jewish Church

The Chief Rabbi	The Very Rev. The Chief Rabbi (*or* The Very Rev. Dr.——	Very Rev. and dear Sir	Dear Chief Rabbi	I am, Very Rev. and dear Sir, Your obedient servant,
Rabbi Doctors	The Rev. Rabbi Dr.——	Rev. and dear Sir	Dear Rabbi ——	I am, Rev. and dear Sir, Your obedient servant,
Rabbis	The Rev. Rabbi ——	Rev. and dear Sir	Dear Rabbi ——	I am, Rev. and dear Sir, Your obedient servant,

Other Denominations

Most Nonconformist ministers should be addressed in speech and referred to as 'Mr. ——." In correspondence they should be addressed (on the envelope) as The Rev. John Blank *or* The Rev. J. C. Blank (see page 155).

Orders of Chivalry

There are *seven* Orders of Knighthood

(1) *The Most Noble Order of the Garter* – given, as a general rule, only to royalties and members of the peerage. It is distinguished by the letters 'K.G.' after the title and name; e.g., The Marquess of Mayfield, K.G. (Scottish peers are given the corresponding *Order of the Thistle* (K.T.), and Irish peers, the *Order of St. Patrick*[1] (K.P.).)

NOTE. These initials should *never* be omitted in correspondence – either social or professional.

(2) *The Most Honourable Order of the Bath* – the highest Order usually given to commoners. This Order has three classes[2] – as also have the following three Orders.

Knight Grand Cross; e.g., Sir John Gilbert, G.C.B.
Knight Commander; e.g., Sir David Welsh, K.C.B.
Companion; e.g., Robert Scott, Esq., C.B.

(It should be noted that a companionship does *not* confer knighthood.)

(3) *The most Exalted Order of the Star of India*[3]

Knight Grand Commander; e.g., Sir Nigel Burton, G.C.S.I.
Knight Commander; e.g., Sir Roger Chase, K.C.S.I.
Companion; e.g., Paul Russell, Esq., C.S.I.

(4) *The Most Distinguished Order of St. Michael and St. George*

Knight Grand Cross .	G.C.M.G.
Knight Commander .	K.C.M.G.
Companion . .	C.M.G.

(5) *The Most Eminent Order of the Indian Empire*[3]

Knight Grand Commander	G.C.I.E.
Knight Commander . .	K.C.I.E.
Companion . . .	C.I.E.

[1] No longer conferred.
[2] Since November, 1970, women have been admitted to the Order of Bath. They are known as: Dame Grand Cross (G.C.B.), Dame Commander (D.C.B.), and Companion (C.B.).
[3] No longer conferred.

(6) *The Royal Victorian Order. Five* classes in this Order, to which women have been admitted since 1936.

Knight or Dame Grand Cross; e.g., Sir George West, G.C.V.O.
Dame Eleanor Hill, G.C.V.O.

Knight or Dame Commander; e.g., Sir James Cooper, K.C.V.O.
Dame Moira Black, D.C.V.O.

Commander; e.g., Peter Armstrong, Esq., C.V.O.
Mrs. (or Miss) Steele, C.V.O.

Member Fourth Class } e.g., Thomas Green, Esq., M.V.O.
Member Fifth Class } Mrs. (or Miss) Brown, M.V.O.

(7) *The Most Excellent Order of the British Empire.* Again *five* classes in this Order, for which women have always been eligible.

Knight or Dame Grand Cross	G.B.E.
Knight or Dame Commander	K.B.E., D.B.E.
Commander	C.B.E.
Officer	O.B.E.
Member	M.B.E.

Order of Merit and Order of the Companions of Honour

Two other important Orders, which do not, however, confer knighthoods, are:

1. *The Order of Merit* (O.M.), which is designed as a special distinction for "eminent men and women" and is limited in number to twenty-four. It ranks in order *after* the first class of the Order of the Bath (i.e., Knight or Dame Grand Cross).

2. *The Order of the Companions of Honour* (C.H.), which is limited to sixty-five in number, and ranks *after* the first class of the Order of the British Empire (i.e., Knight or Dame Grand Cross).

General Rules regarding Orders of Chivalry

The following rules governing the use of Orders should be carefully observed:

1. *All* Orders must be included in business or professional correspondence.

2. A knighthood of a lower Order is shown *before* the companionship of a higher. For example, if Robert Brown were a Knight Commander of the Order of the British Empire (the *lowest* Order) and also a Companion of the Order of the Bath (the *highest* Order usually given to commoners) *and* a Commander of the Royal Victorian Order, he would be addressed as follows: Sir Robert Brown, K.B.E., C.B., C.V.O.

3. 'V.C.' and 'G.C.' have precedence over *all* Orders, Decorations and Medals.

Forms of Address: Some General Rules

1. A clergyman is addressed (in correspondence) as: The Rev. David Clark *or* The Rev. Mr. Clark (if his Christian name or initials are not known) – but *never* as 'The Rev. Clark.'

2. When writing to a Member of Parliament, 'M.P.' must appear *after* any Orders or Decorations he may hold; e.g., John Smith, Esq., D.S.O., O.B.E., M.P.

NOTE. The decoration 'D.S.O.' (Distinguished Service Order), which ranks immediately *before* the fourth class of the Royal Victorian Order, takes precedence of 'O.B.E.' (Officer of the Order of the British Empire).

3. 'M.P.' would also follow all university degrees; e.g., John Smith, Esq., M.A., B.Sc., M.P.

4. 'J.P.' should be used only when writing to the Justice of the Peace in his official capacity – never socially.

5. A professional title precedes other titles, e.g.:

> The Rev. The Hon. Peter Marsden.
> Field-Marshal The Right Hon. Lord Montgomery.
> Rear-Admiral Sir David Heaton.

6. 'Mr.' (or 'Esq.') is never used with a superior title – e.g., Sir, The Hon., The Right Hon., Professor, Councillor, etc. (Note that a woman Councillor would be addressed: Councillor Mrs. Jones *or* Councillor Martha Jones.)

7. A son who was in the habit of using the designation 'Junior' would be addressed: James Brown, Jun., Esq. .

8. A married woman is usually addressed (in correspondence) by her husband's name or initials; e.g., Mrs. John

Smith *or* Mrs. J. C. Smith. A widow may resume her own Christian name if this is necessary to distinguish her from her son's wife.

9. A Government Department may be addressed through the Secretary; e.g., The Secretary, Department of Overseas Trade.

10. *Use of Messrs.* The prefix 'Messrs.' should be used in addressing a partnership; e.g., Messrs. Brown & Co. *or* Messrs. Smith & Jones. It should *never* be used:

(*a*) when the name of the firm includes another courtesy title, e.g. *Sir*: Sir John Graham & Co.;

(*b*) when the name is preceded by the word *The*: The James Grant Furnishing Company;

(*c*) when the firm's name does not consist of personal names: Modern Dry-cleaning Company;

(*d*) when the firm is a *limited* company: Brown & Co. Ltd

NOTE. When writing to a limited company one should address the letter to The Secretary, or other official of the company; e.g., The Contracts Manager, The General Manager, The Accountant, etc.

Foreign Forms of Address (in Correspondence)

The following table will be found helpful when writing to foreign customers:

	Mr. (envelope)	*Mr.* (letter)	*Mrs.*	*Miss*
French	Monsieur	Monsieur	Madame	Mademoiselle
German	Herr	Herr	Frau	Fräulein
Dutch	De Heer	Weledele Heer	Mevrouw	Mejuffrouw
	Den Weledelen Heer (*Doctors and Magistrates only*)			
Italian	Signor	Signor	Signora	Signorina
Spanish	Señor	Señor	Señora	Señorita
Danish	Hr.	Hr.	Fru	Frøken
Norwegian	Herr	Herr	Fru	Frøken
Swedish	Herr	Herr	Fru	Frøcken

12

Correspondence

Business Letters – Parts of a Business Letter – Types of Business Letter – Memorandums – Report-writing – Indexing Précis of Correspondence – Telegrams – Telegraphic Codes – Invitations and Replies – Business Announcements.

Business Letters

IT has been said that the ABC of a good business letter is: *Accuracy*, *Brevity*, and *Clarity*. To these essential qualities might be added: *Courtesy*, *Consistency*, and *Completeness.*

Accuracy. The information you convey in a business letter must be accurate. In order to ensure accuracy, you should cultivate the habit of reading carefully through your letters and checking all figures, prices, and dates.

Brevity. A business letter should be as brief as possible compatible with clarity and courtesy. Long, involved sentences should be avoided.

Clarity. The meaning must be clear. Moreover, the letter must convey the same meaning to both the sender and the receiver. Ambiguity is best avoided by the use of good plain English and short, well-constructed sentences.

Courtesy. A business letter, if it is to create a favourable impression, must be courteous in tone. Do not therefore, in attempting to be brief, let your letter sound abrupt. Remember, too, that it is a form of politeness not only to spell a correspondent's name correctly but also to add after his name any honours or degrees he may have.

Consistency. One statement in your letter should not contradict another statement. It is important also to be consistent in the use of person and tense. Do not, for instance, start a letter in the first person singular and finish it in the first person plural.

Completeness. When you have written your letter see that you have not overlooked a single point. It is both time-consuming and a reflection on your efficiency to have to write a second letter because of something you omitted to mention in the first.

Parts of a Business Letter

The various parts of a business letter are dealt with in detail in *Shorthand and Typewriting Hints*, pp. 55–60.

Types of Business Letter

1. *Letters of Application*

See Chapter I, pp. 13–14.

2. *Letters of Inquiry*

A letter of inquiry may take the form of a request for information regarding prices or terms, etc.; or it may be in the form of a confidential letter requesting information about an employee or a customer's financial position (*status* inquiry). Such letters should be clear, concise, and to the point.

If your correspondent is doing you a favour in carrying out your request it would be only courteous to enclose a stamped addressed envelope.

3. *Quotations*

A quotation, which is an offer of goods at certain prices, is usually sent in reply to an inquiry received. When submitting quotations, the following points should be noted:

(*a*) A clear description of the goods offered must be given. (If possible, samples should be sent.)

(*b*) Prices and terms (together with discounts, if any) should be stated.

(*c*) Terms of delivery (e.g., whether 'carriage paid' or 'carriage forward') should also be indicated.

(*d*) If the quotation is valid for a limited period only this should be stated; e.g., 'subject to acceptance within ten days,' 'subject to market fluctuations,' etc.

4. *Orders*

Orders are usually made out on printed forms, but they may take the form of a letter. When ordering goods it is important to state clearly all the relevant information, including quantity, quality, price, catalogue references, etc. Particulars of delivery and payment should also be given.

NOTE. When an order is received it should be acknowledged promptly. (The acknowledgment may be made by letter or by printed card.) If a remittance has accompanied the order an official receipt should be sent promptly with the acknowledgment.

5. *Letters of Complaint*

Letters of complaint should be carefully and tactfully worded. They should neither threaten nor rebuke. It is always more charitable to assume, if goods have been wrongly supplied or prices incorrectly charged, that a mistake has been made which the firm in question will be only too anxious to rectify once it has been brought to their notice. The keynote of all such letters is *courtesy*.

6. *Letters of Apology*

Letters of apology should be courteous and straightforward, but not servile in tone. You should explain fully how the mistake arose, and state the action you intend to take in order to rectify the matter. Note that it is not necessary to apologize more than once. The apology may be contained in either the first paragraph or the last – but not normally in both.

7. *Letters of Introduction*

A letter of introduction may be given by a person to a business acquaintance with the object of introducing him to another acquaintance, either because (*a*) the one is going to be in the other's district, on business or for pleasure; or because

(*b*) both are engaged in a similar line of business, and their meeting may prove mutually beneficial.

NOTE. Letters of introduction should not be sealed unless, of course, they are sent through the post.

8. *Circular Letters*

A circular letter is either duplicated or printed, as it is intended to be read by a number of correspondents. Its purpose is to give information (e.g., a change of address, the opening of a new branch, etc.) or to gain custom. Such letters should be carefully worded, stereotyped phrases being avoided. In particular, the first few words are of great importance. They should seek to attract and hold the reader's attention so that he is persuaded to read further.

9. *Letters requesting Payment of Overdue Accounts*

The composition of 'dunning' letters, as they are sometimes called, requires great care and skill. In most cases the writer will have two objects in view:

(1) to receive payment of the money due; and
(2) to avoid antagonizing the debtor.

The tone of the letter should be dignified and courteous. It may be necessary to write a series of such letters, and it should be noted that only as a last resort (and in the *final* letter) should 'forcible measures' be adopted, and then only with extreme reluctance; e.g., " . . . if this is not paid within seven days we shall be reluctantly compelled to start legal proceedings" (*or* " . . . we shall have no alternative but to instruct our solicitors to recover the amount due").

10. *'Standard,' or 'Form,' Letters*

Many firms use 'standard,' or 'form,' letters, which are intended primarily to save time in dictating. Such letters (each of which is carefully composed in order to meet certain circumstances of a recurring nature) are numbered and filed, and the employer merely quotes the reference number of a particular letter, leaving his secretary to type it from the file copy.

'Standard' paragraphs (which are also numbered and filed) are used in many offices, thus permitting part of the letter to be dictated, if desired. (*Note.* Both the employer and the secretary will have copies of these numbered paragraphs.)

Memorandums

A *memorandum* (or 'memo') is a short informal message or report, which is usually written on a specially printed memorandum form (size A5). Its use should be restricted to internal or inter-departmental communications, as the general use of the memorandum would suggest lack of courtesy.

It will be seen from the specimen memo shown below that both salutation and complimentary close are dispensed with.

MEMORANDUM

From: General Manager	To: Advertising Manager
Reference: ADV/136/F	Date: 5th May, 19--

The attached report is submitted for your attention and comments.

Enc.

Report-writing

A private secretary may be called upon to prepare a report for her employer. The essential qualities of a good business letter apply equally to reports – namely, *accuracy*, *brevity*, and *clarity*. In addition, the facts submitted in a report must be carefully arranged in logical order.

The following suggestions regarding the preparation of reports will be found helpful:

(*a*) The ordinary rules of composition must be obeyed.

(*b*) The information conveyed should be expressed in clear and simple language.

(*c*) Indirect or reported speech should be used. (Note, however, that a *personal*, or individual, report – e.g., from the secretary to her chief – may be written in the first person.)

(*d*) A suitable heading and introduction explaining the nature of the report should be given.

(*e*) The arrangement, or layout, of the report should be carefully planned, special attention being paid to headings, sub-headings, and numbering of paragraphs.

(*f*) The report should be dated, and should be signed by the person submitting it.

Types of Report

Reports may be divided into two main classes:

(*a*) Ordinary Reports.
(*b*) Special Reports.

(*a*) *Ordinary Reports.* These reports are usually submitted at stated intervals; e.g., Directors' Annual Report to the Shareholders of a Company; monthly Financial or Sales Reports, etc. As a rule, they contain merely a statement of facts arranged according to subjects. A separate paragraph should be devoted to each subject in the report, and each paragraph should be given a suitable marginal heading.

(*b*) *Special Reports.* These are reports on subjects of special inquiry (e.g., fires, accidents, etc.) or reports of sub-committees appointed for special purposes. Careful attention should also be paid to paragraphing and marginal headings. (See specimen report on p. 163.)

The contents and scope of Special Reports are decided by the *Terms of Reference*, which are simply the instructions of the person or authority requiring the report.

In presenting such a report the Terms of Reference would be quoted first; then would follow the *findings* or facts presented, and the *conclusions* drawn from those facts; and, finally, the *recommendations* of the person or subcommittee making the report.

Example of a Special Report

The following example of a *Special Report* is taken from *English Exercises for Secretaries* by R. A. Kelly (Harrap):

REPORT OF THE HOUSING COMMITTEE ON THE DEVELOPMENT OF GRAYS MEAD ESTATE

Terms of Reference	In accordance with a resolution passed at the Main Committee Meeting held on the 12th April, 19 . . , the Housing Committee was instructed to examine the possibility of building a housing estate on the plot of land known as Grays Mead.
Proceedings of the Committee	The Housing Committee met on three occasions – the 16th April and the 10th and 16th May – and reports were received from their solicitor and surveyor. Various members of the Committee visited the site and submitted their findings at the final meeting.
Findings	(*a*) The site is suitable for the construction of two-storey houses. Main services are already available and a negligible amount of levelling will be required. (*b*) There are no restrictive covenants on the land, but the provisions of the local by-laws require that the building line be set back 5.5 metres from the present roadway. (*c*) The shape of the site precludes the building of more than fifteen houses.
Conclusions	The maximum number of houses which can be built on the site is fifteen, and this may prove uneconomic in view of the capital expenditure involved.
Recommendations	(*a*) That the Main Committee should determine the maximum grant available for building. (*b*) That the cost of building be investigated by provisional tenders. (*c*) That such cost be considered in relation to the estimated income over the next ten-year period.

[*Signed*] Paul Smith
Chairman

19th May, 19 . .

Indexing

Indexing is the name given to the method of listing a series of letters or documents of which a précis is to be made. The object of an index is to enable the reader to refer immediately to a particular letter.

In many Government departments, and in business offices where the letters on a subject are often very numerous, indexing of correspondence is essential.

NOTE. If a précis is to be made of only one letter or document an index is not required.

When preparing an index the following points should be observed:

1. Number each letter or document (after arranging in date order), and enter in the index.
2. In the last column indicate the subject-matter of the letter or document. This should consist of a single statement, and should begin with a present participle – e.g., stating, complaining, enclosing, etc.
3. The subject-matter must always be expressed in the third person, the tense being the same as that of the letter itself.
4. Enclosures, if any, should be treated as separate items in the index. They would be numbered as follows: "Enclosure 1, in No. 3," "Enclosure 2, in No. 3," and so on; or, in the case of only *one* enclosure in the letter, as "Enclosure in No. 3."

Précis of Correspondence

Précis-writing, as applied to correspondence, is the art of summarizing a series of letters or documents so that their meaning can be quickly and easily understood.

When making a précis, the following hints will be found useful:

1. Read carefully through the whole correspondence, and note the main points in each letter. If possible, read through the correspondence twice.
2. Before beginning the précis, make an index of the correspondence.

3. Follow the order of events, but do not draw up the précis letter by letter. (*Note.* If a letter is not wholly material it may be ignored.)

4. Use indirect speech (i.e., the past tense and the third person) throughout the précis.

5. Let your précis be a continuous and concise narrative, written in good plain English.

Specimen Index

NO. OF LETTER	DATE	NAMES OF CORRESPONDENTS	SUBJECT-MATTER
1.	14th May, 19..	John Smith & Co. to Quality China Co. Ltd.	Complaining about quality of tea-sets and requesting replacement.
2.	17th May, 19..	Quality China Co. Ltd. to John Smith & Co.	Acknowledging receipt of consignment returned, and explaining that tea-set ordered (No. 128) will be available within a fortnight.
3.	19th May, 19..	John Smith & Co. to Quality China Co. Ltd.	Agreeing to replacement of tea-set No. 128 within a fortnight.
4.	27th May, 19..	Quality China Co. Ltd. to John Smith & Co.	Advising dispatch of tea-set No. 128 by rail and apologizing for any inconvenience caused.

Specimen Précis

On the 14th May, 19–, John Smith & Company complained that the consignment of china tea-sets received by them, and which they were returning that day, was below the standard of the previous consignment ordered, and requested replacement. It was explained to them that the tea-set ordered previously (No. 128) was temporarily out of stock, but that replacement should be possible within a fortnight. Smith & Company expressed their willingness to await replacement of the original consignment, provided delivery could be effected within a fortnight, failing which the order would have to be cancelled. The consignment was, in fact, dispatched to Smith & Company ten days later.

Telegrams

A telegram should contain as much information as possible in the fewest possible words. Under no circumstances, however, should clearness of meaning be sacrificed to brevity.

In a telegram both salutation and complimentary close are dispensed with, and all superfluous words should be omitted. It should be remembered, too, that in a telegram, as distinct from a précis, the ordinary rules of composition are disregarded.

NOTE. A telegram is typed entirely in capitals, and should always be confirmed by letter.

Full details regarding telegrams (both Inland and Overseas) are given in the *Post Office Guide.*

Examples of Telegrams. The message "Please meet me at 15 30 hrs. on Friday at Bideford Station." might be reduced to: "Meet me Bideford Station 15 30 Friday."

As another example, the message "I wish you to cancel my order of the 10th June. A further order is in course of preparation and will be sent to you shortly." might be reduced as follows: "Cancel order tenth June await further order."

Telegraphic Codes

Telegraphic codes – e.g., *ABC*, *Bentley's*, *Marconi's*, etc.– have been devised in order to reduce the cost of telegraphing. In these codes one word may be used to represent a whole sentence. In the *ABC Code*, for instance, the words are alphabetically arranged and numbered, so that each word or number indicates a complete sentence, and the message is decoded simply by referring to the code.

A great variety of information can be conveyed by means of the published codes which have been designed to meet the needs of both commerce and industry.

Many firms indicate in their note-paper heading the code or codes regularly used by them.

Cypher Codes. Where absolute secrecy is called for (e.g., in messages between Governments and their representatives abroad) cypher codes are used, these being composed wholly or in part of figures having a secret meaning. Each group of five figures is charged as one word. Cypher code messages can, of course, be deciphered only by the holders of the key.

Invitations and Replies

When required in quantity formal invitations are printed,

the guest's name being handwritten (usually at the top left-hand corner of the card, but practice varies). For small functions, however, typewritten invitations are quite usual.

The style of reply to an invitation will, of course, depend on the invitation itself – i.e., whether formal or informal.

Formal invitations, and the replies to such invitations, are usually written in the third person. The following points should be noted:

1. Salutation, complimentary close, and signature are omitted.
2. The date usually appears at the bottom left-hand corner of the reply.
3. The reply should state day, date, time, and place of the function concerned. (The *time* may, however, be omitted in the *refusal*.)
4. The third person must be used throughout. (*Note. He* (or *she*) should be used instead of *I*, and *they* instead of *we*.)
5. When refusing an invitation, remember that it is more courteous to give a reason than merely to state the bare fact of refusal.
6. When the formal invitation is a joint one from husband and wife the envelope in reply should be addressed only to the wife.

Examples

(*a*) *Invitation*

Amstel,
Palmyra Road,
Newlands.

Mr. and Mrs. Robert Brown request the pleasure of

.... company at a Dinner-Dance

to be held at Kenilworth House on Saturday, 17th November,

19. . , at 7.45 p.m.

R.S.V.P.

(*b*) *Acceptance*

1 Sunninghill Road,
Claremont.

Mr. John Smith has much pleasure in accepting Mr. and Mrs. Robert Brown's kind invitation to a Dinner-Dance to be held at Kenilworth House on Saturday, 17th November, 19.., at 7.45 p.m.

2nd November, 19..

(*c*) *Refusal*

1 Sunninghill Road,
Claremont.

Mr. John Smith thanks Mr. and Mrs. Robert Brown for their kind invitation to a Dinner-Dance to be held at Kenilworth House on Saturday, 17th November, 19.., but regrets that, owing to a previous engagement, he is unable to accept.

2nd November, 19..

Business Announcements

Business announcements may take many forms – e.g., change of address or change of firm name; the announcement of the death of a partner; the taking into business of a new partner. Such announcements are frequently written in the third person.

Examples

(*a*) *Taking in a New Partner*

Messrs. Digby, Mortimer & Jones have pleasure in announcing that, as from 1st July, 19 . . , they are taking into partnership Mr. John Smith, C.A. The name of the firm will remain unchanged.

(*b*) *Announcing the Death of a Partner*

Messrs. Digby, Mortimer & Jones much regret to announce the death, on 10th February, of their senior partner, Mr. Wilfred Martin Digby, LL.B. They also wish to announce that the business will be continued by the remaining partners as hitherto.

13

Receptionist Duties: The Telephone; Callers and Interviewing

Receiving Calls – Telephone Messages – Making Calls – Telephone Index – Cleansing of Telephone – Post Office Services – Receiving Callers – Interviewing Callers – Performing Introductions

THE TELEPHONE

A great deal of business is transacted over the telephone, and it is therefore essential for the secretary not only to be able to handle the telephone efficiently but also to convey a favourable impression of her firm every time she receives or makes a call. It should be remembered that a firm is often judged by the telephone manner of its staff.

Receiving Calls

The following hints will help you to answer the telephone efficiently:

1. Always answer the telephone *promptly.*
2. Do not say "Hello." (This is time-wasting because it conveys no information to the caller, but compels him to ask who you are.)
3. Begin by saying "Good morning" (or "Good afternoon"). Then state your firm's name or telephone number; e.g., "Good morning. Smith & Jones Ltd."
4. If the call has been put through to your office by the firm's switchboard operator, state the name of your department; e.g., "Sales Department" (*or* "Mr. Smith's office").

5. If you recognize the caller's voice address him pleasantly by name, thus: "Good morning, Mr. Brown. Can I help you?"

6. If the person required by the caller is not available, you should ask the caller whether he wishes to leave a message or to speak to someone else; alternatively, whether he wishes to be called back or to call again later.

7. If it is necessary to call someone back, make a careful note of his name and telephone number and, if necessary, his address. Also inquire the best time to call him. (Take down this information while you are receiving the call.)

8. Always write down *at once* every telephone message. Never trust telephone calls and messages to your memory.

9. Be courteous and helpful at all times – even when it is a 'wrong number'! If the call has been wrongly directed to your office extension, apologize to the caller and have the call transferred at once.

10. Remember to speak directly into the mouthpiece in an even, pleasant tone. Emphasize consonants, and do not pitch your voice too high. Speak clearly but not loudly. Be brief but courteous.

Telephone Messages

See that a message pad and pencil are always available beside the telephone. Pads of printed forms are used by many firms for this purpose.

In addition to taking down accurately the actual message, make a careful note of the caller's name and address and telephone number – remembering to add the date and time of the call.

If the message is a fairly long one, read it back to the caller to ensure its accuracy. Repeat unfamiliar names, using the Telephone Code (e.g., *A for Andrew*, *B for Benjamin*, *C for Charlie*, etc.), and take care to record telephone numbers correctly. Note that telephone numbers should be repeated as follows:

64788 – Six Four Seven Double Eight
6100 – Six One Double Oh
4000 – Four Thousand
999 – Nine Double Nine
66638 – Six Double Six Three Eight
4883 – Four Eight Eight Three

Type out the message as soon as possible, and place it in a conspicuous position on your employer's desk.

Making Calls

If your chief has asked you to make a call on his behalf, see that you have the correct number. Then, when you have been connected, say: "Mr. Brown of Wilson & Brown wishes to speak to Mr. Jones, please." If Mr. Jones is not in, however, arrange to ring back later, or leave a message requesting Mr. Jones to telephone your employer when he returns – in which case do not forget to leave Mr. Brown's telephone number.

Before making a call that is likely to be lengthy or involved, it is helpful to make brief notes of what you want to say, or to have at hand a file on the subject to which you can refer. Again, do not trust to your memory.

NOTE. Important telephone calls should always be confirmed by letter.

Telephone Index

As a secretary, you will find it helpful to keep an index or reference book of telephone numbers frequently required by the firm. These might include your chief's personal telephone numbers (home, doctor, dentist, clubs, etc.); the firm's bank, solicitors, and insurance company; taxi services, restaurants, etc.; as well as the home telephone numbers of the office staff. Such an index makes for greater efficiency in that it saves time and trouble in looking up the number each time you need to make a call; but it must, of course, be kept up to date.

Cleansing of Telephone

Wipe the instrument regularly with a clean cloth. Pay particular attention to the mouth- and ear-pieces by cleansing these parts with a piece of cotton-wool to which a drop of disinfectant has been added. Alternatively a small spray for this purpose may be purchased. In large firms this 'service' may be provided by an outside agency.

Post Office Services

In order to become thoroughly familiar with these services, the secretary should study carefully the first few pages of the *Telephone Directory*, including the 'Green Pages' Section. The Telephone Code has already been referred to. You should make a copy of this list and keep it in an accessible place near the telephone. You will find it most useful for the purpose of checking unfamiliar names and addresses given over the telephone, or for that matter any part of a message that is difficult to hear.

Personal Calls

If you wish to make a trunk call to a particular person – for example, a member of a large firm – a 'personal' call may be advantageous. Such a call (which is subject to an additional charge known as a 'personal fee') is timed from the moment the person required (or an acceptable substitute) is ready to speak. If, however, the person required cannot be traced, only the personal fee is payable.

International Calls

There is now a fairly extensive Telephone Overseas Service. This includes a *Continental Service*, which makes communication possible with the chief towns and cities of Europe; an *International Service*, which covers countries outside Europe; and a *Ship's Telephone Service*. Full particulars of all these services are given in the *Post Office Guide.*

Subscriber Trunk Dialling (S.T.D.)

At many exchanges subscribers can dial trunk calls. Local and dialled trunk calls from lines with dialling facilities are charged in *units of* 1p (2p for calls from coin-box lines), the charge being based on the duration of the call and (in the case of dialled trunk calls) the distance between the charging centres.

NOTE. Details of charges and dialling instructions will be found in *Subscriber Trunk Dialling* issued by the Post Office to all telephone subscribers.

Telephone Credit Cards

Subscribers may be supplied, on application to their Telephone Manager and payment of the appropriate fee, with *telephone credit cards.* The holder of such a card is able, by quoting his card number to the operator, to make a call from any telephone (including a call office), at any time, *on credit.*

Credit-card calls are charged to the subscriber's telephone account, an additional charge per call being payable.

Telegrams by Telephone

Inland and overseas telegrams may be dictated from subscribers' telephones, or from kiosks or other call offices.

Telegrams may also be delivered to telephone subscribers by telephone, and may be addressed to subscribers' telephone numbers; e.g., Fraser, 221 2468, Glasgow. (*Note.* The name of the town is not required for telegrams originating in the same town; e.g., "Jones, 674 1211," would be sufficient for a telegram originating in London.)

Again the secretary is reminded to speak clearly and to make use of the telephone code for difficult or unusual words or names.

Tracing Telephone Numbers

When asking for telephone numbers to be traced through *Directory Inquiries* it is necessary to give the surname, initials, and address of the person you wish to call.

Service Faults

Service inquiries or faults (e.g., failure to get ringing tone, or connection to a wrong number) should be reported to the operator after dialling the appropriate service code.

CALLERS AND INTERVIEWING

Receiving Callers

Whether as secretary to a doctor or dentist or to a business executive, one of the more responsible duties of the private secretary is the receiving of callers. Just as the right telephone manner helps to give the caller a favourable impression of a firm, so can the secretary's manner when receiving personal callers either confirm or destroy that impression. Her manner, therefore, while not lacking in dignity, should be pleasant and welcoming, and her voice warm and friendly.

Callers may be divided into two classes: those *with* appointments and those *without* appointments; but to all callers the secretary must be unfailingly polite and helpful, while avoiding any suggestion of self-importance.

Callers with Appointments

The day's appointments will, of course, have been recorded in both your diary and your chief's diary. In addition to reminding him of each appointment, you must also prepare in good time any material he may require, or have ready for him any papers likely to have a bearing on the visit.

When a caller arrives for his appointment with your employer, greet him pleasantly by name, take his hat and coat, and see that he is comfortably seated before announcing his arrival. Never show the caller straight into your principal's office, as he may still be engaged on some other matter or speaking on the telephone, or may wish to consult some papers before receiving the caller.

If for any reason the caller is required to wait some time, you should apologize for the delay and offer him a newspaper or magazine to read while he is waiting.

Callers without Appointments

Such callers usually need to be handled with care and, in some cases, with considerable tact. It should be borne in mind that your employer is a busy man and cannot possibly see everyone that calls without an appointment; it is therefore your duty to shield him from casual or unwelcome callers.

You should tactfully inquire the nature of the caller's business and, if you consider it is not sufficiently important to warrant an interview with your chief, you might say: "I am afraid Mr. Brown is rather busy just now and cannot be disturbed, but perhaps I could help you?" Let the caller see that you are genuinely trying to assist him; therefore, be patient, sympathetic, and polite.

Should the caller, however, remain stubbornly insistent on seeing your employer, you might suggest his writing in, briefly stating his business and requesting an appointment. But if you should be in any doubt as to the importance or otherwise of the call, you could say: "If you will wait a few moments I shall find out whether Mr. Brown can possibly fit in a short interview before his next appointment."

NOTE. A stranger should never be left alone in a room where there is ready access to confidential papers or documents. (This applies also to members of the staff who should not have access to the information in question.) Such papers should be slipped unobtrusively into a file or drawer before the secretary leaves the room.

Interviewing Callers

During your chief's absence it may be necessary for you to interview callers on his behalf. Considerable tact is called for here, so that you do not convey an impression of self-importance. Your manner, as always, should be pleasant and courteous while you tactfully obtain such particulars as name and address and the nature of the caller's business. If you find that you cannot handle the matter yourself, assure the caller that you will inform your principal of his visit as soon as he returns. Do not, however, be persuaded to make a decision on your employer's behalf, or commit him to any course of action, without being absolutely certain that you are acting in accordance with his wishes.

Remember to make a brief written note of every interview, both for your employer's information and for the files. It is also advisable to enter in your diary the name and address of each caller, together with the time and purpose of the call.

As you will have many other duties to attend to, especially during your chief's absence, it is necessary to limit the time spent on interviewing by making each interview as brief as possible without, of course, giving offence to the caller.

Performing Introductions

When a secretary is required to perform introductions she should remember the following basic rule: *the person whose name you mention first is the one you wish to honour.* For example, a man is presented to a woman caller, thus: "Mrs. Jones, may I introduce Mr. Brown?" Or: "Mrs. Jones, this is Mr. Brown."

A person of lower rank would be presented to one of higher rank, thus: "Lady Smith, may I present Miss Clark?" Or: "Mr. Willoughby [head of your firm], this is Mr. Simpson [the visiting sales representative of a local typewriter agency]."

A younger person is presented to an older person; but in the case of two people of similar age, sex, and rank, it is immaterial whose name is mentioned first.

Should an employer introduce his secretary to a visitor, it is not necessary for her to rise when acknowledging the introduction – unless the visitor is elderly or of higher social rank. She should just smile pleasantly and say: "How do you do?" (*not* "I am pleased to meet you") and then continue quietly with her work.

14

Proof-reading

Preparing Matter for Press – Galley Proofs – Page Proofs – Proof-correction – Useful Reference Books – Common Printing Terms – Proof-correcting Symbols – Example of Proof-correcting.

Preparing Matter for Press

MOST private secretaries, even if not actually engaged on literary work, will at some time or other be called upon to prepare *copy* for printing – 'copy' being the term used for the manuscript or typescript prepared for this purpose. The copy should be clear and legible – therefore preferably typewritten; correctly spelt and punctuated; grammatically correct; and free from typing or other errors. It should be carefully checked, before being submitted to the printer, to ensure its accuracy.

Typewritten copy should be well displayed on A4 paper (*using one side only*), with wide margins and double-line spacing. Footnotes, etc., should, however, be typed in single-line spacing. (See section on Literary Work, Chapter 4, pp. 66–68.)

In order to indicate to the printer the use of any special kind of type, it should be noted that a single line under a word or letter in the copy indicates that italic type is to be used; two lines indicate small capitals; three lines, large capitals; and a wavy line, bold type.

Galley Proofs

After the typewritten MS. has been set up in type, the first proofs submitted by the printer are often in 'galley' form – i.e., in long sheets measuring about half a metre in length. Two 'pulls,' or sets of proofs, taken on inferior paper, are sent to the author for proof-reading and correction, after which one set is returned to the printer, the other being retained by the author for reference. (In the case of a book, the publisher, of course, acts as intermediary between the printer and the author.)

Page Proofs

When the author's corrected proof is received by the printer he divides the galley and arranges the type in the form of pages. The page proofs in turn are proof-read and corrected, and finally the matter is printed on better-quality paper.

Proof-correction

Once a book or other matter has been set up in type, it is most important that alterations other than the correction of printing errors (e.g., broken and inverted letters, letters of the wrong *fount*,[1] misprints, etc.) should be kept to a minimum. Alterations made on the proofs *that represent a change from the original copy* (i.e., the typewritten MS.) can prove most expensive, as the cost of correcting type is very much greater than the cost of setting it up. If, however, alterations require to be made the new matter should, where possible, fit *exactly* into the space made by removing something on the same page to make room for it.

It will be appreciated that the cost of alterations when the book is in page proof is even greater than the cost of alterations to galley proofs.

In correcting proofs the following hints will be found helpful:

(1) The corrections should be made in ink, using the standard proof-correcting symbols as shown on pp. 183–186.

[1] See page 181.

(2) When an alteration requires to be made the existing letter or word should be struck through and the letter or word to be substituted should be written in the *margin* and followed by a stroke (/), which is intended to show that the marginal mark is concluded.

(3) In the case of extensive additions or alterations it is better to type these on a separate sheet of paper and attach to the proof at the appropriate place.

(4) In addition to correcting typographical errors, broken letters should be marked, and also letters out of alignment, inverted letters, letters of the wrong fount, etc.

(5) After the proofs have been carefully checked one set should be returned to the printer clearly marked "Press" (if the printed matter may now be run off) or "Revise" (if the printer is required to submit further corrected proofs).

(6) As a general rule, only matter actually to be printed should be written on the proofs. Any special instruction intended for the printer may, however, be written in the margin, encircled, and preceded by the words "To Printer" – which should be *underlined.*

NOTE. Because proof-reading requires a great deal of concentration, it may be found that the most satisfactory way to carry it out is to have someone read aloud the original copy while you proof-read and correct.

Useful Reference Books

The Writers' and Artists' Year Book (A. and C. Black) contains much useful information and advice to authors and their secretaries on the subject of "Preparation and Submission of Manuscripts." Details (and examples) of type-faces and sizes of type, sizes of books and paper, etc., are also given.

Similar information regarding styles of type, books and paper, etc., will be found in *Rules for Compositors and Readers*, by H. Hart (Oxford University Press), and in *Whitaker's Almanack.*

The *Authors' and Printers' Dictionary* (Oxford University Press) is a useful reference book to anyone concerned with the preparation of printed matter. In addition to a very helpful introductory article entitled "Author and Printer," this book deals with points of spelling (including place-names), punctuation, and pronunciation, etc.; sizes of type, books, and paper; and contains a complete list of printing terms. A selection of the more common of these is given below.

Common Printing Terms

Bold-face Type: **as this**; indicated in MS. by wavy underlining ～～; abbr. *b.f.*

Break. The division into a fresh paragraph.

Chase. Metal frame holding composed type.

Copy. Matter to be reproduced in type.

Dropped Heads: The first pages of chapters, etc., beginning lower than others.

Fair Copy. Transcript free from corrections; abbr. *f. co.*

Fount. A complete set of type of one particular face, or design, and size.

Galley. A flat oblong tray for holding composed type; *galley proofs*, those supplied in 'slips' about half a metre long (see *proof*).

Half-tone Block. One in which the various tones are made by dots.

Hanging Paragraph. First line full out, following ones
indented, as this.

Head-page. The one beginning a book, chapter, etc.

Italic. A style of type as this, in which the letters slope upwards to the right. Marked in MS. by one line underneath; abbr. *ital.*

Justification. The even and equal spacing of words and lines to a given measure.[1]

Keep Standing. The type not to be distributed pending possible reprinting.

Line Block. One in which the various tones are represented by lines.

Linotype. A machine for casting lines or bars of words, etc., as a substitute for type-setting by hand.

[1] This is to ensure that both left- and right-hand margins will be perfectly even.

Literal. A literal error: those of the compositor in substituting one character for another, including 'turns,' 'wrong founts,' and defective types.

Make-up. Arrangement of matter into pages.

Matter. MS. or copy to be printed; type that is composed.

Offset. Transfer of ink from its proper sheet (now commonly *set-off*, q.v.); *also* name of a printing technique.

Overrun. To turn over words from one line to the next, for several or many lines.[1]

Pagination. The paging of a book; also the act of paging.

Preface. The introductory address of the author to the reader, in which he explains the purpose and scope of the book.

Proof. A trial impression from composed type, taken for correction.

- *Author's Proof.* A clean proof, or one returned with his corrections; abbr. *a.p.*
- *Clean Proof.* One having very few printers' errors.
- *First Proof.* The 'clean' proof, as corrected by the compositor, which the author first receives.
- *Foul Proof.* One marked with many errors.
- *Galley* or *Slip Proof.* A proof taken before the matter is made up into pages: usually about half a metre long. (By having the first proof in this form, alterations can be effected much more cheaply when the corrections are likely to be numerous.)
- *Page Proof* (or *Proof in Sheets*). Those made up into pages.
- *Press Proof.* The final one passed by author, editor, or publisher, for the press.

Proof-reader. One who reads and corrects printers' proofs.

Roman. This style of type, or ordinary as distinct from fancy and italic.

Set-off. The transfer of ink from one printed sheet to another.

Spaces. Blanks for placing between letters, words, or lines.

[1] This usually happens when additional matter is inserted in the proofs without space having been allowed for it. (See first paragraph of section on *Proof-correction*, p. 179.)

Proof-correcting Symbols

	MARGINAL SIGN	CORRESPONDING MARK IN TEXT	MEANING
1.	[delete mark]	/ (e.g., hee)	Delete (take out).
2.	[delete and close up mark]	/ (e.g., comeing)	Delete and close up.
3.	#	⅄ (e.g., itis here)	Insert space.
4.	eq.#	⅄ between words (e.g., it was only)	Make spacing equal.
5.	# >	is required. > It should . . .	Space between lines or paragraphs.
6.	less #	⅄ between words	Reduce space.
7.	stet	it is ~~true~~ (dotted underneath)	"Let it stand"; ignore correction dotted underneath.
8.	caps.	≡ under letters or words to be altered.	Change to capital leters.
9.	s.c.	= under letters or words to be altered.	Change to small capitals.
10.	l.c.	Encircle letters to be altered; e.g., It Takes time.	Change to lower case (small letters).
11.	bold	~~~ under letters or words to be altered.	Change to bold type.
12.	ital	___ under letters or words to be altered.	Change to italics.
13.	rom	Encircle words to be altered	Change to roman type.
14.	w.f.	Encircle letter to be altered.	Wrong fount. Replace by letter of correct fount.

Proof-correcting Symbols (*continued*)

MARGINAL SIGN	CORRESPONDING MARK IN TEXT	MEANING
15. 9	Encircle letter to be altered.	Letter inverted. Turn right way up.
16. X	Encircle letter(s) to be altered.	Replace by undamaged letter(s).
17. ⁀‿	⁀‿ linking words or letters (e.g., bec‿ause).	Close up; delete space between letters.
18. *trs.*	⊔⊓ between letters or words (numbered if necessary).	Transpose as indicated.
19. *centre*	Indicate position with ┌ ┐	Place in centre of line.
20. □	E.g.: is required. It should . . .	Indent the first word.
21. ┌	]	Move to the left.
22. ┐	[	Move to the right.
23. *take over*	⊏	Take letter or word from end of one line to beginning of next.
24. *take back*	⊐	Take letter or word from beginning of one line to end of preceding line.
25. ↑	↑ over lines to be moved.	Raise lines.
26. ↓	↓ under lines to be moved.	Lower lines.
27. ǁ	ǁ	Straighten uneven margin.

Proof-correcting Symbols (*continued*)

MARGINAL SIGN	CORRESPONDING MARK IN TEXT	MEANING
28. //	once more	Straighten lines (type unevenly set).
29. ⊥	It is usual.	Push down space (printer's).
30. N.P.	an end. [At last	Begin a new paragraph here.
31. run on	they arrived. The last . . .	No new paragraph here.
32. spell out	Encircle words or figures to be altered.	The abbreviation or figure to be spelt out in full.
33. space out	Underline words or figures to be altered.	Spread words or letters further apart.
34. out see copy	⋏	Insert omitted portion of copy.
35. ⋏ (e.g.: very⋏)	⋏ e.g.: It was early.)	Caret mark. Insert matter indicated in margin.
36. k/	trade mare	Substitute letter or word indicated in margin.
37. ,⋏ ;⋏	⋏	Insert comma/semicolon.
38. ,/ ;/	/ through punctuation sign to be altered	Substitute comma/semicolon.
39. ⊙ (:)	⋏	Insert full stop/colon.
40. ⊙ (:)	/ through punctuation sign to be altered.	Substitute full stop/colon.
41. ?⋏ !⋏	⋏	Insert interrogation/exclamation mark.

Proof-correcting Symbols (*continued*)

MARGINAL SIGN	CORRESPONDING MARK IN TEXT	MEANING
42. ?/ !/	/ through punctuation sign to be altered.	Substitute interrogation/exclamation mark.
43. (/)	⁁ ⁁	Insert parentheses.
44. [/]	⁁ ⁁	Insert square brackets.
45. |-|	⁁	Insert hyphen.
46. /em/	⁁	Insert em rule or dash.
47. ʼ/	⁁	Insert apostrophe.
48. ʻ/ ʼ/	⁁ ⁁	Insert single quotation marks.
49. "/ "/	⁁ ⁁	Insert double quotation marks.
50. ....⁁	⁁	Insert ellipsis.
51. *insert rule*	—— under words affected.	Underline word or words.
52. (?)	Underline words, etc., affected.	Doubtful material. Is this correct or suitable?

Example of Proof-correcting

Caps.	The Wind in the Willows	centre	19
s.c.	III. The Wild Wood		
☐	The Mole had long wanted to make the aquaintance of the	c/	35
,/	Badger. He seemed, by all accounts to be such an imp	#	3
take back	ortant personage and, though visible rarely, to make his	trs.	18
stet	unseen influence felt by every~~body~~ (one) about the place. But	¶	1
Cap.	whenever the mole mentioned his wish to the water rat he	caps.	8
run on	found himself put off.		
,/	"Its all right," the Rat would say. "Bapger'll	ᑫ	15
⊥	turn up some day or other—he's always turning up and	/em/	46
l.c.	then I'll introduce you. The Best of fellows But you	!/	42
⌒	mus t not only take him as you find him, but when you	itals.	12
eq. #	find him.		
w.f.	"Couldn't you ask him here—dinner or something,"	?/	42
¶	said the Mole ~~eagerly~~. "He wouldn't come," replied the	N.P.	30
caps.	rat simply. "Badger hates society, and invitatinos, and	trs.	18
,/	dinner and all that sort of thing"	⊙	. 39
"/	Well, then, supposing we go and call on *him* suggest-	"/ take over	23
N.P.	ed the Mole. "Oh, I'm ~~quite~~ sure he wouldn't like that	¶ ¶	2/1
ital.	at all," said the Rat, quite alarmed. "He's so very shy,	×	16
out see copy	he'd know him ~~quite~~ well. Besides, we can't. It's quite	so/	36
‖	out of the question, because he lives in the very middel	# trs.	3/18
‖	of the Wild Wood.	"/	49

Below is a correct copy of the passage.

THE WIND IN THE WILLOWS

III. THE WILD WOOD

The Mole had long wanted to make the acquaintance of the Badger. He seemed, by all accounts, to be such an important personage and, though rarely visible, to make his unseen influence felt by everybody about the place. But whenever the Mole mentioned his wish to the Water Rat he found himself put off. "It's all right," the Rat would say. "Badger'll turn up some day or other – he's always turning up – and then I'll introduce you. The best of fellows! But you must not only take him *as* you find him, but *when* you find him."

"Couldn't you ask him here – dinner or something?" said the Mole.

"He wouldn't come," replied the Rat simply. "Badger hates Society, and invitations, and dinner, and all that sort of thing."

"Well, then, supposing we go and call on *him*," suggested the Mole.

"O, I'm sure he wouldn't like that at *all*," said the Rat, quite alarmed. "He's so very shy, he'd be sure to be offended. I've never even ventured to call on him at his own home myself, though I know him so well. Besides, we can't. It's quite out of the question, because he lives in the very middle of the Wild Wood."

15

Banking

Advantages of a Banking Account – Bank Accounts – Bank Lodgments – Bank Loans and Overdrafts – Cheques – Endorsements – Cheques with Endorsed Receipts – Crossing of Cheques – Dishonoured Cheques – Letters of Credit – Travellers' Cheques – Credit Cards – Standing Orders – Direct Debiting – Bank Giro Credits – Bank Reconciliation Statement – Negotiable Instruments – Bills of Exchange – Promissory Notes – IOU – Clearing House System – Bank of England – Bank Rate – Legal Tender.

Advantages of a Banking Account

THE chief advantages of operating a banking account are:

(1) Accounts may be paid in the safest and most convenient way – i.e., by cheque.

(2) Bank cheques may be produced, in the event of dispute, as evidence of payment.

(3) Money may be placed on deposit with a bank, thus enabling interest to be earned.

(4) Loan and overdraft facilities are available if required.

(5) The bank's name may be given as a reference to traders when opening a credit account.

(6) Valuables, deeds, securities, etc., may be deposited with the bank for safe custody.

(7) Approved Bills of Exchange may be discounted at the bank before the date of maturity in return for a small charge (i.e., 'discount') made by the bank.

(8) Financial advice can always be obtained, free of charge, from a bank.

Bank Accounts

There are two types of account commonly used at a commercial bank – the *Current Account* and the *Deposit Account.*

The Current Account is one into which payments are periodically made, and on which cheques are regularly drawn. A half-yearly charge is usually made by the bank for keeping its customers' current accounts.

Money placed on Current Account can be withdrawn without notice (i.e., on demand) by the simple expedient of drawing a cheque; but money placed on Deposit Account may be withdrawn only after a specified period of notice has been given to the bank.

The Deposit Account may be regarded as a reserve to which are transferred amounts that are not immediately required to meet the expenses of the business. Because the bank has the use of this money for a definite period, it will pay interest on balances on Deposit Account. (In Scotland money lodged on Deposit Account, on which interest is allowed on the minimum monthly balance, may be withdrawn without notice.)

Unlike Current Accounts, Deposit Accounts cannot be drawn upon by cheque – the normal procedure being to instruct the bank to make the necessary transfer from Deposit to Current Account, upon which cheques are then drawn in the usual way. The agreed period of notice should, of course, be given to the bank. (In Scotland money may be withdrawn from Deposit Account, without notice, on completion of a simple form of receipt known as a Withdrawal Form.)

Bank Lodgments

When paying money into a current account a *pay-in slip* should be completed and presented to the banker with the money. A form of paying-in slip with counterfoil is shown on p. 191 – the counterfoil being retained by the customer after the bank has stamped and initialled it.

Details of the bank's account with the customer are recorded in a bank *pass book* or a periodical *statement of account.* The specimen on p. 192 is a typical form of bank statement.

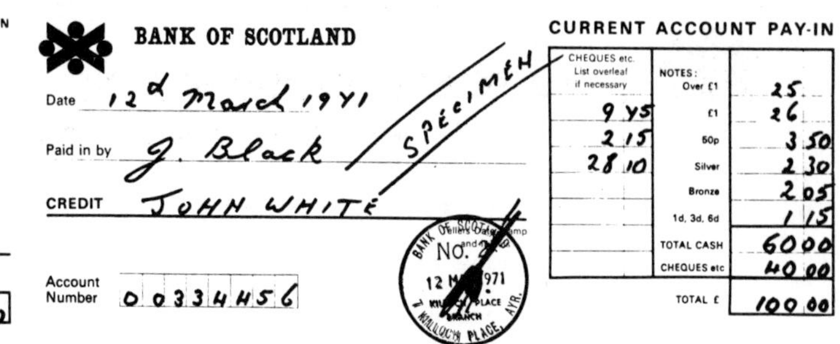

CURRENT ACCOUNT PAY-IN ACKNOWLEDGMENT
Tellers date Stamp and Initials
SPECIMEN
No. 2 12 MAR 71 KILLOCH PLACE BRANCH AYR
A/c JOHN WHITE
Subject to verification of all items other than cash
£ 100 00
Form No. 101

BANK OF SCOTLAND
Date 12th March 1971
Paid in by J. Black
CREDIT JOHN WHITE
SPECIMEN
Account Number 00334456
Tellers Date Stamp and Initials No. 2 12 MAR 1971 KILLOCH PLACE BRANCH AYR

CURRENT ACCOUNT PAY-IN

CHEQUES etc. List overleaf if necessary	NOTES:	
	Over £1	25
9 75	£1	26
2 15	50p	3 50
28 10	Silver	2 30
	Bronze	2 05
	1d, 3d, 6d	1 15
	TOTAL CASH	60 00
	CHEQUES etc	40 00
	TOTAL £	100 00

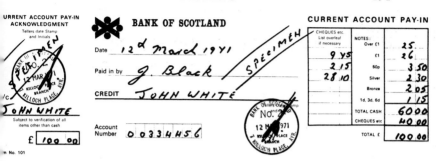

Fig. 6. Pay-in slip

Bank Loans and Overdrafts

Subject to approved security or guarantee, a bank will lend money to its customers either on loan account or by means of overdrafts. On *loan* account an agreed sum is lent for a fixed period, interest being charged in advance on the whole amount for that period. In the case of an *overdraft* the customer is allowed to overdraw his account to an agreed limit, and is charged interest only on the day-to-day balance of the overdraft.

Cheques

A *cheque* is an order to a banker for the payment of a certain sum of money on demand to, or to the order of, a specified person or to bearer.

Each cheque issued by a bank is numbered, but (since February, 1971) no longer requires to bear stamp duty.

Great care should be exercised in making out ('drawing') a cheque, so that there is no possibility of alteration by an unauthorized person. The following points should be noted when filling in a cheque form:

(1) The date must be completed in full.

(2) The payee's name and should be written clearly and accurately, and as close as possible to the word '*Pay*.'

(3) The cheque must be signed by the drawer with his usual signature (i.e., the specimen signature previously given by him to the bank).

STATEMENT OF CURRENT ACCOUNT

BRANCH 1244 ACCOUNT No. 00334456 IN ACCOUNT WITH BANK OF SCOTLAND

PAGE 1

John White Esq.,
Clark Road,
Ayr.

DATE	DESCRIPTION	DEBITS	CREDITS	BALANCE
1 Mar71		Fwd.		£1,000 .00
3 Mar71	678910	12. 04		
	678911	54. 36		
	678912	27. 50		
	678913	20. 10		£ 886 .00
4 Mar71	Div Shell		30. 46	£ 916 .46
5 Mar71	s/o SSEB	25. 20		£ 891 .26
8 Mar71	678914	223. 10		
	678916	146. 02		£ 522 .14
12 Mar71			100 .00	£ 622 .14

SPECIMEN

STATEMENT DATE	* NO VOUCHER FOR THIS ITEM	TOTAL DEBITS TO DATE	TOTAL CREDITS TO DATE	BALANCE ('DR'- OVERDRAWN A

Fig. 7. Bank statement

(4) The amount (in words and in figures) must be written as near as possible to the left-hand edge, in the space provided, and in accordance with the following directions:

(*a*) The amount in *words* should show the number of pounds in words and the pence in figures, thus:

Twenty-five pounds only
Twenty-five pounds 75

NOTE. If the amount is less than £1, *words* must be used to express the number of pence, thus:

Seventy-five pence

(*b*) The amount in *figures* should show the pounds separated from the pence by a *hyphen*, instead of a decimal point, thus:

£25–75

NOTE. If the amount is less than £1, a nought must come after the £ sign and before the hyphen, thus:

£0–75

(*c*) There should always be *two* figures after the hyphen, even if they are noughts, thus:

£25–00

(Alternatively, a dash may be written after the number of pounds, thus: £25——.)

In addition to completing the *cheque proper*, the drawer should also record on the *counterfoil* (i.e., the portion to the left of the perforation) the date, the amount (in figures), the name of the payee, and brief particulars as to the nature of the payment – the counterfoil being retained in the cheque book for reference.

Bankers issue two kinds of cheque – 'order' and 'bearer.'

Order Cheques

An *order* cheque bears the words "or Order" (see specimen cheque on p. 194) and means that the cheque is payable to a specified person, or to such person as the payee may order to receive the money. An order cheque requires to be *endorsed* (i.e., the payee must sign his name on the back of the cheque) before it can be cashed over the counter.

Bearer Cheques

A *bearer* cheque has the words "or Bearer" (instead of "or Order"), indicating that the cheque is payable to the person specified or to *bearer* – i.e., anyone presenting it at the bank. A bearer cheque does not require endorsement.

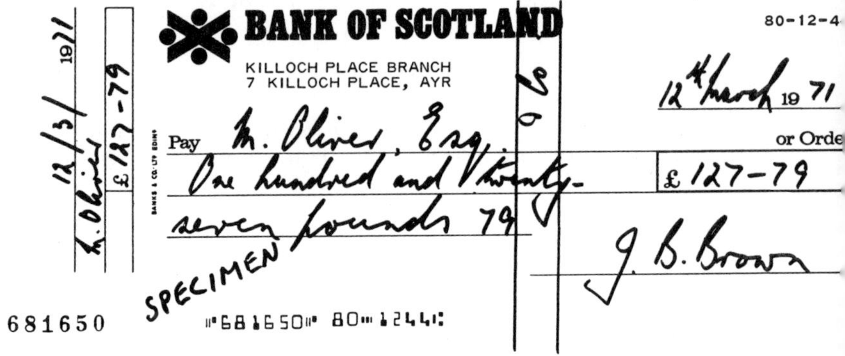

Fig. 8. Order cheque

Parties to a Cheque

There are three parties to a cheque:

(1) *Drawer:* the person who signs the cheque (e.g., J. B. Brown);
(2) *Drawee:* the bank on which the cheque is drawn (e.g., Bank of Scotland);
(3) *Payee:* the person to whom the cheque is made payable (e.g., M. Oliver).

Endorsements

As has been stated, to *endorse* a cheque means to sign one's name across the back of the cheque. An 'order' cheque requires to be endorsed by the payee before it can be cashed over the counter. Endorsement is not necessary, however, in the case of a *crossed* cheque, which cannot, of course, be cashed over the counter but must be paid into a banking account. (See "Crossing of Cheques," p. 196.)

Although a 'bearer' cheque does not normally require to be endorsed before being cashed, the banker may ask for endorsement as proof of identity.

A cheque payable to M. Oliver "or Order" (see specimen above) would be endorsed as shown on p. 195.

This is known as a *general* or *blank* endorsement. Note that the endorsement must always agree with the name or names

Back of Cheque:

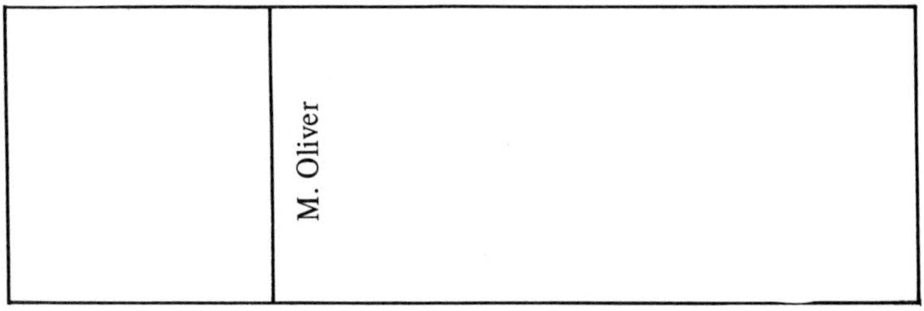

	M. Oliver

used on the face of the cheque. In the foregoing example, had the payee's name been incorrectly spelt "Olivier," the cheque would require to be endorsed thus:

M. Olivier
M. Oliver

If, instead of cashing or banking the cheque, the payee (M. Oliver) wished to pay it to another person (e.g., R. Jones) he would require to endorse it as follows:

Pay R. Jones or Order
M. Oliver

This is termed a *special* endorsement and requires the new endorsee (R. Jones) to endorse the cheque before he can cash it.

A cheque endorsed "Pay R. Jones only" has what is known as a *restrictive* endorsement, because it prevents further negotiation – i.e., R. Jones cannot transfer the cheque to anyone else.

Cheques with Endorsed Receipts

Some companies and corporations require the payee to sign a receipt which is printed on the back of the cheque. Because it is no longer necessary to endorse cheques paid into a banking account, drawers of cheques with endorsed receipts must indicate by means of a prominent capital "R" on the face of the cheque that the banker should look for the receipt on the back of the cheque.

Crossing of Cheques

When making out a cheque it is a wise precaution to 'cross' it by drawing two parallel lines across the face of the cheque, with or without the words "& Co." written between them. This means that such a cheque cannot be cashed, but must be paid into a banking account.

NOTE. A crossed cheque may be converted into an 'open' cheque by the addition of the words "Please pay cash" written on the face of the cheque by the drawer and followed by his signature.

A cheque that is not crossed is known as an *open* cheque, and such a cheque may be cashed over the bank counter. An open cheque is obviously not as 'safe' as a crossed cheque for the reason that, in the event of its going astray, it could be fraudulently cashed by an unauthorized person.

There are two types of crossing:

(1) General.
(2) Special.

(1) The following are examples of *general* crossings:

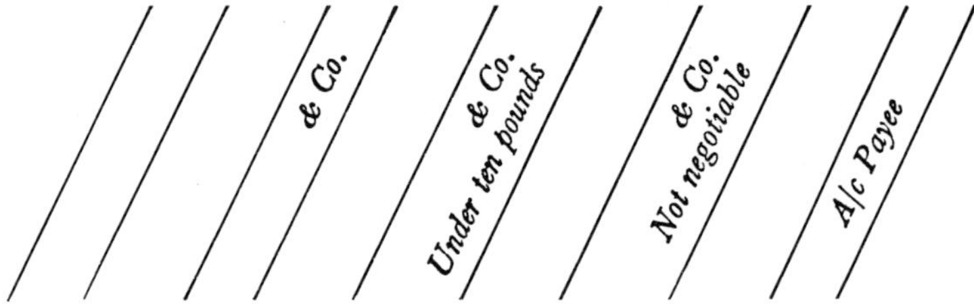

Fig. 9. General crossings

(2) A cheque is crossed *specially* when the name of the payee's bank is written between the parallel lines, thus:

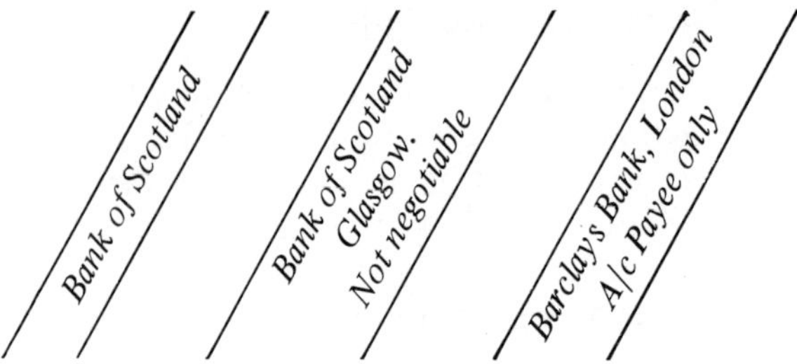

Fig. 10. Special crossings

A cheque that bears a *special* crossing can be paid only to the banker whose name appears in the crossing.

The words "A/c Payee" or "A/c Payee only" appearing in a crossing indicate that the cheque must be paid into the *payee's* account (i.e., the person to whom the cheque is made payable).

Negotiability of Cheques

A cheque is a *negotiable instrument* (i.e., an instrument by delivery of which the legal right to the money it represents is transferable from one person to another).

When a cheque is crossed "Not Negotiable," however, it simply means that the holder of the cheque has no better title or right to it than the person from whom he received it. A crossed cheque marked "Not Negotiable" in effect ceases to become freely negotiable, and thus provides a strong safeguard against fraud.

Dishonoured Cheques

When a cheque is *dishonoured* (i.e., returned by the banker unpaid) it is marked in one of the following ways:

R/D ("Refer to Drawer")
N/F ("No Funds")
I/F ("Insufficient Funds")
"*Not in Order*" (which means that an error has been made in making out the cheque, such as a difference between the amount in figures and that in words).

Other examples of irregularity are: "*Effects not Cleared*" (the cheques, etc., lodged having not yet been credited to the account as a result of the slight delay in passing through the Clearing House), "*Endorsement Irregular*," "*Post-dated*," "*Payment Stopped*," etc.

Stopping Cheques

In the event of a cheque going astray, or being lost or stolen, it is advisable to cancel it and issue a fresh cheque. The cheque may be 'stopped' by instructing the banker (in writing) to stop payment of the missing cheque should it be presented.

Such an instruction must be signed by the drawer, and should indicate the date and number of the cheque, the name of the payee, and the amount.

Post-dated Cheques

A *post-dated* cheque is one that bears a date later than the current date. Such a cheque will not be paid by the banker until the date stated on the cheque.

Ante-dated Cheques

An *ante-dated* cheque is one that bears a date earlier than the current date.

Stale Cheques

A *stale* cheque is one that has not been presented for payment within six months of the date of issue, after which date it lapses.

Letters of Credit

A *Letter of Credit* is a document in the form of a letter given by a bank to a client. It serves to introduce the client to that bank's branches or correspondents (i.e., agents), to whom the letter is addressed, and authorizes them to make payments in favour of the client up to the amount stated in the Letter of Credit. On the back of the letter columns are ruled for details of the payments made, and after payment of the last amount the Letter of Credit is returned to the issuing bank.

Issued simultaneously with the Letter of Credit (but carried separately) is a *Letter of Indication*, which quotes the number of the Letter of Credit and bears a specimen signature of the client. Both the Letter of Credit and the Letter of Indication must be produced before any payment can be obtained.

Travellers' Cheques

Travellers' cheques are also obtainable from a bank and are usually issued in denominations of £2, £5, £10, £20, and £50.

They may be cashed at any bank, and are accepted by many hotels and large stores, as well as shipping lines, airlines, etc.

NOTE. Before her employer leaves on a journey the secretary should see that he has signed all his travellers' cheques *once.* A second signature is required before the cheques can be cashed, but this must be given in the presence of the paying cashier.

Credit Cards

Credit Cards (e.g., Diners Club, American Express, and Barclaycard) may be used in hotels and restaurants and for travel, as well as for day-to-day shopping. When making a purchase or paying a hotel bill, the card is simply presented and a monthly account sent to the cardholder for the amount spent.

The main *advantages* of credit cards are:

(1) The use of a card obviates the need to carry large sums of cash.

(2) A number of bills may be settled with one cheque once a month, with a consequent saving in bank charges.

(3) Business expenses can be kept separate from personal expenses, and are easier to claim as they are all itemized on a monthly account.

(4) Cash (up to about £30) may be drawn at any branch of certain specified banks, or cheques may be cashed upon presentation of the card.

The main *disadvantage* of credit cards is that, in the event of loss, the cardholder is liable for all fraudulent expenses until the company is notified.

NOTE. In addition to credit cards, *cheque cards* (or travel cards) are issued by all the big banks except Barclays. These cards do *not* give credit but are intended to guarantee the cardholder's cheques up to a certain amount. (For details of *G.P.O. credit cards*, see p. 174.)

Standing Orders (Banker's Orders)

Where payments are required to be made periodically (e.g., monthly instalments or annual subscriptions) arrangements may be made for the bank to make payment direct on the due date. In this connection the customer will give his banker the appropriate instructions by completing a *standing order*, which may take the following form:

To: Bank of Scotland 15th August, 19 . .

Please pay to Barclays Bank, for Account Johnson & Smith Ltd., a sum of £6·50 on the 31st August and each following month, until otherwise ordered.

J. B. Brown

The bank will, of course, make the appropriate entry in the pass book or bank statement; and as soon as the statement is received the secretary, or other person responsible, should credit the cash book with the amount of the standing order plus the small charge made by the bank for this service.

Direct Debiting

A more recent banking service is *Direct Debiting*, which has a greater flexibility than the older Standing Order system. Standing Orders can be used only for *fixed* payments at *fixed* intervals, whereas Direct Debiting provides a system for paying fixed *or* varying amounts at fixed *or* varying dates, and therefore combines the benefits of the cheque and the Standing Order services.

Under the Standing Order system, the *bank* makes payment to the recipient (Johnson & Smith Ltd. in the specimen shown above), whereas under Direct Debiting the recipient himself passes the debit to the bank through the cheque-clearing system, and thus receives immediate credit.

No charge is made by the bank for this service.

Bank Giro Credits

The *Bank Giro Credit System* provides an alternative to the settlement of accounts or the payment of salaries, etc., by individual cheques. Under this system a Bank Giro credit slip is completed for each account (or each employee having a bank account), the credit slips being sent to the bank together with a cheque for the *total* sum to be paid. The credits to be distributed are then sent through the Giro Credit Clearing to the banks and branches indicated on the various slips, and each payee's account is credited with the appropriate amount.

Bank Giro credits are also used by those firms (e.g., multiple stores) whose principal bank account is in some other town. Such a firm may make lodgments at any branch of any bank, the money being then transferred through the Giro Credit Clearing to the firm's principal bank account, which is usually held in the town in which the head office of the company is based.

Bank Reconciliation Statement

It rarely happens that the bank balance shown in the cash book at any particular time agrees with the amount shown in the bank statement or pass book at the same date. This disagreement may be due to the fact that

(*a*) there is frequently a short lapse of time between the issue of a cheque and its subsequent payment by the bank on which it is drawn; *or*

(*b*) the bank may not yet have credited to the account all the cheques lodged with it.

It is therefore necessary to reconcile these two balances by preparing a *Bank Reconciliation Statement*, which, for reference purposes, is usually entered (in red ink) as a memorandum in the cash book. Before preparing the reconciliation statement the following procedure is necessary:

(1) Go through the cash book very carefully with the bank statement, and mark with a pencil tick corresponding items in the cash book and bank statement. (The unticked items will account for the difference between the two balances.)

(2) Make a list of *outstanding* cheques – i.e., those shown on the credit side of the cash book as having been drawn but which have not yet been presented at the bank and, consequently, do not appear in the bank statement. Next make a

list of *credits* outstanding – i.e., cash and cheques which have been paid into the bank but not yet credited to the account, and which do not therefore appear in the bank statement.

(3) Bank charges, etc. (which have already been deducted by the bank and are shown in the bank statement as a debit) will require to be entered on the credit side of the cash book, but meanwhile must be included in the reconciliation statement.

The *Bank Reconciliation Statement* is then prepared on the lines of the specimen example which has been compiled from the information given below:

Cash at Bank as shown by Cash Book (Bank Column)	£351·32
Cash at Bank as shown by Bank Statement	£370·42
Cheques drawn but not yet presented:	
J. Brown	£35·34
R. Jones	£19·52
F. Smith	£6·46
Cheques, etc., paid in but not yet credited:	
R. S. West	£16·28
S. Green	£22·69
Bank Charges not yet entered in Cash Book	£3·25

Method (1)*

BANK RECONCILIATION STATEMENT

as at 31st December, 19 . .

Balance shown in Bank Statement:			£370·42
Deduct cheques drawn but not yet presented:			
J. Brown:	£35·34		
R. Jones:	£19·52		
F. Smith:	£6·46		
			£61·32
		c/f	£309·10

* In Method (1) it will be seen that the reconciliation statement begins with the balance shown in the *bank statement*, whereas in Method (2) it begins with the balance shown in the *cash book*.

		b/f	£309·10
Add cheques paid in but not yet credited:			
R. S. West:	£16·28		
S. Green:	£22·69		
Bank Charges:	£3·25		
			£42·22
Balance shown in Cash Book:			£351·32

Method (2)*

BANK RECONCILIATION STATEMENT
as at 31st December, 19 . .

Balance shown in Cash Book:		£351·32
Add cheques drawn but not yet presented:		
J. Brown:	£35·34	
R. Jones:	£19·52	
F. Smith:	£6·46	
		£61·32
		£412·64
Deduct cheques paid in but not yet credited:		
R. S. West:	£16·28	
S. Green:	£22·69	
Bank Charges:	£3·25	
		£42·22
Balance shown in Bank Statement:		£370·42

NOTE. When there is an *overdraft* at the bank the procedure in each case is the reverse of that shown above.

Negotiable Instruments

It has already been stated that a cheque is a 'negotiable instrument' (see p. 197). Two further examples of negotiable instruments are Bills of Exchange and Promissory Notes.

* See footnote on p. 202.

Bills of Exchange

A *Bill of Exchange* is an unconditional order in writing addressed by one person to another, signed by the person giving it, requiring the person to whom it is addressed to pay on demand, or at a fixed or determinable future time, a sum certain in money to, or to the order of, a specified person or to bearer.

This *legal definition* of a Bill of Exchange also includes cheques, which are simply Bills of Exchange drawn on a banker and payable on demand.

The following is a specimen Bill of Exchange (inland):

No. 123 £140·53 16 West Street,
Glasgow.

5th August, 19 . .

Three months after date pay to our order the sum of One hundred and forty pounds fifty-three pence for value received.

W. Brown & Sons

To: Messrs. Cook & Lane,
51 North Street,
Glasgow.

There are three parties to a Bill of Exchange:

(1) *Drawer:* the person (or firm) who makes out and signs the bill (W. Brown & Sons); i.e., the creditor.
(2) *Drawee:* the person (or firm) on whom the Bill is drawn (Messrs. Cook & Lane); i.e., the debtor.
(3) *Payee:* the person (or firm) to whom the bill is to be paid (W. Brown & Sons).

In the foregoing example the "drawer" and the "payee" are one and the same (W. Brown & Sons); but Brown & Sons, had they so wished, could have made the bill payable to a third party – e.g., John Smith, in which case they would have specified "Pay to John Smith or order."

Acceptance of a Bill of Exchange

Before a Bill of Exchange can be drawn there must be a clear understanding between the creditor and the debtor that the creditor will draw the bill upon the debtor. Once the amount of the bill and the time limit for payment (i.e., the 'tenor' of the bill) have been agreed upon, the creditor 'draws' (i.e., writes out and signs) the bill. He then sends it to the debtor (or 'drawee') for *acceptance*, which is simply an acknowledgment of the bill and indicates willingness to pay it when it becomes due.

This 'acceptance' is written across the face of the bill in a similar position to the crossing on a cheque, e.g.:

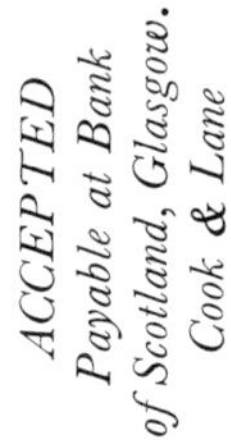

ACCEPTED
Payable at Bank
of Scotland, Glasgow.
Cook & Lane

Fig. 11. 'Acceptance' on bill

The drawee (who is now known as the *acceptor*) then returns the accepted bill to the drawer, who retains it until the due date, or, if he is in need of ready cash before that date, takes it to someone (usually his banker) who will 'cash' it for him.

Days of Grace

In calculating the due date of an inland Bill of Exchange three days ('days of grace') are added. In the foregoing example the bill (which is dated on the 5th August) matures or becomes payable on the 8th November – i.e., three months and three days after date. Days of grace do not, however, apply to bills payable on demand, at sight, or on some fixed date.

Advantages of Bills of Exchange

The chief advantages of a Bill of Exchange are:

(1) It fixes beyond dispute the amount owing and the date on which it is to be paid.

(2) It may be discounted at a bank (i.e., cashed in advance), a small charge known as 'discount' being levied by the bank.

(3) It enables a trader to obtain the use of the goods or to resell them before payment becomes due.

(4) Because a Bill of Exchange is negotiable, it can be transferred from one person to another without the actual transmission of money.

NOTE. A bill may be transferrred from one person to another by the act of endorsement – the person signing his name on the back of the bill being called the *endorser*, while the person to whom it is endorsed is known as the *endorsee.*

An endorsement may be written on the bill itself or on a slip of paper attached to the bill, known as an 'allonge.'

Dishonour of a Bill of Exchange

A Bill of Exchange may be dishonoured either by non-acceptance or by non-payment. Dishonour by non-acceptance occurs when the bill is presented by the drawer to the drawee for acceptance and acceptance is refused or cannot be obtained. Dishonour by non-payment occurs when the bill is presented for payment on maturity (i.e., the date on which it is payable) and payment is refused or cannot be obtained.

Noting a Bill

An *inland* bill, when dishonoured, may be 'noted' – that is, presented a second time by a Notary Public on the day of its dishonour, or not later than the next succeeding business day. If still unpaid, the Notary affixes his note to that effect, stating the reason for dishonour, and in a court of law this is accepted as proof that the bill was presented and dishonoured.

Protesting a Bill

A *foreign* bill, in the event of non-acceptance or non-payment, must be 'protested,' a *protest* being a formal certificate issued by a Notary Public to the effect that the bill has been dishonoured.

Accommodation Bill

An *Accommodation Bill* is a Bill of Exchange that has been issued *without value having actually been received*, as would be the case if given in exchange for a loan. It is sometimes known as a 'fictitious bill,' a 'kite,' or a 'windmill.'

Promissory Notes

A *Promissory Note* is an unconditional promise in writing made by one person to another, signed by the maker, engaging to pay on demand, or at a fixed or determinable future time, a sum certain in money to, or to the order of, a specified person or to bearer.

The following is a specimen Promissory Note:

£140·53 51 North Street,
Glasgow,

5th August, 19 . .

Three months after date, we promise to pay to Messrs. W. Brown & Sons, or order, the sum of One hundred and forty pounds fifty-three pence for value received

Payable at
Bank of Scotland,
Glasgow.

Cook & Lane

There are *two* parties to a Promissory Note – the *maker* (Cook & Lane) and the *payee* (W. Brown & Sons).

It will be seen that a Promissory Note is a *promise* to pay, whereas a Bill of Exchange is an *order* to pay.

As in the case of Bills of Exchange, three days of grace are allowed in calculating the due dates of Promissory Notes.

IOU (*I owe you*)

An IOU, on the other hand, is *not* a negotiable instrument. It is merely a written acknowledgment of a debt given by the person who owes the money to the person advancing the loan. The IOU is retained by the lender as proof of the indebtedness.

Clearing House System

The *Clearing House System* may be described as the method by which the cheques and bills paid into the banks of the country for collection are brought together in central establishments and the various claims of each bank against the others are settled.

The members of the Clearing House (known as 'clearing banks') all have accounts with the Bank of England, which is also a member of the Clearing House.

All the cheques and bills that pass through the Clearing House on any day are settled simply by means of debit and credit entries in the books of the Bank of England – which entries adjust the differences as between the clearing banks – the whole transaction being carried through without the exchange of actual cash.

Bank of England

The *Bank of England*, which was incorporated in 1694 under Royal Charter, is both the bankers' bank and the Government's bank. Its chief functions are as follows:

(1) To 'manage' the Note Issue of the country.

(2) To safeguard the Gold Reserves of the country.

(3) To act as the Bankers' Bank.

(4) To act as a Clearing Agent for the settlement of differences between the various banks.

(5) To deal with the receipt of bullion (i.e., gold or silver in bars) and specie (minted coins) from the Mint.

(6) To 'manage' the National Debt.

(7) To conduct the main banking business of the State (i.e., the proceeds of Income Tax, Customs and Excise, etc.).

(8) To 'fix' the Bank Rate, etc.

Bank Rate

Bank Rate is the official minimum rate per cent of discount charged by the Bank of England for discounting approved Bills of Exchange. Bank Rate controls all rates of interest throughout the country. For example, an *increase* in Bank Rate means an increased interest charge for mortgages, more expensive hire-purchase transactions, and dearer bank overdrafts.

Legal Tender

Legal Tender is any form of money that can be used in legal settlement of a debt, and that cannot be refused by the creditor. In the British Isles one cannot be compelled to accept, in settlement of a debt, more than £5 in 5p or 10p coins; £10 in 50p coins; or 20p in the lower denominations of ½p, 1p, or 2p.

Bank notes (i.e., those notes issued by the Bank of England) are legal tender for *any* amount, which means they are on exactly the same footing as coined money. Notes issued by Scottish and Irish banks (and usually referred to as 'country' notes) are not legal tender, but are regarded as 'good' tender if not objected to at the time of tender.

NOTE. Each Scottish bank has its English 'correspondent,' and in the event of difficulty country notes can always be exchanged for English notes at the correspondent bank.

16

Payment of Wages and Accounts

Paying Wages and Salaries – Preparation of the Weekly Pay Roll by Accounting Machine – Paying Accounts – Receipts – Methods of Payment – National Giro – Paying Subscriptions.

Paying Wages and Salaries

A LARGE firm usually includes within its organization a Wages Department, which is concerned solely with the preparation and payment of wages. In the smaller office, however, the secretary is frequently responsible for performing this task. The procedure is normally as follows:

On the Day before Pay Day

(1) Enter up the weekly or monthly Wages Book in accordance with the specimen ruling given below.

1. Date	2. Name	3. Rate of Pay	4. Gross Wage (week or month)	5. National Insurance Deduction	6. P.A.Y.E. Deduction

7. Graduated Pension Contribution	8. Super-annuation Deduction (if any)	9. Net Wage Payable	10. Employer's National Insurance Contribution	11. Remarks

(2) Calculate the appropriate deductions for National Insurance contributions, P.A.Y.E. Income Tax, and Graduated Pension contributions. (See Chapters 17 and 18.)

(3) Enter the wages and the appropriate deductions on each employee's Deduction Card.

(4) Draw a cheque for the total wages and the total value of insurance stamps. (*Note.* The amount of the cheque drawn must agree with the total amount shown in the Wages Book for "net wages payable" plus the *total* insurance stamps.)

(5) Make an analysis of the cheque, divided into notes, silver, and copper, to enable each employee to receive his exact wage. (The analysis may be made on the back of the cheque.) For example, a wage of £9·95 would require one £5 note, four £1 notes, one 50p, one 5p, and four 10p coins.

(6) Purchase from the Post Office the requisite number of National Insurance stamps.

On Pay Day

(1) Affix the appropriate insurance stamp to each employee's National Insurance card, and cancel the stamp by writing or stamping the date across it.

(2) Obtain each employee's signature as he is paid (if this is the usual practice), remembering to exercise discretion to ensure that one employee does not see how much another is receiving.

NOTE. It is the practice of many firms to pay their employees by cheque.

Preparation of the Weekly Pay Roll by Accounting Machine

Instead of entering up the Wages Book by hand, as is usual in a smaller firm, the preparation of the weekly Pay Roll in a large organization is frequently carried out by accounting machine.

In addition to the Pay Roll – which is simply a register of employees showing how the wages for each employee are calculated, and providing at the same time a permanent record of each week's wages – the employer must also keep the following essential records:

(*a*) Deduction Card for each employee (see Chapter 17);

(*b*) the employee's Pay Slip, which is inserted in (or printed on) the pay envelope, and which shows how the employee's wage is calculated and made up.

The Pay Roll or Wages Sheet is inserted in the machine at the back, while the employee's Deduction Card and Pay Slip are inserted at the front of the machine. As each item is entered in turn, including the necessary deductions, the machine carriage is automatically tabulated and the machine computes and prints the cumulative gross wage to date, taxable pay, tax payable for the week, and the net wage payable.

The great advantage of machine operation is that the individual records and the Pay Roll are prepared simultaneously, thus ensuring speed with complete accuracy.

Paying Accounts

When paying accounts the following points should be observed:

(*a*) Ensure that the goods or services charged for have actually been received, and that the account has not already been paid;

(*b*) check the accuracy of the account or invoice;

(*c*) check that any discount allowed has been deducted;

(*d*) if payment is being made by cheque, ensure that the cheque is correctly drawn, that it is properly crossed, and that the counterfoil is completed.

NOTE. Do not forget to number and file the receipted account when it is returned.

Receipts

Receipts should be numbered consecutively and filed. A box file (see Chapter 8) is useful for this purpose.

Methods of Payment

Business accounts may be paid by

(*a*) cash;
(*b*) postal order;
(*c*) money order;
(*d*) cheque;
(*e*) bill of exchange;
(*f*) promissory note;
(*g*) Bank Giro credit;
(*h*) National Giro.

Cheques, Bank Giro credits, bills of exchange, and promissory notes have been dealt with in Chapter 15.

Cash

If cash (whether in the form of coin or notes) is sent through the post it should be registered – the special envelope supplied by the Post Office being used for this purpose.

Postal Orders

Small amounts, up to £5 in value, may be sent through the post by means of postal order. When paying accounts by postal order it is important to retain the counterfoil in order to support any claim for repayment should the postal order be lost. It is a wise precaution also to cross postal orders, in which case payment will be made only through a bank.

Money Orders

Money orders are issued for amounts up to £50 in value.

For certain classes of payment, such as payment of Income Tax, money orders are issued free of poundage. Details will be found in the *Post Office Guide.*

Application for a money order must be made upon the printed requisition form issued by the Post Office and requiring the following information.

(1) the full name of the payee;
(2) the name and address of the sender;
(3) the name of the Post Office at which the money is to be paid;

(4) the amount of the order and the method of payment – i.e., whether at the Post Office specified, through a bank, or by telegraph.

The money order, issued by the Post Office to the sender, states only the amount of the order and the name of the paying office. It is sent by the purchaser to the payee, who will present it at the paying office, where he will be asked to sign the order and to state the name of the sender.

Telegraphic Money Orders. An inland money order may be transmitted to the payee by telegraph, in which case the words "By Telegraph" should be written across the completed requisition form. In addition to paying the poundage (which is the same as that on an ordinary money order), the sender is required to pay the cost of the telegram of advice sent by the issuing office to the paying office.

National Giro

The *National Giro* is a banking service operated by the Post Office and offering current account facilities. (Full details of the Giro Service are given in the *National Giro Handbook.*)

Once an account has been opened with the initial deposit the account-holder is sent a supply of Giro stationery: (*a*) appropriate forms for use when making transfers or deposits; (*b*) payment orders; (*c*) postage-paid envelopes addressed to the National Giro Centre.

Facilities offered by the National Giro Service are:

(1) *Automatic Debit Transfer* (ADT) between Giro accounts, whereby arrangements may be made for the payment from one holder's account to another holder's account of varying amounts at fixed or varying dates.

(2) *Standing Orders* for transfers between Giro accounts; i.e., regular payments may be made by transfer from one holder's account to another holder's account.

(3) *Giro Drafts* – a Giro draft being a special type of Giro payment order drawn by the Post Office.

Inpayments. Payments may be made into the Giro account of one person by any other person without a Giro account. An 'inpayment' form (obtainable at the Post Office is merely completed by the person making the payment and handed over the counter together with the amount to be credited and the appropriate fee.

Statements of Account. As in the case of a bank, statements of account are rendered periodically to the account-holder, or will be submitted more frequently upon request. (*Note.* No holder of a Giro account may overdraw his account.)

Giro Directories. A directory of account-holders is published at regular intervals. The complete directory consists of eight sections, six of which contain the names (in alphabetical order), addresses and account numbers of both private and business account-holders for the six geographical centres. The seventh section lists (in alphabetical order) all *business* account-holders, while the eighth section lists all account-holders in order of *account number.*

Paying Subscriptions

Where subscriptions are regular and *few in number* (e.g., club subscriptions or charitable subscriptions) they may be dealt with as follows:

(*a*) *By Banker's Standing Order*, which authorizes the bank to make payment direct on the due date. (See pp. 199–200.)

(*b*) *By making a note in the Secretary's Diary* under the appropriate date.

(*c*) *By making a note on Reminder ('Tickler') Cards*, which are placed behind the appropriate guide cards in order of date. (See section on Diaries and Memory Aids, Chapter 6, p. 97.)

If, however, subscriptions are rather more numerous it will be found helpful to keep a small card index, containing the names and addresses (in alphabetical order) of the organizations concerned, amount of subscription, and date due.

This method may also be used where the secretary is responsible for the collection of subscriptions from others, in which case a card is made out for *each subscriber*, giving name and address, amount of subscription, date due, and date paid. (See section on Card Indexing, p. 117.)

17

Income Tax and P.A.Y.E.

Assessment and Collection of Income Tax – "Pay as You Earn" (P.A.Y.E.) – Income Tax Year – Graduated National Insurance Contributions – Deduction Cards – Code Numbers – Emergency Code (Code 'E') – Tax Tables – Deduction or Refund of Tax – Remitting Tax – Employee Leaving – Emergency Code Table – Employer's Certificate of Pay and Tax Deducted – Employer's Annual Statement Declaration and Certificate – "Employer's Guide to 'Pay As You Earn'" – P.A.Y.E. Forms – Mechanization of P.A.Y.E. – Allowances – Surtax – Selective Employment Tax – Corporation Tax – Capital Gains Tax – Confidential Nature of Income Tax Matters.

INCOME Tax was first introduced in 1798 as a temporary war tax; it was reintroduced in 1842 and has since become a permanent part of the taxation structure of this country. Originally very wide in scope, covering the incomes of all types of entities – whether companies, partnerships, or individuals – it is now concerned primarily with the income of the individual, whether self-employed or in the employment of another.

Income Tax is reimposed annually through the medium of the annual Finance Act. In the spring of each year the Chancellor of the Exchequer presents to Parliament his Budget, in which he estimates the taxation requirements of the Government for the ensuing year and proposes the measures by which he wishes to collect such taxes. These measures are incorporated in the annual Finance Bill which, after debate, becomes the

Finance Act for the year and gives the force of law to the proposals of the Government.

The rate of Income Tax for the year is fixed by the annual Finance Act, and is known as the "Standard Rate." This rate (at present 39p in the £, or 38·75%) is levied on the *taxable* income of the taxpayer, which is his income for the year calculated according to certain rules and after various *allowances* (see p. 226) have been deducted to provide relief appropriate to his circumstances.

Assessment and Collection of Income Tax

The Government Department responsible for the assessment and collection of Income Tax is that of the Commissioners of Inland Revenue, normally referred to as the Board of Inland Revenue. Under the Commissioners are the local Inspectors, permanent civil servants. Collectors are concerned for the most part only with the collection of tax, and are not to be confused with Inspectors.

Inspectors have an expert knowledge of tax law, and are responsible for making most assessments (other than Surtax) and dealing with claims and allowances. The country is divided into 'districts,' with one or more Inspectors in charge of each. All inquiries concerning Income Tax should be addressed to the Inspector of the district in which the taxpayer is normally resident, or (in the case of an employee) in which his income arises; e.g., a sales representative who is paid from Head Office will have his tax matters dealt with by the district to which Head Office makes its returns, irrespective of where *he* lives and works.

If a taxpayer disagrees with an assessment of tax, he may appeal against it. His appeal will, in the first place, be addressed to the Inspector who raised it; but as the Inspector is, of course, a party to the dispute the appeal is heard and determined, not by the Inspector, but by the General Commissioners (local persons appointed on a voluntary basis by the Lord Chancellor or, in Scotland, by the Local Authority).

Schedules

Income Tax is assessed under various 'schedules' according to the nature of the income assessed:

Schedule A – Rents receivable from lands, houses, buildings, etc.

Schedule B – National income from the *occupation* of woodlands (namely, one-third of the annual value of the land) which are managed on a commercial basis for profit, where no election is made for assessment under Schedule D.

Schedule C – Income arising from interest and dividends on certain Government stocks, etc., such income having been taxed at source.

Schedule D – Income *not* taxed at source arising out of the following 'cases':

Case I: Trades, commercial activities on land, including cattle dealers and milk sellers, and woodlands commercially managed where the taxpayer so elects.

II: Professions and vocations.

III: Untaxed War Loan and other Government Stocks, Deposit Interest, Treasury Bills, etc.

IV: Foreign and Colonial securities.

V: Foreign and Colonial possessions, including foreign pensions.

VI: Sundry profits not included in other Cases, such as letting furnished accommodation, guaranteeing a loan, underwriting, etc., where not a trade assessable under Case I.

VII: Short Term Gains (see p. 227.)

Schedule E – Deals with income from an office or employment, and applies to salaries and wages, bonuses, commissions, directors' fees, pensions (other than foreign pensions), etc. The method used for deducting Income Tax under Schedule E is known as "Pay As You Earn."

Collection of Tax

Schedules A, B & D – Inspectors issue to tax-payers 'Assessment Notices' stating the amount of income assessed to tax and the tax payable. A pay-slip and instructions for payment are added. Collectors are informed, and it is their duty to ensure that the tax is paid on time.

Schedule C – The payer, or paying agency in the United Kingdom, deducts tax at the Standard Rate and pays this over to the Inland Revenue. If the taxpayer thereby pays more tax than is due, procedures exist for reclaiming the excess.

Schedule E – The employer, or other person responsible for payment of the wage, salary, pension, or other emolument, calculates the tax due – according to the P.A.Y.E. regulations – and pays this over to the Inland Revenue authorities.

"Pay As You Earn" (P.A.Y.E.)

The P.A.Y.E. method of collection of Income Tax was first devised during the 1939–1945 War and has been in operation ever since. It is also used nowadays as a vehicle for the collection of National Insurance Graduated Contributions; but this is simply a matter of clerical machinery and has nothing to do with Income Tax as such. Graduated Contributions are dealt with in Chapter 18 (p. 236).

Under the P.A.Y.E. scheme, the employer is responsible for making the appropriate deductions of Income Tax, *before* payment of wages or salaries to his employees, and remitting the amount of tax thus deducted to the Collector of Taxes once a month.

The amount of tax to be deducted by the employer each pay day depends on:

(1) the employee's total gross pay since the beginning of the Income Tax year (6th April);

(2) his Income Tax allowances (or 'free pay') for the same period as determined by his 'code number'; and

(3) the total tax deducted on previous pay days.

Operation of the P.A.Y.E. Scheme

The P.A.Y.E. scheme operates as follows:

(*a*) The employer first calculates the amount of pay due to the employee.

(*b*) To this amount he adds the total of all previous payments made to the employee since 6th April.

(*c*) He then refers to Table A (Free Pay Table) and calculates the amount of 'free pay' to which the employee is entitled in accordance with his code number.

(*d*) The amount of 'free pay' is subtracted from the total gross pay to date – referred to in (*b*) – in order to arrive at the amount of taxable pay due.

(*e*) The employer then refers to Table B (Taxable Pay Table) in order to calculate the total tax due to date.

(*f*) Finally, he subtracts the amount of total tax already deducted from the figure of total tax shown in Table B (see (*e*)), thus arriving at the amount to be deducted from the employee's gross pay on the pay day in question.

Sometimes (as, for example, when the employee has worked a short week) the figure of total tax shown by the Tax Tables may be less than the tax already deducted – in which case the employer must *refund* the difference to the employee instead of making any deduction.

NOTE. It is the employer's duty to keep records of the figures of pay given and tax deducted at each pay day. (See pp. 210–212.)

A list of forms used in operating "Pay As You Earn" is given on p. 225.

Income Tax Year

The tax year runs from 6th April to 5th April, and is divided into 52 weeks, 6th to 12th April being week *one*; and twelve months, 6th April to 5th May being month *one*.

Each year, prior to 6th April, the Inland Revenue Authorities issue each employer with:

(*a*) a set of Tax Tables;

(*b*) a Deduction Card for each employee earning £5·25 or more a week (*or* £22·75 or more a month);

(*c*) a Blue Card of Instructions for weekly-paid employees;

(*d*) a Yellow Card of Instructions for monthly-paid employees;

(*e*) a pay-slip (P30) for the payment of tax to the Collector of Taxes;

(*f*) a current copy of the *Employer's Guide to "Pay As You Earn"* (see p. 224), or any necessary amendments to it.

Graduated National Insurance Contributions

Under the National Insurance Act, 1959, *graduated pension contributions* must be deducted by employers from the wages or salaries of their employees, through the P.A.Y.E. system in conjunction with Income Tax, and forwarded together with the tax deductions to the Collector of Taxes at the end of each tax month. (See Chapter 18, pp. 236–237.)

Deduction Cards

When the employer deducts Income Tax and graduated pension contributions from the wages or salaries of his employees, both the graduated contribution and the tax deducted are entered on a Deduction Card – each employee being given a separate P11 card (see p. 225).

The Deduction Card is divided into eight columns, which are headed as follows:

NAT. INS. Employee's Graduated Contributions (1)	Gross Pay in the week (*or* month) (2)	Total Gross Pay to date (3)	Total Free Pay to date as shown by Table A (4)
Total Taxable Pay to date (5)	Total Tax due to date as shown by Table B (6)	Tax deducted in the week (*or* month) (7)	Tax refunded in the week (*or* month) (8)

Tax Tables are supplied by the Board of Inland Revenue for use with the Deduction Cards, and at the end of the Income Tax year (5th April) all the Deduction Cards must be returned to the Collector of Taxes.

Code Numbers

In the space at the top of the Deduction Card marked "Code," there is entered either a number (which may be any number from 1 to 728) or the letters "C",[1] "D",[2] "S.R."

[1] *Code C* – Standard rate *less* earned income relief at the normal rate appropriate to the amount of pay.

[2] *Code D* – Standard rate *less* earned income relief at the lower rate of one-ninth only.

(Standard Rate) or "N.T." (No Tax). Where the Code is a number from 1 to 728, this indicates the place in Table A of the Tax Tables to which reference must be made in order to find the amount of the employee's free pay to be entered on his Deduction Card.

A person's *code number* is determined by the allowances to which he is entitled, and which must be indicated on a Tax Return form (P1) to be completed annually by the employee. The more allowances a person has, the higher is his code number – e.g., a single man might be allotted Code Number 205, and a married man Code Number 505.

Emergency Code (Code 'E')

Where the *Emergency Code* is used, the employer should prepare a Deduction Card and enter 'E' in the code space at the top of the card. The Emergency Code Table is provided for use where Code 'E' applies (see p. 224).

Tax Tables

Tax Tables are issued to the employer for both weekly- and monthly-paid employees. Each Tax Table consists of two parts:

Table A: Free Pay Table. This shows for each code number the total free pay to date – i.e., the fixed weekly (or monthly) free pay multiplied by the appropriate number of weeks (or months).

Table B. Taxable Pay Table. This shows the total tax due on the taxable pay to date – i.e., the total gross pay to date less the total free pay to date.

NOTE. Copies of the Tax Tables are available for reference in public libraries, tax offices, etc. In addition, the employer should make available for reference by his employees a copy of the Tax Tables to enable them to check the deductions made from their pay, if desired.

Deduction or Refund of Tax

Tax must be deducted or refunded in accordance with the Tax Tables whenever any pay is paid to the employee, *irrespective of the period over which the pay was earned and even if that period fell into a previous Income Tax year.*

Tax deductions must be calculated by reference to the gross pay of the employee before any deductions are made, "gross pay" for tax deduction purposes including the following: salary, wages, fees, overtime, bonus, commission, pension, sick pay, holiday pay, etc.

Remitting Tax

In addition to making the appropriate Income Tax deductions from the wages or salaries of his employees, the employer is also responsible for remitting the amount of tax thus deducted to the Collector of Taxes not later than the 19th day of each month – i.e., within fourteen days of the end of each Income Tax month (ending on the fifth day of each calendar month). A pay-slip is used for this purpose, the slip being returned to the employer with an official receipt. Pay-slips are issued each month, showing the total remittances made from 6th April to date.

If there is no remittance due in any month the pay-slip should still be sent in but marked "Nil."

Employee Leaving

When an employee for whom the employer holds a Deduction Card leaves, a certificate on form P45 ("Particulars of Employee Leaving") must be prepared in accordance with the directions on that form.

Form P45

When form P45 has been completed, part 1 must be detached and sent to the Tax Office immediately, and *parts 2 and 3 of the form handed to the employee when he leaves.* The employee must not separate parts 2 and 3 of the form, but must hand both parts to his new employer as soon as he begins his next employment, so that the correct deductions of tax may be continued. The new employer then detaches part 3, which he should complete and send to the Tax Office immediately, retaining part 2 for reference.

If the new employee fails to produce form P45 – possibly because he has lost it, or because he has not previously been employed – form P46 must be completed by the employer and sent to the Tax Office immediately. In addition, he should prepare a Deduction Card and apply the Emergency Code Table (Pink Card).

Emergency Code Table

Instructions for use of the Emergency Code are given on an *Emergency Code Table* (P15) which is sent to employers for use:

(*a*) for any employee liable to tax for whom no Deduction Card or form P6 has been received;
(*b*) for certain new employees.

Tax should be deducted by reference to the Emergency Code Table (P15) and in accordance with the instructions on that Table.

Employer's Certificate of Pay and Tax Deducted

After 5th April each year the employer is required to give a certificate (P60) to every employee who is in his employment on that date and from whose pay tax has been deducted. The certificate should show the total amount paid to the employee during the year and the total tax (less refunds) deducted.

Employer's Annual Statement Declaration and Certificate

At the end of each Income Tax year, and not later than the 19th April, all the Deduction Cards must be returned to the Collector of Taxes. The employer's Annual Statement Declaration and Certificate (form P35) must also be completed and sent to the Collector of Taxes with the cards.

"Employer's Guide to 'Pay as You Earn'"

The *Employer's Guide to "Pay as You Earn"* issued by the Board of Inland Revenue is a useful booklet which should be referred to when queries arise in connection with P.A.Y.E. procedure.

NOTE. There is also a *Farmer's Guide to "Pay As You Earn."*

P.A.Y.E. Forms

The following is a list of forms likely to be needed for normal P.A.Y.E. procedure:

P1	Tax Return Form.
P6	Notice to employer of code number or amended code number.
P8	Blue Card. Instructions to employers – weekly-paid employees.
P10	Yellow Card. Instructions to employers – monthly-paid employees.
P11	Combined weekly and monthly Deduction Card.
P15	Emergency Code Table (Pink Card).
P30	Pay-slip – employer's remittances.
P35	Employer's Annual Statement Declaration and Certificate.
P45	Part 1: Particulars of employee leaving.
	Part 2: Employee leaving – copy of employer's certificate.
	Part 3: New employee – particulars of old employment.
P46	Particulars of employee for whom no code number has been notified to employer.
P47	Employer's application for authority to refund tax exceeding £10 to new employee.
P48	Authority to refund tax exceeding £10 to new employee.
P50	Refund during unemployment – employee's application.
P60	Employer's Certificate of Pay and Tax Deductions to be given to employee at end of tax year.
GPF1	Graduated Contribution Tables (weekly).
GPF2	Graduated Contribution Tables (monthly).

Mechanization of P.A.Y.E.

The operation of P.A.Y.E. is essentially a mechanical one, and is being increasingly carried out today by computer or semi-computerized machines, such as the I.B.M. or Burrough's 'magnetic stripe' system.

Allowances

In order to graduate the amount of tax payable according to the financial position of each tax-payer, certain personal allowances (which vary with individual circumstances) are granted. The most important of these allowances are:

(*a*) Earned Income Allowance.
(*b*) 'Personal' Allowance.
(*c*) Child Allowance.
(*d*) Dependent Relative Allowance.
(*e*) Age Allowance.
(*f*) Life Assurance (and Building Society Interest) Allowance.

The appropriate allowances – the amounts of which vary from time to time, as laid down in the annual Finance Act – are deducted from a person's total income, the remainder being called his *taxable* income. These allowances must be claimed at the time the Income Tax Return is completed.

Surtax

Surtax[1] is an additional rate of tax levied at a scale rate on those whose total income exceeds a specified level, the rate of tax being governed by the annual Finance Act. The tax, which is a personal one, is assessed and collected separately from Income Tax and is due on the 1st January following the year of assessment.

Selective Employment Tax (S.E.T.)[2]

Since 5th September, 1966, all employers have been required to pay *Selective Employment Tax* in respect of every employee for whom they are liable to pay National Insurance contributions. The tax is payable together with the National Insurance contribution in one combined stamp. (See leaflet NI 157 for current rates.)

NOTE. No part of the tax is borne by the employee.

[1] In 1973 – instead of computing Surtax and Income Tax separately, as hitherto – a *single* graduated personal tax will be introduced. A complete P.A.Y.E. recoding will therefore come into effect on 6th April, 1973.

[2] Cut by half in 1971, and to be abolished entirely in 1973. (NOTE. Purchase Tax will also be abolished in 1973, at which time both S.E.T. and Purchase Tax will be replaced by a *single* "Value Added" Tax (V.A.T.), which is a tax on spending.)

Selective Employment Tax is, in certain cases, offset by a system of refund and premiums, but in no case can the tax be excused *before* payment.

Corporation Tax

Corporation Tax is a tax levied on the profits of limited liability companies and other corporate bodies in the United Kingdom. It is *not*, however, charged on profits earned by sole traders or partnerships.

Capital Gains Tax

Capital Gains Tax is a tax on gains made by speculation.

Under the provisions of the Finance Act, 1965, and subsequent amending Acts, capital profit realized on the purchase and sale of any chargeable asset held for a period of less than twelve months was subject to Short Term Gains Tax[1] (see Case VII, Schedule D, p. 218), while that realized on chargeable assets held for a period of more than twelve months is now subject to a Capital Gains Tax.

A gain realized on the sale of a person's dwelling-house is not, however, subject to Capital Gains Tax; nor are goods and chattels on which a gain of £1000 or less is realized. The sale of securities to the value of £500 or less in any one year is also not subject to Capital Gains Tax.

Confidential Nature of Income Tax Matters

As a great deal of confidential information is likely to come into the secretary's hands when dealing with her employer's Income Tax affairs, it is imperative that she should observe absolute silence and discretion in all such matters.

[1] Under the Finance Act, 1971, *Short Term Gains Tax* has been abolished.

18

Insurance

Insurance Policy – Premium – Days of Grace – Proposal Form – Insurable Value – Types of Insurance: Fire, Life, Accident, Marine – National Insurance Scheme – Industrial Injuries Scheme – Combined Weekly Contribution – Alternative Methods of Payment of Insurance Contributions – Types of Insurance Card – Currency of Card – Emergency Cards – Custody of Insurance Cards – Return of Card at End of Employment – Employer's Guides to National Insurance – Graduated National Insurance Contributions – Employer's Guide – National Health Service.

INSURANCE has been defined as

> a contract whereby a person called the insurer or assurer (and in the case of marine insurance, the underwriter) agrees, in consideration of either a single or a periodical payment called the premium, to indemnify another person called the insured or assured against loss resulting to him on the happening of certain events, or to pay him a sum of money on the happening of a specified event.

Insurance Policy

The document which sets out the terms and conditions of the contract between the Insurance Company (the "insurer") and the insured person is called an *insurance policy*. In addition to setting out the conditions of insurance, it shows the value covered, the premium payable, and the date on which payment is due.

Premium

The periodical payment to the Insurance Company is called a *premium*. It is usually paid annually. The dates for renewals of policies should be carefully noted by the secretary in order to avoid the lapse of benefits. (See *Diaries and Memory Aids*, pp. 96–97.)

Days of Grace

It is customary for most Insurance Companies to hold their clients 'covered' against loss by allowing them certain 'days of grace' pending payment of the premium. Days of grace do not, however, normally apply in the case of 'short-term' policies or motor[1] insurance, which must be renewed on the date of expiry.

Proposal Form

When entering into a contract of insurance it is necessary for the 'proposer' (i.e., the person taking out the policy) to complete a 'proposal form,' which contains a large number of questions to be answered and is the basis of the contract between the insurer and the insured. In completing the proposal form it is the duty of the proposer to disclose clearly and accurately all material information relating to the proposed insurance. Any incorrect answer given in the proposal form may render the contract null and void.

Insurable Value

The basis of insurance should always be the *true* value of the article or property to be insured. In cases of doubt it may be necessary to obtain the services of a valuer.

[1] Days of grace may, however, apply to motor policies for a period of fifteen days; but the cover for this period is restricted to the *minimum* cover required under the Road Traffic Act – that is, *third party injuries only*. If the *full* cover under the policy – whether Comprehensive, Third Party, etc. – is to be continued, the renewal premium must, of course, be paid by the date of expiry.

Types of Insurance

The various types of insurance may be divided into four main classes:

(*a*) Fire Insurance.
(*b*) Life Assurance.
(*c*) Accident Insurance.
(*d*) Marine Insurance.

Fire Insurance

Fire insurance may cover not only material property, such as buildings and contents, but also "Loss of Profits" or "Consequential Loss" insurance, whereby trading losses incurred as a result of the destruction of business premises by fire may be guarded against.

Life Assurance

Life assurance includes pension schemes in addition to "Whole Life" and "Endowment" assurance. *Whole Life* assurance provides the payment of a stipulated sum at death only; while *Endowment* assurance provides for this payment – in consideration of a higher premium – either at death or at the expiration of a stated period.

Accident Insurance

This branch of insurance covers a wide field and includes Personal Accident, Motor Vehicles, Plate Glass, Burglary, Cash or Wages in Transit, Public Liability (which provides indemnity in respect of legal liability for accidental bodily injury to, or damage to the property of, third parties as a result of negligence on the part of the insured or his employees, or through defects in his premises), Fidelity Guarantee (which protects the employer against loss of money through embezzlement), etc.

Marine Insurance

Marine insurance is divided into two main sections:

(i) Hull insurance (i.e., the vessel itself).
(ii) Cargo insurance.

Comprehensive Insurance

The best type of insurance for buildings and contents of private houses and offices is a Comprehensive, or "All In," policy, which combines in one contract fire, burglary, third party, and other risks.

Car Insurance

Here too a 'comprehensive' policy may be taken out to cover (within certain limitations) the following risks:

Damage to the car itself as a result of accident.
Theft.
Fire.
Injury to Insured.
Third Party risks, etc.

NATIONAL INSURANCE

National Insurance Scheme

The National Insurance Act, 1946, which came into force on 5th July, 1948, introduced a comprehensive scheme of national insurance which applies to everybody in Great Britain from school-leaving age to pensionable age.

The scheme is administered by the Department of Health and Social Security, and provides, in return for regular weekly contributions, the following cash benefits:

Sickness Benefit.
Unemployment Benefit.
Maternity Benefits.
Widow's Benefit.
Guardian's Allowance.
Child's Special Allowance.
Retirement Pension.
Death Grant.

Under the National Insurance Scheme insured persons are divided into three classes:

Class 1: Employed persons.
Class 2: Self-employed persons.
Class 3: Non-employed persons (i.e., all those who are not in Class 1 or Class 2).

Insurance contributions are payable in every case, and in Class 1 contributions are paid by the employer also.

The benefits for which an insured person is covered depend on the class of contribution paid.

Class 1: Contributions give cover for *all* benefits.

Class 2: Contributions give cover for all benefits *except* Unemployment and Industrial Injury.

Class 3: Contributions give cover for all benefits *except* Sickness, Unemployment and Industrial Injury benefits, and Maternity Allowance.

Contributions are paid by means of National Insurance stamps, which are obtainable only at Post Offices, and are affixed to a National Insurance card.

Industrial Injuries Scheme

The National Insurance (Industrial Injuries) Act, 1946, provides for a system of insurance against personal injury by accident arising out of and in the course of a person's employment, and also covers certain industrial injuries. It does not cover the self-employed or the non-employed.

This compulsory insurance scheme, which replaces the Workmen's Compensation Acts, is financed by contributions from employer, employee, and the State, and provides the following benefits:

(*a*) Injury Benefit.
(*b*) Disablement Benefit.
(*c*) Death Benefit.

Combined Weekly Contribution

The contributions due under the main National Insurance Scheme and the Industrial Injuries Scheme from employers and employees are generally paid together as a single contribution. Each employee has a card to which a stamp of the appropriate value, covering the combined weekly contribution, is to be affixed. This stamp also includes a separate National Health Service contribution (see p. 237).

NOTE. Contributions are not payable during unemployment or incapacity for work due to sickness or industrial injury.

Full details of the rates of contribution applicable are given in the *Employer's Guide to Flat-rate National Insurance Contributions* (NI20).

Time for Payment of Insurance Contributions

As a general rule cards are stamped not later than the time of payment of the wages or salaries for that period – e.g., weekly or monthly.

An employer is responsible for seeing that his employees have handed to him their insurance cards, and that such cards are stamped each pay day and the employee's share of the contribution deducted from his pay.

Self-employed and non-employed contributors must stamp their own cards week by week.

Cancellation of Stamps

Immediately after affixing a stamp to a card the employer is required to cancel it by stamping or writing in ink across the face of the stamp the date on which it was affixed.

Alternative Methods of Payment of Insurance Contributions

(*a*) *Direct Payment – Schedule System.* Employers with at least 100 employees may, subject to certain conditions, pay contributions by cheque. Contribution cards continue to be held but are not stamped. At the end of their currency the cards are endorsed by the employer with the number of contributions paid and sent to the local Social Security Office. The employer completes a schedule showing particulars of the individual employees and of the contributions noted on their cards.

(*b*) *Direct Payment – Invoice System.* Subject to similar conditions, an employer may,[1] as an alternative to the use of a schedule, submit the cards to the local Social Security Office with an invoice showing bulk entries for groups of cards on

[1] Since 1969 the invoice system has *not* been available to new applicants.

which the same number and rate of contributions have been noted as paid.

(*c*) *Impressed Stamping.* An employer may, under certain conditions, be permitted to pay contributions by impressing stamps on insurance cards by means of a stamp-impressing machine, instead of using adhesive stamps.

(*d*) *Yearly, Half-yearly, or Quarterly Stamping.* A few employers have continued to use the arrangement whereby cards are stamped at yearly, half-yearly, or quarterly intervals by using special stamps representing up to 13 weeks' contributions. This method of paying contributions existed before the schedule or invoice system came into operation, but in view of its limited use fresh applications are no longer being invited.

Types of Insurance Card

There are six types of card, each indicating the sex and age group of the insured person, and the contribution payable for him, viz.:

Men aged 18 years and over.
Women aged 18 years and over.
Boys under 18 years of age.
Girls under 18 years of age.
Men (Special Card).
Women (Special Card).

Special cards are for employees who are retired from regular employment; for those who have reached the age of 70 (men) or 65 (women); or for married women or widows who have chosen not to pay National Insurance contributions.

Currency of Card

Contribution cards cover a period of 52 or 53 weeks and must be exchanged annually. In order to spread the work involved in the exchange evenly over the year, everyone, when first registering for insurance, is allocated (and retains permanently) one of four different 'contribution years,' viz.:

A. Commencing on first Monday in March.
B. Commencing on first Monday in June.
C. Commencing on first Monday in September.
D. Commencing on first Monday in December.

The symbol "A," "B," "C," or "D" is printed boldly at the end of the National Insurance number on the front of each card, and, in addition, distinctive colours are used for the cards of the four contribution years.

Emergency Cards

If an employee fails to produce an insurance card, or if for any reason the employee is not in possession of a card for stamping, the employer must apply to the local Social Security Office for a card. In certain circumstances the local Social Security Office may issue an *emergency* card instead of an ordinary card. The emergency card covers a period of thirteen weeks and must be returned by the employer to the local Social Security Office from which it was issued as soon as the employee produces his ordinary card for stamping.

If the employment ends, or the emergency card expires before the employee produces his ordinary card, the emergency card should be returned at once to the local Social Security Office.

Custody of Insurance Cards

The employer is responsible for the safe custody of an insurance card so long as the employment continues. If it is lost, destroyed, or defaced while in his custody he must inform the local Social Security Office immediately.

Return of Card at End of Employment

The employer must return an insurance card to an employee immediately his employment ends, unless the employment is terminated by the employee without giving any notice to the employer, in which case the employer must return the card within fourteen days.

Employer's Guides to National Insurance

Full details of the National Insurance Scheme and the Industrial Injuries Scheme are given in the *Employer's Guide to Flat-rate National Insurance Contributions.*

Everybody's Guide to National Insurance (including Graduated Contributions and Pensions) is also a useful booklet, which explains briefly how the revised system of National Insurance operates.

Additional information may be obtained from the National Insurance Acts and Regulations, copies of which may be purchased direct from H.M. Stationery Office or through any bookseller.

In all cases of doubt inquiries should be made at the local office of the Department of Health and Social Security.

Graduated National Insurance Contributions

Under the National Insurance Act, 1959, *graduated pension contributions* require to be collected by employers from the earnings of their employees, through the P.A.Y.E. system, along with Income Tax. This Government Pension Scheme, which came into force on 6th April, 1961, provides for retirement pensions being paid in accordance with earnings throughout working years.

Contributions are payable by *all* employed persons between the ages of 18 and 70 (65 for a woman) earning over £9 a week.

The employer is liable for the same amount as he deducts from each employee, graduated contributions being calculated on each week's (or month's) gross pay separately – and *not* (as with Income Tax under P.A.Y.E.) on a cumulative basis.

Payment of Graduated Contributions

The employer is responsible for remitting to the Collector of Taxes, after the end of each tax month, the total graduated contributions due in respect of his employees and himself for that month, together with their P.A.Y.E. Income Tax. The Inland Revenue Authorities are responsible for forwarding the graduated contributions to the Department of Health and Social Security.

Use of P.A.Y.E. Deduction Cards, etc.

The P.A.Y.E. deduction cards provide space for entering the employee's graduated contributions. (The *employer's* contributions are *not* entered on these cards.) Where, however, no graduated contributions are due, no entry should be made in column (1) of the card.

Completion and Return of Cards

At the end of the tax year the employer should:

(1) see that the employee's surname and initials, together with his National Insurance number, are on every tax deduction card;

(2) add up each employee's graduated contributions in the tax year and enter the total on his tax deduction card in the space provided;

(3) complete form P35 (Employer's Annual Statement Declaration and Certificate), which covers both graduated contributions and Income Tax;

(4) return to the Collector of Taxes all the completed tax deduction cards, together with form P35 and any balance of contributions or tax due.

Employer's Guide

Full particulars of this scheme will be found in the *Employer's Guide to Graduated National Insurance Contributions*, copies of which may be obtained from the local office of the Department of Health and Social Security.

National Health Service

The *National Health Service*, with its medical, hospital, dental, and other services, is available to everyone including those who are not liable to pay weekly contributions. It is administered by the Department of Health and Social Security and the Scottish Home and Health Department.

The Health Service is sometimes confused with the National Insurance Scheme; but there is in fact an entirely separate National Health Service contribution, which, for convenience, is collected with the National Insurance contribution in one combined stamp.

19

Conduct of and Procedure at Meetings

Requisites of a Valid Meeting – Notice of Meetings – Agenda – Committee Meetings – General Meetings – Rules governing Procedure at Meetings – Motions and Resolutions – Amendments – Voting – Adjournment of Meetings – Minutes – Reports – Secretary's Duties – Company Meetings – Technical Terms relating to Meetings – Specimen Agenda and Minutes: Committee Meeting; Annual General Meeting.

A *MEETING* has been defined as "an assembly of people for a specific purpose." The word 'meeting' therefore implies the coming together of at least two people.

Requisites of a Valid Meeting

In order that the business transacted at a meeting may be *valid* (i.e., legally effective and binding), it must be:

(1) *properly convened* – i.e., the proper notice must have been sent to every person entitled to be present;

(2) *properly constituted* – i.e.,

(*a*) the right person must be in the chair, and
(*b*) a proper *quorum* (see p. 252) must be present;

(3) held in accordance with the rules or regulations of the particular organization.

Notice of Meetings

A *notice* of the meeting must be sent by the secretary to every person entitled to attend. It should state clearly the day, date, time, and place of the meeting, and must be served in the proper manner as laid down in the Constitution. It must be issued the required length of time before the meeting (at least twenty-one *clear* days' notice being given of all annual general meetings, and seven to fourteen days' notice of other meetings), and must state clearly the purpose for which the meeting has been called. Furthermore, it must be issued under the proper authority, as laid down in the regulations. For example, the notice of a general meeting of the shareholders of a company would be signed as follows:

By order of the Board
JAMES BROWN
Secretary

Clear Days' Notice. "Twenty-one *clear* days' notice," in the case of an annual general meeting, means twenty-one days *excluding* the date of posting and the date of the meeting. If the meeting is to be held on, say, 31st July, the notices should be sent out not later than 9th July.

Agenda

The preparation beforehand of the *agenda* is another important secretarial duty. The agenda is a list (or programme) of the various items of business to be transacted at a meeting, in the order in which they are to be dealt with.

If the agenda is prepared in good time, and sent out in advance of the meeting, it usually incorporates the notice convening the meeting and gives the day, date, time, and place of the meeting. (See specimen agendas on pp. 252–254.)

The agenda is prepared by the secretary in consultation with the chairman. It should be typed with a wide *right*-hand margin to enable the members to make notes. The chairman's agenda paper, in conjunction with the secretary's shorthand notes, will form a useful basis for the preparation of the minutes of the meeting.

In the specimen agendas given on pp. 252 and 254, it will be seen that the reading of the minutes of the previous meeting (after "Apologies for absence") forms the first business of the meeting. If, however, it is necessary to elect a chairman, that will, of course, be the first item on the agenda. A temporary chairman is chosen to take the chair while the election of chairman takes place; but it should be noted that under no circumstances can the secretary act as chairman.

The secretary will find it helpful to prepare additional copies of the agenda to enable her to hand one to each member on his arrival at the meeting. Alternatively, she may put one in each place round the table before the meeting actually begins. An agenda book, in which the agenda of each meeting is inserted, is usually placed before the chairman.

It is the secretary's duty to make a note of any matters requiring the attention of the committee that may be brought to her notice beforehand, so that they may be included in the agenda for the next meeting.

Committee Meetings

The secretary should be thoroughly conversant with the standing orders or rules of the particular organization she represents. These regulations usually lay down, for example, the number of clear days' notice required to be given of any meeting – i.e., whether seven, fourteen, or twenty-one days. The minimum number required to form a *quorum* (see p. 252) is also stated.

In addition, she should see that the arrangements made for the meeting are such as will ensure its smooth working. These arrangements will include: ensuring that the accommodation is ample and the seating arrangements satisfactory; that the room is suitably heated; that there is an adequate supply of stationery, etc., for the use of members; and that any books or papers needed for reference are ready to hand.

The chairman will occupy the seat at the head of the table (with the secretary at his right hand and the treasurer on his left), while the members of the committee will sit round the table. As the members enter the room the secretary will ask them to sign the Attendance Book. She should also see that they are supplied with copies of the agenda.

Before the chairman opens the proceedings the secretary should make sure that a quorum of members is present.

Order of Business

The business dealt with at the meeting must follow the order set out on the agenda, and the chairman should not vary the order of business without the consent of the meeting.

Normally, the business dealt with at a *committee* meeting would be in the following order:

(1) Apologies for absence.
(2) Minutes of the last meeting to be read and confirmed (i.e., verified as correct).
(3) Business arising out of the minutes.
(4) Correspondence.
(5) Secretary's report and Treasurer's financial statement.
(6) Reports of subcommittee (if any).
(7) Special business which has been notified.
(8) Any other business.
(9) Date of next meeting.

The minutes of the previous meeting are usually read by the secretary. (If, however, the minutes have been circulated to members beforehand, together with the notice of meeting, they are taken 'as read' at the meeting.) When the secretary is called upon by the chairman to read the minutes of the last meeting she should do so promptly, remembering to read clearly and fluently.

During the course of the meeting the secretary may be asked to give any information required concerning the matters under discussion. In addition, she should take notes of the proceedings to enable her to write up the minutes afterwards in the Minute Book.

General Meetings

The *general* meeting of an association or club is open to *all* its members and is usually an annual meeting. The proceedings must be conducted in accordance with the standing orders or rules of the particular organization, but usually take the following form:

(1) Apologies for absence.
(2) Minutes of the last general meeting to be read and confirmed.
(3) Business arising out of the minutes.
(4) Correspondence.
(5) Annual reports and accounts presented for adoption.
(6) Election of officers and committee for the year.
(7) Special business – e.g., alteration of rules, appointment of standing subcommittees, etc.
(8) General discussion of the society's affairs and the programme of arrangements for the year (e.g., lectures, debates, demonstrations, etc.).
(9) Any other business.

The secretary again is responsible for the arrangements and for seeing that the notice of meeting is sent out in good time – twenty-one clear days' notice being required for the annual general meeting of a club or association.

Rules governing Procedure at Meetings

The following general rules apply to procedure at meetings of all types of organization – whether association, club, or company.

1. All remarks must be addressed to the chairman, and not to other members present. A member wishing to speak should rise (or, when in committee, turn) and address the chair. The form of address ("Mr. Chairman") that is used when addressing the chair may also be applied to a woman in the chair, although it is more usual for her to be addressed as "Madam Chairman"; and during the course of the proceedings the chairman would be referred to as "Sir" (or "Madam"). Should more than one member rise to speak at the same time, the chairman must be quick to notice the first speaker and ask the others to wait.

2. As it is the chairman's primary function to exercise control over the meeting, it is important that members should support the chair and under no circumstances argue with the chairman or question the propriety of his ruling.

3. The order of business, as set out on the agenda, should not be varied without the consent of the meeting.

4. As a general rule, the business conducted at a meeting should be dealt with by motion and resolution (see below). At 'question time,' however, members are permitted to put questions to the chairman or other office-bearer for the purpose of obtaining information on certain matters of interest. Questions may also be raised by members at any time during the discussion on 'points of order' (see p. 251).

5. Discussion, which should at all times be relevant, should be confined to the motion before the meeting. A member is permitted to speak only once on each motion, with the exception of the proposer, who has the right to reply before the motion is put to the vote.

6. Once a motion is before the meeting, it may not be withdrawn without the consent of the meeting; nor may a motion, once it has been passed or rejected, be brought up again at the same meeting.

7. If an amendment to a motion is proposed, this immediately takes precedence and must be put to the meeting by the chairman before the original motion. If the majority are in favour of the amendment it becomes the resolution. If not, the amendment is dropped and discussion resumed on the original motion.

8. Discussion on a motion may be terminated in one of the following ways:

(*a*) by putting the motion to the vote after everybody has had an opportunity to speak;

(*b*) by the lapse of time allowed for the discussion (known as the 'Guillotine Closure'), after which the motion is put to the vote;

(*c*) by passing a formal motion – such as "to proceed to the next business" – which is intended to end discussion of undesirable or frivolous motions.

Motions and Resolutions

The word 'resolution' is commonly used to describe a 'motion'; but a *motion* is strictly a proposal put forward at a meeting, and it becomes a *resolution* only when it has been adopted (i.e., voted upon and passed). When the motion is put to the meeting it is often referred to as 'the question.'

It is customary for a motion to be seconded, but a chairman may put an unseconded motion to the vote if he so desires, provided there is no rule or regulation to the contrary. The person who puts the motion to the meeting is known as the *proposer*; and if someone seconds, or signifies his approval of, the motion proposed that person is called the *seconder*.

In addition to speaking first on the motion, the proposer also has the right to reply at the close of the discussion before it is put to the vote; but the seconder may speak on the motion only once.

A motion should be framed clearly and in definite terms; and it is desirable (if the motion is not on the agenda) that the proposer should write it out clearly on a slip of paper, so that the chairman may be able to read the exact wording when putting it before the meeting.

The proposer of a motion should rise and say: "I move (*or* I propose) that . . .," followed by the actual words of the motion; e.g., "That a subcommittee, consisting of Miss White, Mrs. Black, and Miss Green, be appointed to deal with catering arrangements for the Flower Show."

The seconder would then rise and say: "I second Mr. Brown's proposal that a subcommittee . . .," after which the chairman would put the motion to the meeting by saying: "It is moved by Mr. Brown, and seconded by Mr. Jones, that a subcommittee . . ."

Finally, the motion would (after discussion) be put to the vote and, if passed, recorded as a *resolution* of the meeting. It would be entered in the Minute Book thus:

> RESOLVED: That a subcommittee, consisting of Miss White, Mrs. Black, and Miss Green, be appointed to deal with catering arrangements for the Flower Show.

Amendments

An *amendment* is a proposed alteration to a motion that is being discussed by a meeting. It must not be a mere negation of the motion, as obviously the same result could be obtained by voting against it, but it may consist of the alteration of some words, or the addition or deletion of certain words. For example, if at a first meeting of a club a member proposed "that the annual subscription be £3·00," another member might move an amendment to add the words "for senior members and £2·00 for junior members."

After discussion the amendment is voted upon and, if passed, the original motion is altered accordingly. The chairman should allow only one amendment at a time to be before the meeting.

Voting

There are *five* usual methods of voting, viz.:

(1) *By voice.* Members should answer "Ay" or "No," and the chairman then declares the result by saying "The ayes have it," or "The noes have it." (This method is used only when there is no doubt about the outcome.)

(2) *By show of hands.* This is the most common form of voting for ordinary meetings. Each person raises one hand when the chairman calls "For" or "Against" the motion, the hands being then counted and the result of the voting obtained.

(3) *By poll.* Although a show of hands is the usual method of ascertaining the views of the meeting, the regulations may give any member the right to demand a poll, which, if demanded, must be granted. (At a Company meeting a group of no fewer than *five* members have the right to demand a poll.) The chairman must then decide when and where the poll will be taken.

The usual method of taking a poll is to ask every member entitled to vote to sign a paper headed "For" or "Against" the motion. If a member is unable to attend he may appoint another person (known as a 'proxy') to vote for him.

(4) *By division*, as in Parliament, where members divide and file into separate rooms or lobbies representing those 'for' and 'against' the proposal. The counting of members is delegated to tellers, one or two being appointed to each side.

(5) *By ballot.* This is the method of 'secret' voting as used at Parliamentary Elections. It is not often used at ordinary meetings; but, if it is, members merely record their vote on the official voting papers and place them in a ballot box, which is

later opened, the votes being counted by scrutineers (or tellers) appointed for the purpose.

Adjournment of Meetings

A meeting may be *adjourned* for various reasons – e.g., if no quorum is present; for the purpose of taking a poll; or when a motion to adjourn has been carried.

It should be noted that a meeting, once it has been called, should *never be postponed*, but should be held and then adjourned if necessary.

Minutes

Minutes are a concise record of the business discussed at a meeting and the decisions arrived at. Minutes are 'confirmed' (or 'approved') at the next meeting by being read by the secretary, after which the chairman obtains the consent of the meeting to his signing them as a correct record of the proceedings.

In order that they may provide a complete and permanent record for future reference, minutes are entered in a Minute Book and should include the date, time, and place of meeting, together with the names of those present or, in the case of large meetings, the numbers present.

The exact wording of resolutions passed should be given, together with the names of the proposer and the seconder in the case of important resolutions.

There are three distinct operations involved in the compiling of minutes:

- (*a*) taking the minutes in note form;
- (*b*) drafting the minutes;
- (*c*) recording the minutes in the Minute Book.

Taking the Minutes

It is desirable to keep a special notebook for minutes, the books when completed being numbered consecutively and dated (on the front cover) with the starting and finishing dates.

Perhaps the most difficult part of the work associated with the preparation of minutes is that of note-taking. It requires both skill and experience. The important thing to remember is that, no matter how full or lengthy a particular discussion may be, it is only those points which have a real bearing on the final issue – and, of course, the actual decision itself – that should be recorded. With experience, the secretary will learn to recognize which matters in the course of the proceedings are vital, and which may be rejected as trivial.

Drafting the Minutes

In drafting the minutes (which should be done as soon as possible after the close of the meeting) care should be taken to express their meaning as clearly and as simply as possible. Long, involved sentences should be avoided, as these can lead to ambiguity or inaccuracies, and punctuation should be kept to a minimum as in legal documents. Indirect speech should always be used.

It will be found helpful to compare the minutes, as drafted, with the agenda for the meeting to ensure that nothing has been omitted. It is usual – and a very good practice – for the secretary to forward the draft minutes to the chairman for his approval before entering them in the Minute Book.

Recording the Minutes

The minutes should be written in a bound Minute Book, which is ruled with a wide left-hand margin to allow for sub-headings, or (in accordance with the more modern practice) typewritten on sheets which are inserted in a loose-leaf Minute Book.

A suitable heading should be given containing the following details: the nature of the meeting, the place, the date, and the time of the meeting, e.g.:

> A Meeting of the Board of Directors of the Transvaal Rubber Co. Ltd. was held at the Registered Office, at 10 Barnett Street, London W1H 7AE, on Monday, 6th March, 19–, at 14 30 hrs.

This should be followed by the chairman's name and the names of those present (if a committee or board meeting) or the number present in the case of a general meeting.

The minutes, which should record the business transacted in the same order as that shown on the agenda, should be numbered, and the subject of each inserted in the margin as a sub-heading. (They may also be indexed under subject-headings at the back of the book.)

Reports

Unlike *minutes* – which it has been stated are "a concise record of the business discussed at a meeting and the decisions arrived at" – *reports* of meetings record (in summarized form) the remarks made by the various speakers in the course of a debate, together with the arguments advanced by them for and against any proposed action. The names of the speakers are given in the report, and the result of the voting is usually included.

A *verbatim* report is not as a rule called for, however. This is a record of a meeting, speech, lecture, etc., which is reported *word for word.*

Secretary's Duties

A private secretary's duties in connection with *any* type of meeting may be summarized as follows:

(1) *Arranging for the Meeting*

Beforehand: (*a*) Issue of notices of meeting.
(*b*) Preparation and serving of the agenda.

On the day: Preparation for the meeting. (See below.)

(2) *Attending the Meeting* – for the purpose of:

(*a*) taking the minutes, and (afterwards)
(*b*) compiling the minutes.

Preparation for the Meeting

Before the meeting actually begins the secretary should ensure that the room is suitably heated and that the seating arrangements are satisfactory. She should see that ash-trays are available and placed at convenient points round the table, and that there is an adequate supply of water and glasses. She should also ensure that each member is supplied with writing paper, and that spare copies of the agenda are available for the use of members.

Finally, she should see that the following items are ready to hand:

(*a*) Minute Book (for the reading and confirmation of the minutes of the previous meeting).
(*b*) Attendance Register.
(*c*) All relevant papers and correspondence.
(*d*) Any books of reference that may be required; also Standing Orders or Constitution of the organization.
(*e*) Shorthand notebook, pens and pencils.

Company Meetings

(*a*) *Directors' or Board Meeting*

This is to a company what a committee meeting is to a club or association. The management of the company is vested in its Board of Directors, the Board being elected by the shareholders of the company. The Board in turn elects a Chairman and appoints a Managing Director and a Company Secretary.

The ordinary business of the company is transacted at its Board meetings which are held at regular intervals, usually monthly or weekly.

(*b*) *Annual General Meeting*

The Annual General Meeting of a company is a compulsory meeting, which must be held once a year in addition to any other general meeting and not more than fifteen months after the preceding Annual General Meeting. It must be announced as the "Annual General Meeting" in the notice of the meeting, which must be sent to all the shareholders of the company, at least twenty-one days' clear notice being given.

At this meeting the routine business of the company is transacted, including presentation of the annual reports and accounts for adoption, retirement and re-election of directors and auditors, and the declaration of dividends.

(*c*) *Extraordinary General Meeting*

In addition to the ordinary general meetings of shareholders, an Extraordinary General Meeting may be called at any time for the purpose of transacting the *special* business set out in the notice.

(*d*) *Statutory Meeting*

This is a compulsory meeting of the shareholders of a joint-stock company, and it must be held not less than one month and not more than three months from the date at which the company is entitled to commence business. The purpose of this meeting is to give shareholders an opportunity of seeing what progress the company has made since its inception, and to enable any special matters requiring their approval to be put before them.

Technical Terms relating to Meetings

Ad hoc. This term, which is of Latin origin, means 'for this purpose.' An *ad hoc* committee or subcommittee is one that has been appointed to report upon or to carry out one particular piece of work. It is sometimes called a 'special' committee.

Casting Vote. An additional vote granted, in accordance with the regulations of an association, club, or company, to the chairman of a meeting. A casting vote must be used only when the votes 'for' and 'against' a motion are equally divided, in order that a decision may be arrived at.

Closure. A formal motion (e.g., "That the question be now put") brought forward with the intention of ending a lengthy discussion on any matter before the meeting. If this formal motion is seconded and carried, the motion or amendment before the meeting must immediately be put to the vote without further discussion. If it is defeated, discussion may be continued.

Co-opted Member. A person specially appointed to act on a committee as an *addition* to the committee, usually because of some specialized knowledge or qualification possessed by the co-opted member.

Ex officio. A Latin phrase meaning 'by virtue of office.' An *ex-officio* member of a committee is appointed to it because of some other office or position he holds. For instance, the president of a club may be an *ex-officio* member of its committee.

Lie on the Table. A motion that a letter or report should 'lie on the table' is equivalent to proposing that no action should be taken in the matter for the time being. Such matters may be raised again at any subsequent meeting.

Memorandum and Articles of Association. The *Memorandum of Association* is a document setting out the objects for which a company is formed; while the *Articles of Association* are the rules governing the internal management of the company and defining the manner in which its business shall be conducted.

Nem. con. An abbreviation of *nemine contradicente* (Latin) meaning 'no one contradicting' (i.e., without opposition). A motion is said to be carried *nem. con.* when there have been no votes against it, although some members have abstained from voting.

Nem. dis. An abbreviation of *nemine dissentiente* meaning 'no one dissenting.' This is sometimes used instead of *nem. con.*

Next Business. A motion "that the meeting proceed with the next business" is a method of ending discussion on any matter brought before the meeting.

Out of Order. A remark or statement made by a member is said to be 'out of order' when it involves a breach of the rules governing the meeting. A person may also be called to order by the chairman for any breach of good manners or good taste.

Point of Order. This is a question relating to the procedure at a meeting (e.g., concerning a breach of the rules or standing orders, absence of quorum, etc.). Points of order may be raised by a member at any time during the discussion and must be decided by the chairman at once.

Proxy. A person appointed in the place of another to represent him at a meeting, such provision being contained in the regulations of the organization.

Put the Question. When concluding the discussion on a motion the chairman 'puts the question' by announcing, "The question before the meeting is . . ."

Quorum. This means the *minimum* number of persons required to be present at a meeting to make it valid. The number is laid down in the rules or regulations of the club, association, or company.

Rider. This is an *addition* to a resolution after it has been passed. It differs from an *amendment* in that it adds to, instead of altering, the sense of the resolution. It must be proposed, seconded, and voted upon in the usual way.

Right of Reply. The right accorded to the proposer (but not the seconder) of a motion to reply at the close of the discussion. He may, however, reply only once.

Status Quo. An abbreviation of *status quo ante* (Latin) meaning 'the existing circumstances.'

Standing Orders. These are the regulations drawn up by an association for the conduct of its meetings. They may also be known as the 'Constitution.' As a general rule, Standing Orders may not be altered except at an annual or special meeting; but they may be *suspended* at any meeting by a majority of two-thirds for the purpose of allowing discussion or a decision on some matter otherwise prohibited.

Subcommittee. A subcommittee is appointed by the committee of an association, club, or society, for a special purpose; e.g., the Entertainments Subcommittee of a club. The subcommittee will meet as required, and must report to the committee periodically.

Teller. A person appointed to count the votes at a meeting.

Unanimously. A motion is said to be carried "unanimously" when *all* members present at the meeting have voted in favour of it. (See also *Nem. con.*)

Specimen Agenda and Minutes

Specimen Agenda (Committee Meeting)

WESTLAKE COMMUNITY ASSOCIATION

A Meeting of the Executive Committee of the Westlake Community Association will be held in the Board Room of the Association, at 100 Main Street, Westlake, on Friday, 7th April, 19–, at 2.30 p.m.

AGENDA

1. Apologies for absence.
2. Minutes of last meeting.

3. Business arising out of the minutes.
4. Treasurer's financial statement.
5. Report on donations received.
6. To consider the establishment of a Sports Club.
7. To consider the question of Life Membership of the Association
8. Any other business.
9. Date of the next meeting.

JANET JONES
Secretary

Specimen Minutes (Committee Meeting)

A Meeting of the Executive Committee of the Westlake Community Association was held in the Board Room of the Association, at 100 Main Street, Westlake, on Friday, 7th April, 19–, at 2.30 p.m.

Present:

Col. R. J. Hamilton (in the Chair)
Miss C. Black
Mrs. J. Brown
Mr. H. T. West
Mr. R. Bain
Miss Janet Jones (Secretary)

Apologies for Absence

A letter of apology was read from Mrs. D. C. Green.

Minutes of last Meeting

The minutes of the meeting of the Executive Committee held on 10th March, 19–, were read, approved, and signed by the Chairman.

Business Arising

The Secretary reported that the repairs specified had been carried out at a cost not exceeding the sum estimated.

Treasurer's Financial Statement

A statement of the current financial position of the Association was read and adopted.

Donations

The Secretary reported the following donations to the Funds of the Association:

	£
Messrs. J. Rogers & Co.	50·00
Mr. & Mrs. John Clarkson	10·00
Anonymous	5·00

Establishment of Sports Club

The Secretary reported that the questionnaire distributed amongst the members had revealed considerable interest in the proposed establishment of a Sports Club.

RESOLVED: That a Subcommittee, consisting of Mr. Bain, Miss Black, and Mr. West, be appointed to arrange for the establishment of a Sports Club, and be authorized to expend £50·00 on suitable equipment.

Life Membership	RESOLVED: That donations of £10·00 and over to the Funds of the Association shall constitute a title to Life Membership.
Any Other Business	The Secretary was instructed to prepare the Annual Report for presentation at the Annual General Meeting of the Association on the 8th May.
Next Meeting	It was decided to hold the next meeting of the Executive Committee on Friday, 5th May, 19–, at 2.30 p.m.

R. J. HAMILTON
Chairman
5th May, 19–

Specimen Agenda (Annual General Meeting)

WESTLAKE COMMUNITY ASSOCIATION

The Annual General Meeting of the Westlake Community Association will be held in the Main Hall, at 100 Main Street, Westlake, on Monday, 8th May, 19–, at 7.30 p.m.

AGENDA

1. Apologies for absence.
2. Minutes of last meeting.
3. Business arising out of the minutes.
4. Secretary's Annual Report.
5. Treasurer's Annual Report and Balance Sheet.
6. Election of Executive Committee for 19–.
7. Appointment of Auditors for 19–.
8. To consider the proposed alteration to Rule 7 of the Constitution as follows:
   (*a*) That the following words be omitted:
   "and shall not be eligible for re-election."
   (*b*) That the following words be substituted:
   "and shall be eligible for re-election after an interval of one year.
   Proposed by Mr. John Clarkson.
   Seconded by Mr. Hugh Kennedy.
9. To consider the establishment of a Junior Social Club.
10. Any other business.

JANET JONES
Secretary

Specimen Minutes (General Meetings)

The Second Annual General Meeting of the Westlake Community Association was held in the Main Hall, at 100 Main Street, Westlake, on Monday, 8th May, 19–, at 7.30 p.m.

Col. R. J. Hamilton was in the Chair, and there were 148 members present.

Apologies for Absence	The Secretary submitted apologies for absence received from Mrs. J. C. Hart, Mrs. R. J. Smith, Miss A. Dell, and Mr. John Tait.
Minutes of Last Meeting	The minutes of the last Annual General Meeting, held on 10th May, 19–, which had been circulated to all members, were taken as read and approved, and were signed by the Chairman as a correct record of the proceedings.
Business Arising out of the Minutes	There were no matters arising out of the minutes.
Annual Report, Financial Report, and Balance Sheet	The Chairman gave a brief survey of the year's progress, after which the adoption of the Reports and Balance Sheet was moved by Mr. J. Burton, seconded by Mr. D. C. Green, and carried unanimously.
Election of Executive Committee	In accordance with Rule 6 of the Constitution, the Executive Committee was re-elected for a further period of twelve months, the formal motion being proposed by Mr. R. J. Smith and seconded by Mr. H. T. McNeil.
Appointment of Auditors	The reappointment of Messrs. Ramsay & Murdoch as Auditors for 19– was moved by Mr. T. West, seconded by Miss V. Clayton, and carried unanimously.
Proposed Alteration to Rule 7 of the Constitution	The following proposal for the alteration of Rule 7 of the Constitution was moved by Mr. John Clarkson and seconded by Mr. Hugh Kennedy: (*a*) That the following words be omitted: "and shall not be eligible for re-election." (*b*) That the following words be substituted: "and shall be eligible for re-election after an interval of one year." After some discussion, the motion was put to the vote and carried *nem. con.*
Establishment of Junior Social Club	RESOLVED: That the Association shall proceed at once to establish a Junior Social Club, and that the Committee be asked to undertake the work of organization. Proposed by: Mr. G. King. Seconded by: Miss L. Mayne.
Vote of Thanks	The meeting closed with a vote of thanks to the Chairman and Committee members for their services during the past year.

Chairman

20

Office Machinery and Equipment

Typewriters – General Hints on Care of the Typewriter – Typewriter Ribbons – Carbon Copying – Continuous Stationery Machine – Cheque-writing Machine – Vari-typer (Variable Typewriter) – Stenotyping Machines – Duplicators – Stencil Process – Spirit Process – Offset Litho Process – Type-setting Machines – Colour Duplication – Copying Machines – Dictating Machines – Adding/Listing Machines – Calculating Machines – Book-keeping and Accounting Machines – Punched Card Systems – Teleprinters (Telex Service) – Addressing Machines – Stapling Machines – Stamping Machines – Franking Machines – Guillotine – Latest Equipment.

OFFICE machines may be classified into eight main groups:

(1) *Writing* – e.g., typewriters, Vari-typer, etc.
(2) *Printing* – e.g., duplicators and type-setting machines.
(3) *Copying* – e.g., "Copycat," "Xerox 3600," "Thermo-Fax," etc.
(4) *Recording* – e.g., dictating machines, tape recorders, etc.
(5) *Calculating* – e.g., adding machines, computers, etc.
(6) *Book-keeping and Accounting* – for the purpose of entering ledger accounts, etc.
(7) *Communication* – e.g., telephones, teleprinters, etc.
(8) *Miscellaneous* – e.g., stamping machines, franking machines, etc.

Typewriters

Typewriters may be *manual* or *electric*, the former being the ordinary type of machine that is in use in many offices.

The *electric* typewriter, although similar in appearance to the manual machine, is electrically operated. The chief advantages of an electric machine are:

(*a*) automatic return of the carriage, thereby saving both time and energy;
(*b*) less fatigue to the typist;
(*c*) greater output of work;
(*d*) evenness of impression.

IBM "82" Electric Typewriter. The IBM "82" ("Selectric") typewriter has no type-bars or moving carriage. Instead there is an interchangeable 'golf ball' typing head (containing all the characters of the keyboard and obtainable in a variety of type styles*) which is mounted on a carrier that glides along a cylindrical rod across the paper. As a key is struck, the typing head rotates and lifts to bring the correct character into position for printing.

A useful feature of this machine is the dual-pitch selector, which enables the typist at the flick of a lever to switch from 10 pitch (10 characters to the inch) to 12 pitch (12 characters to the inch).

Cleaning the Typewriter

No matter how efficient she may be, the secretary cannot possibly produce first-class work on the typewriter unless her machine is kept in good condition and cleaned daily. She should be provided with a cleaning kit which comprises the following:

(*a*) a hard type-brush;
(*b*) a long-handled soft dusting brush;
(*c*) a soft duster.

* There are 'golf ball' elements for technical symbols, OCR (Optical Character Recognition type, which can be read by computer OCR readers) and elements in most foreign languages.

The Type. The type should be brushed first thing every morning, the hard type-brush being used for this purpose. In addition, the type-brush should be used when there are visible signs of clogging as, for example, when cutting stencils. Brush firmly, but not too heavily, in order to avoid straining the type-bars; and always brush outwards from back to front – not from side to side. A plastic cleaner, such as "Typeclean" or the "Parker" roller, will help to keep the type spotless. (The type-brush itself should be cleaned periodically by dipping into methylated spirits and cleaning off on a piece of waste cloth or blotting-paper.)

The Inner Parts. The long-handled soft brush will be found useful for dusting the delicate parts of the mechanism and for removing paper-fluff, etc., from inside the frame. It may also be used for cleaning underneath the machine.

The Outer Casing. The soft duster should be used for the outer casing of the machine and for the platen-roller. If the platen has become shiny it can be wiped over with a clean cloth that has been moistened with methylated spirits.

Oiling the Typewriter. If the machine is in constant use – and provided it is kept well dusted – it will not need much oil. As a general rule, it is better to under-oil than to over-oil. Note that the type-bars should *never* be oiled.

General Hints on Care of the Typewriter

(1) Always cover the typewriter when not in use.

(2) If it is necessary to move your machine, always lift it by the base from the back, and never by any other part.

(3) Before lifting always stabilize the carriage by bringing the margin stops together in the centre of the scale. (This will prevent the carriage from running to one end if the machine is tilted.)

(4) Never leave your typewriter

(*a*) near a hot radiator, or

(*b*) too near the edge of the desk where it could easily be knocked off by a passer-by.

(5) At the end of a line return the carriage briskly but not violently.

(6) Do not depress the tabulator key unless you have set some stops; otherwise damage to the mechanism may be caused.

(7) Strike full stops, commas, and hyphens – in fact, *all* punctuation marks – rather more lightly than the other keys.*

(8) Always use a backing sheet, as this will not only protect the platen but also improve the appearance of your work.

(9) Should the machine not be in use for some time (e.g., week-ends and holidays) it is a good idea to move the paper-release lever forward, in order to take pressure off the platen.

(10) Never erase over the ribbon vibrator, as this will cause particles of rubber and paper dust to fall into the type-basket. Before erasing always depress the margin-release key and draw the carriage out to its fullest extent – either to the left or to the right, as required.

(11) If your machine develops a fault the cause of which is not apparent, do not try to repair it yourself but call in a trained mechanic to attend to it.

(12) Finally, do remember that the life of your machine will be prolonged by regular servicing.

Typewriter Ribbons

Typewriter ribbons are of various kinds. They may be:

(*a*) Cotton, silk, or nylon.

(*b*) 'Monochrome' (single-colour), 'bichrome' (two-colour), or 'trichrome' (three-colour).

For general typewriting work, the black record ribbon is the most widely used as it has the advantage of being absolutely permanent.

There are also *special-purpose* ribbons, the more important being as follows:

(*a*) *Copying ribbons* – for use with a letter-copying book.

(*b*) *Transparent plastic ribbons* – which are intended to improve the quality of stencil-cutting.

(*c*) *Litho-inking ribbons* – for use when typewritten work requires to be photographed.

(*d*) *Carbon or acetate ribbons* – which are fitted on a special attachment to the typewriter – give an excellent finish

* This, of course, refers to manual, not electric, typewriters.

to typewritten work and are becoming increasingly popular for all types of private secretarial work. They measure approximately 198 metres in length as against 11 to 13 metres for an ordinary record ribbon, but can be used only once.

Carbon Copying

Carbon paper may be:

Single – coated on one side only.

Double – coated on *both* sides, so that each sheet of carbon gives two impressions – on the front of one sheet of copying paper and on the back of another, thereby reducing the normal number of carbon sheets required by half. Double carbon is useful when a large number of copies is required; but since half the copies will give a 'mirror' impression, the copying paper must be sufficiently transparent to enable one to read *through it*.

NOTE. A typewriter with a fairly hard platen is desirable if a large number of carbon copies is called for, and it will also be found necessary to strike the keys a little more sharply. (This does not, however, apply to *electric* typewriters where key depression is electrically controlled.) As many as *twenty* carbon copies can be taken at one time on an electric machine.

Carbon paper may be obtained in a variety of colours, in order

(*a*) to match the colour of the ribbon;

(*b*) to produce distinctive colours for various departments, etc.; *or*

(*c*) to draw attention to one or more items by means of a contrasting colour.

Care of Carbon Paper

The following points should be noted in the care and handling of carbon paper:

(*a*) It should be stored in a flat box to prevent creasing.

(*b*) It should be handled lightly so that smudging is avoided. (NOTE. Carbon paper is obtainable with cut-off corners, so that it can be separated easily from the copying paper without causing smudges.)

(*c*) It should be turned regularly from top to bottom to ensure that the most economical use is made of each sheet.

(*d*) It should be kept away from hot pipes or radiators.

(*e*) When taking a number of copies, a backing sheet with a fold-over top will be found useful for keeping the top edges even and preventing the carbons from slipping when inserting them into the typewriter.

Correction of Errors on Carbon Copies

(1) Move the carriage to the extreme left or right, so that eraser dust does not fall into the delicate mechanism of the machine.

(2) Turn up two or three line-spaces.

(3) Insert a piece of stiff paper or thin card between each sheet of carbon and of copying paper at the appropriate point.

(4) After erasing the top copy, lift each sheet of carbon in turn and erase the copies. (An eraser shield will help to prevent smudging.)

(5) Make sure that all the pieces of paper or card have been removed, and turn back the platen.

(6) Switch the ribbon to *stencil* position, and type in the correction. Then switch the ribbon to normal position, and type lightly *over* the correction. (This will ensure that the correction on the carbon copies is as clear as that on the top copy.)

NOTE. If the typewriter ribbon is fairly new it will be found helpful to erase *first* with a soft pencil rubber and then with the typewriter rubber.

N.C.R. ("No Carbon Required") Paper

This is a chemically treated paper that produces the same impression as carbon paper and makes it unnecessary to interleave sheets of carbon.

Continuous Stationery Machine

With a continuous stationery machine it is possible to feed invoices or forms into a typewriter from the rear and tear them off as completed. As each set of forms is finished, the next set automatically follows on. At the flick of a lever the carbon from the completed set is automatically fed into the next set at the correct position for typing. The use of such a machine in a busy office would obviously result in a considerable saving of time and, consequently, increased output.

Cheque-writing Machine

This machine operates in much the same way as an ordinary typewriter, but instead of merely printing on the surface of the paper the type-face cuts impressions into the paper, thus making alteration of the writing impossible.

Vari-typer (Variable Typewriter)

In the Vari-typer – which is electrically operated – the typist is provided with a variety of changeable styles and sizes of type, as well as the means of obtaining a perfectly even right-hand margin (automatic 'justification'), thus enabling her to produce typewritten work that closely resembles print. The use of a carbon ribbon further enhances clarity of impression.

The Vari-typer is similar in appearance to an ordinary typewriter, and is operated in much the same way. A complete fount of type is contained on a small segment (instead of on a set of type-bars), and this spins round to present the appropriate character to the paper when a key is struck. Segments can be changed in a matter of seconds, thus allowing a wide variety of type styles to be used on the one machine.

The Vari-typer will set up 'masters' suitable for any method of duplication – stencil, spirit, or offset litho.

Stenotyping Machines

Stenotyping (the British system is known as "Palantype") is a method of note-taking by machine. The machine is operated by touch; but instead of striking each key separately, as in typewriting, several keys are struck at the same time. Words are recorded phonetically on a band of paper, which moves on automatically as the machine is operated. The machine, which is noiseless in operation, is small and light enough to rest on the knees of the operator.

The main advantages claimed for this system are:

(1) Notes are always legible, whether taken at verbatim speed or very slowly.

(2) The notes may be transcribed as easily by one person as by another.

(3) The multi-lingual keyboard permits the machine to be operated in any language with which the operator is familiar.

Duplicators

Duplicating is a process whereby a 'master' copy is prepared initially, the 'master' being then fitted to a duplicator to enable the requisite number of copies to be produced.

There are three methods of duplicating:

(*a*) stencil;
(*b*) spirit;
(*c*) offset litho.

Stencil Process

In this process the stencil (which is a sheet of special wax tissue) is 'cut' by typing on to it the matter to be reproduced, or it may be cut by hand by means of a stylus pen.

The stencil, or 'master,' is attached to the rotary drum of a duplicator, paper being then fed into the machine so that it passes between the drum and a roller which presses the paper against the stencil, resulting in an impression being made on the paper. The inking process in most duplicators is similar, the ink being fed from the rotating drum through the stencil and on to the paper.

NOTE. The larger duplicating firms provide an electronic stencil-cutting service, which enables 'masters' to be made from forms, photographs, drawings, etc.

Preparation of Stencils

The following points should be observed when 'cutting' a stencil:

(1) Clean the type thoroughly.
(2) Switch the typewriter ribbon out of action, so that the type will strike directly on to the stencil.
(3) Insert a sheet of carbon paper between the stencil and the backing sheet, with the coated side uppermost. (This improves the legibility of the stencil while typing.)
(4) Insert the stencil into the typewriter, adjusting margin stops in accordance with the scale at the top of the stencil.
(5) Strike the keys with a sharp, staccato touch. (*Note*. The letters *m* and *w*, fractions, and capital letters require a slightly heavier stroke, while the letters *o*, *c*, and *e*, the underscore, and all punctuation marks should be struck more lightly.)*
(6) Errors may be corrected by brushing lightly over the letter or word with correcting fluid, allowing it to dry for a few moments, and then typing in the correction.
(7) For signatures (or drawings) a stylus pen is used, the carbon sheet being first removed and a stylus plate inserted between the stencil and the backing sheet.
(8) After completing the stencil, check it very carefully before removing it from the typewriter.
(9) Clean the type with a hard brush in order to remove any traces of wax.

Duplicating Procedure

The various duplicating 'steps' are briefly dealt with as follows:

(1) Remove the carbon from between the stencil and the backing sheet.
(2) Attach the head of the stencil to the drum of the duplicator; then turn the handle slowly with one hand, while holding the bottom of the stencil with the other, until the stencil falls into position on the cylinder.

* This, of course, refers to *manual*, not electric, typewriters.

(3) Tear off the backing sheet and inspect the stencil for possible creases, which should be carefully smoothed out.

(4) Prepare the duplicating paper by 'fanning' it in order to separate the sheets, then place in feed tray.

(5) Adjust the receiving tray according to the size of paper being used.

(6) Run off a test copy, and note what adjustments may be required – e.g., more or less 'head' space or equalizing of margins. (Several test copies may be necessary before the stencil is ready to be run off.)

(7) Set the register, or automatic counter, to the number of copies required.

(8) Switch on electricity.

(9) After completion of the 'run'

(*a*) switch off electricity;

(*b*) drop the feed tray and remove unused paper;

(*c*) remove duplicated copies from the receiving tray;

(*d*) remove stencil from duplicator by detaching it at the head. (If it is intended to use the stencil again, clean it off and store away carefully. If not, place on backing sheet, fold up, and dispose of it.)

(*e*) When machine is in daily use, dust regularly to prevent accumulation of paper fluff.

(*f*) Always replace dust cover after use.

Spirit Process

In the spirit duplicator the rotary principle is also employed. Instead of ink being used as the printing medium, however, a specially prepared spirit (which dries very rapidly) is used.

A 'master' copy is prepared by using special carbons (hectograph) on a special type of glossy paper. These carbons may be obtained in a variety of colours, and colour work by the spirit process is therefore an easy matter. When the master copy has been prepared it is fitted to the machine and the requisite number of copies produced.

The chief disadvantage of the spirit process is that only about three hundred copies can be obtained from one 'master,' whereas in the stencil process several thousand copies may be obtained from a good-quality stencil.

Offset Litho Process

In the 'offset' process the printing medium is a thin metal or paper sheet which can be typed upon (a special 'copying' ribbon, however, being necessary) or hand-written with special inks. The sheet is fastened to the drum of a rotary duplicator, the impression being picked up by a rubber blanket and then transferred to the paper that is to be printed – hence the term 'offset.' Up to fifty thousand copies can be obtained from one metal sheet. Two well-known examples of this type of duplicator are Rotaprint and Multilith.

Type-setting Machines

In the printing-machine method of duplication (e.g., Multigraph) the 'master' from which the copies are made consists of metal type, which is set up on a circular drum. The machine is electrically operated and is capable of running off an unlimited number of copies at the rate of approximately six thousand an hour. Such a machine would obviously be of value only in an office where it could be used regularly for large quantities of duplicating, in which case it would probably necessitate a full-time operator.

Colour Duplication

It has already been mentioned that colour work by the spirit process is a comparatively simple matter. It is, however, also possible to carry out colour duplication by the ink process, the simplicity or otherwise of the operation depending on the manner in which the ink change is made. In some duplicators the change is made in a few seconds merely by removing the rotary drum and replacing it with another drum containing a different colour of ink. In other machines, however, the drum requires to be thoroughly cleaned before ink of another colour can be used.

Where colour work is carried out it is necessary to cut a separate stencil for each part of the work that has to be reproduced in a particular colour. Care must be taken, of course, to ensure that each colour registers in the correct place on the duplicated copy.

Copying Machines

Where it is necessary to reproduce a *replica* of an original document a copying process must be used. In most copying machines the basic principle is the same – the action of light on chemically treated paper.

Copying by machine is now carried out extensively in many offices, the chief advantage being the combination of speed and accuracy. For the best results in copying typewritten matter, a special ('photo-copy') ribbon should be fitted to the typewriter; and if handwritten matter is to be copied black or indian ink should be used.

There are many copying machines on the market, the majority of which adopt one of the following processes:

(1) Transfer process, which may be

(*a*) diffusion transfer;
(*b*) gelatine transfer; or
(*c*) heat transfer.

(2) Reflex process.
(3) Direct Positive process.
(4) Dyeline process.
(5) Xerographic process.
(6) Electro-photographic process.

Dictating Machines

Dictating machines are of two main types:

(1) those that use a *magnetic* medium;
(2) those that use a *non-magnetic* medium.

Magnetic Media

Dictating machines that use a magnetic medium do not provide a permanent record. There are various kinds of magnetic media in use, viz.:

(*a*) *Tapes.* Tapes, which are used on tape recorders, are made of magnetically coated plastic material, and are capable of recording twenty-five minutes or more of continuous dictation.

(*b*) *Sheets.* Some machines use sheets, these being made of magnetically coated plastic or paper. A sheet will record approximately twelve minutes of dictation, and a copy may be taken of the recording by placing two sheets together on the machine instead of one.

Sheets containing recorded messages may be sent through the post at ordinary letter rate; and it should be noted that folding or even crumpling of the sheet does not damage the recording in any way.

(*c*) *Discs.* Discs, which are also magnetically coated, may be obtained in various colours. The playing time ranges from six to twenty minutes, and after transcription the disc may be wiped clean with an eraser magnet.

(*d*) *Plastic Belts.* A belt will record approximately twelve minutes' dictation, and after transcription it too may be wiped clean with an eraser magnet. Belts may be folded and sent through the post.

(*e*) *Wire.* Where very long periods of dictation require to be recorded, *wire* dictating machines will be found most useful. A number of these machines record up to approximately five hours of continuous dictation.

NOTE. All the magnetic media mentioned above can be used indefinitely, corrections being made by dictating over the original dictation. It has already been stated that magnetic media do *not* provide a permanent record, and, moreover, there is always the danger of the recording being cleared before it has been transcribed by the typist.

Non-magnetic Media

A permanent record can, however, be made on the non-magnetic type of dictating machine; and there is the further advantage that the amount of dictation recorded can be clearly seen by both the dictator and the typist. It is, however, necessary for the dictator to note on an index slip any correction or instruction to the typist regarding additional copies, etc.

Non-magnetic media may take the form of plastic belts or discs.

Plastic Belts. A plastic belt provides a permanent and non-erasable record, the playing time being about twenty minutes.

The belts, which are small and light in weight, can be sent through the post or retained in a filing cabinet.

Discs. The playing time of a plastic disc is also about twenty minutes. Like the plastic belt, it provides a permanent record, although a special heat process enables it to be resurfaced for further use.

NOTE. It is essential to assess the length of each letter before typing to ensure that the correct size of paper is used.

Remote Dictation System

In large offices, where it is not always practicable to supply individual dictating machines to each person likely to dictate, a *remote dictation system* may operate. Under this system the dictator has access to a microphone, or some other form of recorder, from which point the dictation is at once transmitted to the typists' room where one or more recording machines are situated.

Adding/Listing Machines

Adding/Listing Machines may be divided into two main classes:

(*a*) Small Keyboard Machines.
(*b*) Full Keyboard Machines.

The following features are common to both *small* and *full* keyboard machines:

(1) Hand or electrically operated.
(2) Keys operated by 'touch,' as in typewriting.
(3) Machine provided with a tally roll on which calculations are printed.
(4) Adds and subtracts.
(5) *Electric* model provided with motorized 'error,' 'non-add,' and 'repeat' keys.
(6) Single and double (and, in some cases, triple) zero keys are provided for rapid entry of figures with multiple noughts.

Small Keyboard Machine

(1) Keys are numbered from one to nine with a zero key. (Also available with the decimal ½p key.)

(2) As each amount is recorded, the operating lever (or motor-bar in the case of electrically operated machines) must be depressed.

(3) Totals are obtained (on manual machines) by depressing the 'total' key and the operating lever, or (on electric machines) the 'total' motor-bar. (*Note.* Totals are, in most cases, automatically printed in red with a distinguishing asterisk, while subtotals (also printed in red) appear without the asterisk.)

(4) Amounts are entered on the keyboard by depressing the appropriate keys in the same order as the figures would be read – i.e., from left to right. (*Note.* When pounds only are recorded, two noughts must be entered for the pence column.)

(5) Error correction can be made by depressing the 'error' key, which cancels the whole amount set up on the keyboard.

(6) Minus amounts and minus ('negative') totals are usually clearly defined in red with a distinctive sign.

Full Keyboard Machine

(1) Amounts are entered on the keyboard by depressing the appropriate keys in the same order as the figures would be read – i.e., from left to right. (*Note.* The amounts recorded are clearly visible before operating the machine.)

(2) Several figures may be entered simultaneously by using two or more fingers and reading the amount as a whole.

(3) Noughts print automatically without operation of the keys.

(4) Error correction can be made (in the case of a *single* key) by depressing the correct key in the appropriate column, or the *whole* amount set up on the keyboard can be cancelled by depressing the 'error' key.

Calculating Machines

Calculating machines have been developed primarily to carry out the processes of multiplication and division. They are of two main types:

(*a*) *flat;*
(*b*) *rotary.*

Bearing in mind that multiplication is merely 'extended addition,' one can see that a calculating machine would deal with multiplication sums as follows:

3 x 3 = 3 + 3 + 3 (i.e., 9)
4 x 3 = 4 + 4 + 4 (i.e., 12)
6 x 3 = 6 + 6 + 6 (i.e., 18) and so on.

The process of division – which of course, is the reverse of multiplication – consists of a series of 'extended subtractions,' the divisor figure being repeatedly subtracted until there is no remainder (or one smaller than the divisor).

'Flat' Type of Calculator

When operating the 'flat' type of calculator the number to be multiplied is repeated by depressing the appropriate keys the number of times indicated by the *units* figure of the multiplier; this operation is repeated for the number of *tens* in the multiplier, and then for the number of *hundreds*, etc. The totals are accumulated in the machine, the answer being recorded on the dials.

Rotary Calculator

The rotary calculator operates on the same principle with the difference that, instead of the keys being depressed manually, the figure to be multiplied is set in the machine and a side handle turned the appropriate number of times (i.e., according to the units figure of the multiplier), this result being recorded on a dial. Part of the machine is then moved along one place to the right, and the process is repeated for the number of tens in the multiplier, and so on, the final result being recorded on the *totals* dial.

Printing Calculator

The printing calculator is an extremely useful office machine, which has the following features:

1. Electrically operated.
2. Automatically adds, subtracts, multiplies, and divides.
3. Operated by 'touch.'

4. Lists results of calculations on a tally roll.

5. Provided with error-correction key, non-add key, and repeat key(s).

6. Available with or without the decimal ½p.

7. Plus and minus amounts clearly defined by colour; e.g., plus totals print in *black*, minus totals in *red*.

8. Capable of calculations involving discounts and percentages, currency conversions, gross pay calculations, etc.

Book-keeping and Accounting Machines

Despite the wide variety of types and sizes of book-keeping machines, resulting in individual differences, the basic principles are the same in nearly every case – *simultaneous entry*, *totalling*, and *balancing*.

The chief advantages of machine accounting are as follows:

(*a*) The amount of work involved in entering up transactions is reduced, resulting in a saving of time and labour.

(*b*) Arithmetical accuracy is ensured as a result of the balancing being done mechanically.

(*c*) Each account is automatically balanced after every entry, thus avoiding delay at the end of the month.

(*d*) Customers' statements (which are prepared simultaneously with their ledger accounts) are ready for dispatch as soon as the postings for the month have been completed, thereby resulting in accounts being settled more quickly.

Punched Card Systems

Punched card systems (e.g., Hollerith) differ from other accounting machines in that the original information, instead of being entered up directly, requires to be transferred initially to punched cards. These cards have holes punched in them in such a manner as to give the desired information – date of transaction, account number, value of goods, etc. The cards are verified for accuracy, sorted automatically, and then fed into a machine which prints the necessary ledger sheets, statements, etc., with speed and accuracy.

Teleprinters (Telex Service)

Telex is a twenty-four-hour teleprinter service supplied by the Post Office for the rapid interchange of printed messages between subscribers in this country and for communication with subscribers in many countries overseas, including the United States of America. It can also be used for sending and receiving inland and overseas telegrams.

Subscribers rent from the Post Office a teleprinter and a line to the nearest Telex exchange. In appearance the teleprinter resembles an ordinary typewriter, and it can be operated by a competent typist after a little practice.

How to make a Telex Call

Calls are made by direct subscriber dialling to all United Kingdom subscribers and to most European countries. When the connection has been made to the other Telex subscriber the caller types his message, which is printed simultaneously on *both* machines. Each copy contains printed confirmation that the connection has been made and the messages and replies from the other subscriber correctly received. These printed messages constitute a permanent record of the information that has been exchanged and can be filed in both offices for future reference.

NOTE. Telex messages may be sent to a subscriber even when his teleprinter is unattended (for example, at night); the message will then be available when the office reopens.

Perforating Attachment and Automatic Transmitter

Difficult messages, such as stock returns or statistical information, can be recorded on punched tape for automatic and consequently more rapid transmission. This necessitates auxiliary equipment (known as an *automatic transmitter*, or "auto sender") which can be rented from the Post Office.

Addressing Machines

Addressing machines, which operate on the same principle as duplicators and can address as many as four thousand envelopes an hour, have a wide variety of uses. In addition to addressing envelopes for circulars, they may be used for inserting addresses on invoices and statements and on wrappers for catalogues and price-lists; for pay envelopes, renewal notices, etc.

Stapling Machines

Staplers, or stapling machines, save time and also give a much neater appearance to papers than when they are fastened by pins or clips.

Stamping Machines

Stamping machines are used for stamping letters or insurance cards. The stamps can be obtained from the Post Office in strips; and the machine in one operation moistens the stamp, records its issue, and affixes it to the envelope. National Insurance stamps are, in addition, cancelled by dating. It should be noted that some machines take stamps of only one value, while others take stamps of any value.

Franking Machines

Franking (Postage Meter) machines are used to frank letters with the correct postage without the use of adhesive stamps, printed impressions being made on the envelopes instead. The machine is provided with a meter which records the number of times the franking die is used. Payments (in advance) in respect of postage must be made from time to time at a specified Post Office, and the machine must be presented at the same Post Office in order that the meter may be 'set.'

A franking machine reduces the number of entries in the postage book and, at the same time, rules out the risk of loss or pilferage of stamps.

Guillotine

A guillotine (which is an extremely sharp cutting device) is most useful in an office for slicing or trimming paper and cards.

Latest Equipment

The field of office machinery and equipment is a rapidly changing one, and it is important for the secretary – in order that she may be in a position to advise her employer at any time – to keep up to date with new developments. She should therefore read the literature and illustrated leaflets supplied by the various manufacturers and, if possible, attend business efficiency exhibitions or visit the showrooms of local firms, where she can inspect the latest equipment.

Appendix A

Metric System—Metric Conversion

WEIGHTS AND MEASURES

Metric System

Length

10 millimetres (mm.) . .	= 1 centimetre (cm.)
10 centimetres	= 1 decimetre (dm.)
10 decimetres	= 1 metre (m.)
10 metres	= 1 dekametre (dam.)
10 dekametres	= 1 hectometre (hm.)
10 hectometres . . .	= 1 kilometre (km.)

Area (Land)

100 sq. metres	= 1 are (a.)
100 ares	= 1 hectare (ha.)
100 hectares	= 1 sq. kilometre

Weight

10 milligrams (mg.). . .	= 1 centigram (cg.)
10 centigrams	= 1 decigram (dg.)
10 decigrams	= 1 gramme (gm.)
10 grammes	= 1 dekagram (dag.)
10 dekagrams	= 1 hectogram (hg.)
10 hectograms	= 1 kilogram (kg.)
10 kilograms	= 1 myriagram
10 myriagrams	= 1 quintal (q.)
10 quintals	= 1 tonne (t.)

(Jewellers weigh gems in carats. 1 carat = 200 mg.)

Capacity

10 millilitres (ml.) . . . = 1 centilitre (cl.)
10 centilitres . . . . = 1 decilitre (dl.)
10 decilitres . . . . = 1 litre (lit.)
10 litres . . . . . = 1 dekalitre (dal.)
10 dekalitres . . . . = 1 hectolitre (hl.)

CONVERSION TABLES

English to Metric

Length

1 inch . . . . . . = 25·400 millimetres
1 foot . . . . . . = 0·30480 metre
1 yard . . . . . . = 0·91440 metre
1 fathom . . . . . . = 1·8288 metres
1 pole . . . . . . = 5·0292 metres
1 chain . . . . . . = 20·1168 metres
1 furlong . . . . . . = 201·168 metres
1 mile . . . . . . = 1·6093 kilometres

Area

1 sq. inch . . . . . . = 6·4516 sq. centimetres
1 sq. foot . . . . . . = 9·2903 sq. decimetres
1 sq. yard . . . . . . = 0·8361 sq. metre
1 perch . . . . . . = 25·293 sq. metres
1 rood . . . . . . = 10·117 ares
1 acre . . . . . . = 0·40468 hectare
1 sq. mile . . . . . . = 259·00 hectares

Volume

1 cu. inch . . . . . . = 16·3870 cu. centimetres
1 cu. foot . . . . . . = 0·02832 cu. metre
1 cu. yard . . . . . . = 0·764553 cu. metre

Capacity

1 gill . . . . = 1·421 decilitres
1 pint . . . . . . = 0·568 litre
1 quart . . . . . . = 1·136 litres
1 gallon . . . . . . = 4·546 litres
1 peck . . . . . . = 9·092 litres
1 bushel . . . . . . = 3·637 dekalitres
1 quarter . . . . . . = 2·909 hectolitres

Avoirdupois

1 grain	=	0·0648 gramme
1 dram	=	1·772 grammes
1 ounce	=	28·350 grammes
1 pound	=	0·454 kilogram
1 stone	=	6·350 kilograms
1 quarter	=	12·70 kilograms
1 hundredweight	=	50·80 kilograms
1 ton	=	1016·05 kilograms
	=	(1·01605 tonnes)

Apothecaries'

1 minim	=	0·059 millilitre
1 fluid scruple	=	1·184 millilitres
1 fluid drachm	=	3·551 millilitres
1 fluid ounce	=	2·841 centilitres
1 pint	=	0·568 litre
1 grain	=	0·0648 gramme
1 scruple (20 grains) . . .	=	1·296 grammes
1 drachm (3 scruples) . . .	=	3·888 grammes
1 oz. (8 drachms)	=	31·1035 grammes

Troy

1 grain	=	0·0648 gramme
1 pennyweight	=	1·5552 grammes
1 troy ounce	=	31·1035 grammes
1 troy pound	=	373·2420 grammes

Appendix B

Commercial and General Abbreviations

&	(ampersand) and
@	at
A1	first class; first rate (at Lloyd's)
a.a.r.	against all risks
A.A.	Automobile Association
A.C.	Alternating Current
A/C	Account Current
a/c, acct.	account
A.C.A.	Associate of the Institute of Chartered Accountants
Acc.	Acceptance *or* accepted
A.C.I.I.	Associate of the Chartered Insurance Institute
A.C.I.S.	Associate of the Chartered Institute of Secretaries
A.C.W.A.	Associate of the Institute of Cost and Works Accountants
a/d	after date
A.D.	*Anno Domini* (in the year of our Lord)
A.D.C.	Aide-de-camp
ad lib.	*ad libitum* (at pleasure)
ad val., a/v	*ad valorem* (according to the value)
adv.	advice
advt.	advertisement
Afft.	Affidavit
agric.	agriculture
Agt.	Agent
A.I.A.	Associate of the Institute of Actuaries
a.m.	*ante meridiem* (before noon)
amp.	ampere

A.M.I.C.E.	Associate Member of the Institution of Civil Engineers
A.M.I.E.E.	Associate Member of the Institution of Electrical Engineers
A.M.I.Mech.E.	Associate Member of the Institution of Mechanical engineers
A.M.I.Mun.E.	Associate Member of the Institution of Municipal Engineers
amt.	amount
anon.	anonymous
ans.	answer, answered
a/o	account of
App.	Appendix
appro.	approval, approbation
approx.	approximate
A.P.S.	Associate of the Pharmaceutical Society
A.R.A.	Associate of the Royal Academy
A.R.A.M.	Associate of the Royal Academy of Music
A.R.C.M.	,, ,, ,, Royal College of Music
A.R.C.O.	,, ,, ,, Royal College of Organists
A.R.I.B.A.	Associate of the Royal Institute of British Architects
arr.	arrive or arrives; arrival
A.R.S.A.	Associate of the Royal Scottish Academy
A.S.A.A.	Associate of the Society of Incorporated Accountants and Auditors
Assn., Assoc.	Association
Asst.	Assistant
A.T.C.	Air Training Corps
B.A.	Bachelor of Arts
bal.	balance
Bart., Bt.	Baronet
B.B.	Bill Book
B.B.C.	British Broadcasting Corporation
B.Ch.	Bachelor of Surgery
B.C.L.	Bachelor of Civil Law
B.Com.	Bachelor of Commerce
b/d	brought down (book-keeping)
B/D	Bank Draft
B.D.	Bachelor of Divinity
bdl.	bundle
B.D.S.	Bachelor of Dental Surgery
bds.	boards (in book-binding)

B/E	Bill of Exchange
B.E.A.	British European Airways
B.Ed.	Bachelor of Education
Beds.	Bedfordshire
B.Eng.	Bachelor of Engineering
Berks.	Berkshire
b/f	brought forward (book-keeping)
bk.	bank; book
bkpt.	bankrupt
B.L.	Bachelor of Law
B/L	Bill of Lading
B.M.	Bachelor of Medicine
B.M.A.	British Medical Association
B.Mus.	Bachelor of Music
B/N	Bank Note
B.O.A.C.	British Overseas Airways Corporation
bot., bt., bght.	bought
B.P.	British Pharmacopoeia; British Public
B/P	Bills Payable
B/R	Bills Receivable
B.R.	British Rail(ways)
B.R.S.	British Road Services
brl.(s)	barrel(s)
Bros.	Brothers
B/S	Bill of Sale
B.S.A.	Birmingham Small Arms (Company)
B.Sc.	Bachelor of Science
B.Sc.(Econ.)	Bachelor of Science (Economics)
B.S.I.	British Standards Institution
B.S.T.	British Summer Time
B.T.C.	British Transport Commission
B.Th.U.	British Thermal Unit
Bucks.	Buckinghamshire
B.U.P.	British United Press
bx., bxs.	box, boxes
c., c/s	case, cases
C., Cent.	Centigrade
C.A.	Chartered Accountant
C/A	Capital Account (book-keeping); Current Account
Cambs.	Cambridgeshire
Cantab.	of Cambridge
caps.	capitals

Capt.	Captain
Carms.	Carmarthenshire
C.B.	Cash Book; Companion of (the Order of) the Bath
C.B.E.	Commander of (the Order of) the British Empire
C.B.I.	Confederation of British Industry
C.C.	County Council
c.c.	cubic centimetre
cc.	copies
cd.	candela (luminous intensity)
c/d	carried down (book-keeping)
C.E.	Civil Engineer; Church of England
Cert.	Certificate
c/f	carried forward (book-keeping)
c. & f.	cost and freight
c.f.i., c.f. & i.	cost, freight and insurance
cf. *or* cp.	compare
cg.	centigram
C.G.M.	Conspicuous Gallantry Medal
ch., chap.	chapter
C.H.	Clearing House (banking); Customs House; Companion of Honour
Ch.D.	Chancery Division
chq.	cheque
C.I.	Channel Islands
C.I.D.	Criminal Investigation Department
C.I.E.	Companion of (the Order of) the Indian Empire
Cie	*Compagnie* (French – company)
c.i.f.	cost, insurance, and freight
c.i.f. & c.	cost, insurance, freight, and commission
c.i.f.c. & i.	cost, insurance, freight, commission, and interest
C. in C.	Commander-in-Chief
C.I.S.	Chartered Institute of Secretaries
C.J.	Chief Justice
ck., cks.	cask, casks
cm.	centimetre
C.M.G.	Companion of (the Order of) St. Michael and St. George
C/N	Credit Note
Co.	Company; county
c/o	care of; carried over
C.O.	Commanding Officer; Colonial Office

C.O.D.	Cash on Delivery; Concise Oxford Dictionary
Col.	Colonel
col.	column
comm.	commission
Consols.	Consolidated Funds
cont.	contract
Co-op	Co-operative Society
Cr.	credit or creditor
C.S.I.	Companion of (the Order of) the Star of India
ctge.	cartage
cu., cub.	cubic
cu.m.	cubic metre
cum div., c.div.	cum (with) dividend
cumec.	cubic metre per second
cum. pref.	cumulative preference
curr.	current – of the present month
C.V.O.	Commander of the (Royal) Victorian Order
C.W.O.	Cash with Order
D/A	Deposit Account (banking); documents against acceptance
D.B.	Day Book
D.B.E.	Dame Commander of (the Order of) the British Empire
D.C.L.	Doctor of Civil Law
D.C.M.	Distinguished Conduct Medal
D.C.V.O.	Dame Commander of the Royal Victorian Order
D/D	Demand Draft
D.D.	Doctor of Divinity
d/d	days after date
Deb.	Debenture
Deft.	Defendant
deg.	degree
deld.	delivered
dep.	depart or departs, etc.
Dept.	Department
D.F.C.	Distinguished Flying Cross
dft.	draft
diam.	diameter
diff.	difference
disc.	discount
dist.	district
div.	dividend; division
D.L.	Deputy Lieutenant

D. Lit.	Doctor of Literature
D. Litt.	Doctor of Letters
D.L.O.	Dead Letter Office
D.Mus.	Doctor of Music
D/N	Debit Note
D.N.B.	Dictionary of National Biography
D/O	Delivery Order
do.	ditto, the same
dol.(s)	dollar(s)
doz.	dozen
D/P	documents against payment
Dr.	debit or debtor; doctor
d/s	days after sight
D.S.C.	Distinguished Service Cross
D.Sc.	Doctor of Science
D.S.O.	Distinguished Service Order
d/y	delivery
E.	East
ea.	each
E.C.	East Central (Postal District, London)
Ed.	Editor; edition
E.E.	Errors excepted
E. & O.E.	Errors and omissions excepted
e.g.	*exempli gratia* (for example)
E.I.S.	Educational Institute of Scotland
enc.(s)	enclosure(s)
Eng.	English
entd.	entered
E.P.N.S.	Electro-plated nickel silver
E.P.T.	Excess Profits Tax
esp.	especially
Esq.	Esquire
E.T.A.	Estimated Time of Arrival
etc.	*et cetera* (and the rest)
et seq. (sing.)	*et sequens* } (and the following)
et seqq. (plur.)	*et sequentes* } (and the following)
ex	from out of (as *ex S.S. "Westward Ho"*)
ex	without (as *ex coupon, ex dividend,* etc.)
exch.	exchange
ex cp.	ex coupon
exd.	examined
ex div. (d.)	ex dividend
ex int.	ex interest

exor.(s)	executor(s)
exx.	examples
f., fr.	franc(s)
F., Fahr.	Fahrenheit
f.a.a.	free of all average (marine insurance)
f.a.q.	fair average quality
f.a.s.	free alongside ship
F.C.A.	Fellow of the Institute of Chartered Accountants
F.C.I.I.	Fellow of the Chartered Insurance Institute
F.C.I.S.	Fellow of the Chartered Institute of Secretaries
fcp.	foolscap
f.g.a.	free of general average (marine insurance)
F.G.S.	Fellow of the Geological Society
F.I.A.	Fellow of the Institute of Actuaries
f.i.b.	free into bunker (coal trade)
fig.(s)	figure(s)
fo., fol.	folio (book-keeping)
F.O.	Foreign Office
f.o.b.	free on board
foll.	following
For.	Foreign
f.o.r.	free on rail
f.p.	fully paid
f.p.a.	free of particular average (marine insurance)
fr.	franc(s)
Fr.	French
F.R.A.S.	Fellow of the Royal Astronomical Society
F.R.C.O.	Fellow of the Royal College of Organists
F.R.C.P.	Fellow of the Royal College of Physicians
F.R.C.S.	Fellow of the Royal College of Surgeons
F.R.G.S.	Fellow of the Royal Geographical Society
F.R.H.S.	Fellow of the Royal Horticultural Society
F.R.Hist.S.	Fellow of the Royal Historical Society
F.R.I.B.A.	Fellow of the Royal Institute of British Architects
F.R.S.	Fellow of the Royal Society
F.R.S.A.	Fellow of the Royal Society of Arts
frt.	freight
F.S.A.	Fellow of the Society of Antiquaries
F.Z.S.	Fellow of the Zoological Society
fwd.	forward
G/a	General average (marine insurance)

Gaz.	Gazette
G.B.	Great Britain
G.B.E.	Knight (or Dame) Grand Cross of (the Order of) the British Empire
G.C.	George Cross
G.C.B.	Knight Grand Cross of (the Order of) the Bath
G.C.I.E.	Knight Grand Commander of (the Order of) the Indian Empire
G.C.M.G.	Knight Grand Cross of (the Order of) St. Michael and St. George
G.C.S.I.	Knight Grand Commander of (the Order of) the Star of India
G.C.V.O.	Knight Grand Cross of the (Royal) Victorian Order
G.H.Q.	General Headquarters
Glam.	Glamorgan
G.L.C.	Greater London Council
Glos.	Gloucestershire
gm.	gramme(s)
G.M.	George Medal
G.M.T.	Greenwich Mean Time
Gov., Govt.	Government
G.P.	General Practitioner
G.P.O.	General Post Office
gr.	gross
gr. wt.	gross weight
ha.	hectare (= 10,000 sq. m.)
Hants.	Hampshire
H.B.	hard black (of pencils)
H.C.	House of Commons
H.E.	His Excellency
Herts.	Hertfordshire
H.H.	His (or Her) Highness; double-hard (of pencils)
hhd.	hogshead
H.H.H.	treble-hard (of pencils)
H.L.	House of Lords
H.M.	His (or Her) Majesty
H.M.C.	Her Majesty's Customs
H.M.S.	Her Majesty's Ship
H.M.S.O.	Her Majesty's Stationery Office
H.O.	Home Office
Hon.	Honourable; honorary
Hon. Sec.	Honorary Secretary

H.P.	Hire Purchase
h.p.	horse-power
H.Q.	Headquarters
hrs.	hours
ib., ibid.	*ibidem* (in the same place)
id.	*idem* (the same)
i.e.	*id est* (that is)
I/F	insufficient funds (banking)
Inc.	Incorporated
incog.	*incognito* (unknown)
I. of M.	Isle of Man
I. of W., I.W.	Isle of Wight
insce.	insurance
inst.	instant (of the present month)
Inst.	Institute
int.	interest
inv.	invoice
IOU	I owe you
i.q.	*idem quod* (the same as)
I.Q.	intelligence quotient
I.R.O.	Inland Revenue Office
It.	Italian
ital.	italics
J/A	Joint Account
J.P.	Justice of the Peace
Jun., Jr.	Junior
K.B.	Knight Bachelor
K.B.E.	Knight Commander of (the Order of) the British Empire
K.C.B.	Knight Commander of (the Order of) the Bath
K.C.I.E.	Knight Commander of (the Order of) the Indian Empire
K.C.M.G.	Knight Commander of (the Order of) St. Michael and St. George
K.C.S.I.	Knight Commander of (the Order of) the Star of India
K.C.V.O.	Knight Commander of the (Royal) Victorian Order
kg., kilo.	kilogram(me)
K.G.	Knight of (the Order of) the Garter
km.	kilometre
K.P.	Knight of (the Order of) St. Patrick
K.T.	Knight of (the Order of) the Thistle

Kt.	Knight
kW	kilowatt
£	*Libra*(*e*) (pound(s) sterling)
l., lit.	litre
Lancs.	Lancashire
lat.	latitude
l.c.	lower case (printing)
L/C	Letter of Credit
L.C.C.	London County Council
L.C.J.	Lord Chief Justice
L.D.S.	Licentiate in Dental Surgery
Led.	Ledger
Lib.	Liberal
lin.	linear
Lincs.	Lincolnshire
Litt.D.	Doctor of Letters
L.J.	Lord Justice
LL.B.	Bachelor of Laws
LL.D.	Doctor of Laws
loc. cit.	*loco citato* (in the place quoted)
long.	longitude
L.R.A.M.	Licentiate of the Royal Academy of Music
L.R.C.P.	Licentiate of the Royal College of Physicians
L.R.C.S.	Licentiate of the Royal College of Surgeons
l/s	litre per second
L.S.	*locus sigilli* (the place of the seal)
Lt., Lieut.	Lieutenant
Lt.-Col., Lieut.-Col.	Lieutenant-Colonel
Lt.-Com.	Lieutenant-Commander
Ltd., Ld.	Limited
m.	metre
M.	Monsieur; mille (one thousand)
M.A.	Master of Arts
Maj.	Major
Maj.-Gen.	Major-General
Mass.	Massachusetts
max.	maximum
M.B.	Bachelor of Medicine
M.B.E.	Member of (the Order of) the British Empire
M.C.	Military Cross; Master of Ceremonies
M.D.	Doctor of Medicine
m/d	months after date
mem., memo.	memorandum

M.Eng.	Master of Engineering
Messrs.	Messieurs, Gentlemen, Sirs
mfg.	manufacturing
M.F.H.	Master of Foxhounds
mfr.	manufacturer
mg.	milligram
Mgr.	Monseigneur; Monsignor
M.I.C.E.	Member of the Institution of Civil Engineers
Middx.	Middlesex
M.I.Mech.E.	Member of the Institution of Mechanical Engineers
min.	minimum; minute
M.I.P.	Marine Insurance Policy
Mlle.	Mademoiselle, Miss
mm.	millimetre
mm/s	millimetre per second
MM.	Messieurs, Sirs
M.M.	Military Medal
Mme	Madame (*plural* 'Mmes')
mo., mos.	month, months
M.O.	Money Order; Medical Officer
M.O.H.	Medical Officer of Health
Mon.	Monmouthshire
M.P.	Member of Parliament
m.p.h.	miles per hour
M.P.S.	Member of the Pharmaceutical Society
m/s	metre per second; months after sight
MS.	manuscript
MSS.	manuscripts
M.V.	Motor Vessel
M.V.O.	Member of the (Royal) Victorian Order
N.	North
N.A.A.F.I.	Navy, Army, and Air Force Institutes
N.B.	*nota bene* (mark well, take note)
N.C.B.	National Coal Board
N.C.O.	non-commissioned officer
n.d.	no date
N.E.	North East
nem. con.	*nemine contradicente* (no one contradicting)
N/F	no funds (banking)
N.F.U.	National Farmers' Union
N/m	no mark (shipping)
No., Nos.	number, numbers

Nom.	nominal
Nom. Cap.	nominal capital
non seq.	*non sequitur* (it does not follow)
Northants.	Northamptonshire
Notts.	Nottinghamshire
N.P.	Notary Public; new paragraph
N.S.W.	New South Wales
N.U.R.	National Union of Railwaymen
N.U.T.	National Union of Teachers
N.W.	North West
N.Y.	New York
N.Z.	New Zealand
o/a	on account
O.B.E.	Officer of (the Order of) the British Empire
o/c	overcharge; out of charge (customs)
O.C.	Officer Commanding
oct. (8vo)	octavo
o/d	on demand
O/D	overdraft
O.E.D.	Oxford English Dictionary
O.H.M.S.	On Her Majesty's Service
O.M.	Order of Merit
o.p.	out of print
op. cit.	*opere citato* (in the work cited)
O.R.	Owner's Risk; Official Receiver
Ord.	Ordinary
O/S	outstanding; out of stock
Oxon.	Oxfordshire; of Oxford
p., pp.	page, pages
p.a., per ann.	*per annum* (for the year)
P/A	Power of Attorney; private account (book-keeping)
P.A.Y.E.	Pay as you earn (Income Tax)
P.C.	Police Constable; Privy Councillor; postcard
P/C	Petty Cash; Prices Current
pc., pcs.	piece, pieces
P.C.B.	Petty Cash Book
pcl.	parcel
pd.	paid
Pembs.	Pembrokeshire
per cent	*per centum*
per pro., p.p.	*per procurationem* (by procuration); on behalf of

Pref.	Preference *or* preferred; Preface
pro	for
Prof.	Professor
pro tem.	*pro tempore* (for the time being)
prox.	*proximo* (of the next month)
P.S.	*postscriptum* (postscript)
P.T.	Physical Training
P.T.O.	please turn over
Q.B.	Queen's Bench
Q.C.	Queen's Counsel
q.e.d.	*quod erat demonstrandum* (which was to be demonstrated)
qto. (4to)	quarto
q.v.	*quod vide* (which see)
qy.	query
R.A.	RoyalAcademy; Royal Artillery
R.A.C.	Royal Automobile Club
R.A.F.	Royal Air Force
R.A.M.	Royal Academy of Music
R.C.	Roman Catholic
R.C.M.	Royal College of Music
R/D	Refer to drawer (banking)
Rd.	Road
Ph.D.	Doctor of Philosophy
pkg.	package
pkt.	packet
P. & L.	Profit and Loss
P.L.A.	Port of London Authority
Pltf.	plaintiff
p.m.	*post meridiem* (afternoon)
pm.	premium
P.M.	Paymaster; Postmaster; Prime Minister
P.M.G.	Paymaster General
P/N	Promissory Note
P.O.	Post Office; Postal Order
P. & O.	Peninsular & Oriental Steam Navigation Company
pop.	population
P.O.S.B.	Post Office Savings Bank
p.p.	*per procurationem* (on behalf of; as agent for)
pp.	pages
P.P.S.	*post postscriptum* (further postscript); Parliamentary Private Secretary

re	in regard to; relating to
recd.	received
rect.	receipt
ref.	reference
reg., regd.	registered
regt.	regiment
retd.	returned
Rev., Revd.	Reverend
R.G.S.	Royal Geographical Society
rm.	ream
R.M.S.	Royal Mail Steamer
R.N.	Royal Navy
R.N.R.	Royal Naval Reserve
R.N.V.R.	Royal Naval Volunteer Reserve
rom.	Roman type
R.P.	reply paid
Rs.	rupees
R.S.A.	Royal Scottish Academy; Royal Society of Arts
R.S.P.C.A.	Royal Society for the Prevention of Cruelty to Animals
R.S.V.P.	*répondez s'il vous plaît* (please reply)
rt.	right
Rt. Hon.	Right Honourable
Rt. Rev.	Right Reverend
Ry.	Railway
$	dollar(s)
S.	South
S.A.E.	stamped addressed envelope
Salop.	Shropshire
S.B.	Sales Book
s.c., s. caps.	small capitals
S.E.	South East
sec.	second
Sec., Secy.	Secretary
sect.	section
Sen., Senr.	Senior
sgd.	signed
S/N	Shipping Note
Soc.	Society
S.O.S.	Wireless code-signal of extreme distress
Sov.	Sovereign
S.P.C.K.	Society for Promoting Christian Knowledge
S.P.R.	Society for Psychical Research

sq.	square
sq. km.	square kilometre
sq. m.	square metre
sq. mm.	square millimetre
S.S.	Steamship
S.S.C.	Solicitor to the Supreme Court (Scotland)
St.	Saint; street
Staffs.	Staffordshire
std.	standard
S.T.D.	Subscriber Trunk Dialling
stg.	sterling
stk.	stock
Supt.	Superintendent
S.W.	South West
t.	tonne (= 1000 kg.)
T.A.	Territorial Army
T.D.	Territorial Decoration
tech.	technical
temp.	*tempore* (in the period of)
T.G.W.U.	Transport and General Workers' Union
T.O.	turn over
tr.	tare
Treas.	Treasurer; Treasury
trs.	transpose
T.T.	telegraphic transfer
T.U.C.	Trades Union Congress
u.c.	upper case (printing)
U.K.	United Kingdom
ult.	*ultimo* (of the last month)
U.N.E.S.C.O.	United Nations Educational, Scientific, and Cultural Organization
U.N.O.	United Nations Organization
U.S.	United States
U.S.A.	United States of America
U.S.A.F.	United States Air Force
U.S.S.R.	Union of Soviet Socialist Republics
U/w	Underwriter
v.	*versus* (against)
V.A.D.	Voluntary Aid Detachment
V.C.	Victoria Cross
V.H.F.	very high frequency
via	by way of
V.I.P.	Very Important Person

viz.	*videlicet* (namely)
vol.	volume
V.S.	veterinary surgeon
W.	West
W.A.A.C.	Women's Army Auxiliary Corps
W.A.A.F.	Women's Auxiliary Air Force
W.B.	way-bill; Warehouse Book
W.C.	West Central (Postal District, London)
w.f.	wrong fount (printing)
Whf.	wharf
W.H.O.	World Health Organization
Whse.	warehouse
W.I.	West Indies
Wilts.	Wiltshire
wk(s).	week(s)
Y.M.C.A.	Young Men's Christian Association
Worcs.	Worcestershire
W.R.A.C.	Women's Royal Army Corps
W.R.A.F.	Women's Royal Air Force
W.R.I.	Women's Rural Institute
W.R.N.S.	Women's Royal Naval Service
W.R.V.S.	Women's Royal Voluntary Service
W.S.	Writer to the Signet
wt.	weight
x.c., x.cp.	ex (without) coupon
x.d., x.div.	ex (without) dividend
x.int.	ex (without) interest
Y/A, Y.A.R.	York-Antwerp Rules (marine insurance)
yr.	your; year
yrs.	yours; years
Y.W.C.A.	Young Women's Christian Association
Zool.	Zoology, etc.
′	feet (as 2′ 6″ – two feet six inches)
″	inches (as 6″ x 3½″ – six inches by three and a half inches)
x	by (as 3 x 2 – three by two)
°	degree (as 90° – ninety degrees)
#	number, numbered (as #66/483)
°C.	degree Celsius (centigrade)
°K.	degree Kelvin (thermodynamic)

Appendix C

Common Business Terms

Account Rendered. A term used when the unpaid balance of an account (full details of which have been previously sent to the customer) is brought forward on a statement of later date; e.g., "To account rendered, £20·00."

Account Sales. A statement sent by an agent to a principal giving full details of the goods sold on his behalf and the price obtained, *less* the agent's commission and all expenses incurred by him in selling the goods – thus showing the net proceeds.

Ad valorem. According to the value.

Advice. Notice, in writing, of something that has been done, or is intended to be done, on one's behalf.

Agent. A person who has authority to act on behalf of another.

Appreciation. Increase in value.

Arrears. Payments overdue.

Assets. Property belonging to and debts owing to a person or firm.

Audit. The examination of accounts in order to verify them.

Auditor. One who carries out an audit.

Bad Debts. Accounts which are irrecoverable, and which should be written off to a 'Bad Debts' Account.

Balance. The difference between the two sides of an account.

Balance Sheet. A statement of the financial position of a trader as at a given date. His assets are recorded on the right-hand side, and his liabilities on the left-hand side.

Bank Certificate. A certificate issued by a bank, for audit purposes, certifying the amount of a company's balance in the bank's books at a certain date.

Bank Draft. A bill of exchange drawn by one bank on another, payable to the order of the person named.

Banker's Order. A written order given by a customer to his banker to make periodic payments on his behalf – e.g., monthly instalments or annual subscriptions. (See p. 199.)

Bank Giro Credits. A system operated by banks for making payments to third parties. (For details see p. 200.)

Bank Rate. The rate per cent charged by the Bank of England for discounting approved bills of exchange.

Bankruptcy and *Insolvency.* A trader is *insolvent* if he is unable to pay his debts in full; he is *bankrupt* when declared so by the Court.

Bill of Exchange (legal definition). An unconditional order in writing addressed by one person to another, signed by the person giving it, requiring the person to whom it is addressed to pay on demand, or at a fixed or determinable future time, a sum certain in money to, or to the order of, a specified person or to bearer.

Bill of Lading. A receipt given by the shipping company for goods put on board a ship. It contains the conditions and terms agreed upon as to freight, etc., and also gives particulars of weights and measurements, shipping marks and numbers. The B/L must be produced by the consignee before he can claim the goods.

Bill of Sale. A document assigning personal property and usually given as security for a loan.

Bill Payable. The term applied to a bill of exchange by the person who has to pay it.

Bill Receivable. The term applied to a bill of exchange by the person who is to receive it.

Bonded Goods. Goods that are liable to customs duty are placed in a Government or bonded warehouse until the duty has been paid. (Such goods are said to be *in bond.*)

Bonus. An extra dividend sometimes paid to shareholders; an additional sum paid to employees in the form of a percentage on results.

Book Debts. Accounts outstanding and owing to the trader, as shown in his books.

Broker. One who buys or sells, on behalf of other persons, for a commission. (There are various kinds of broker: Bill Broker, Insurance Broker, Stock and Share Broker, etc.)

Brokerage. The commission payable to a broker for his services.

Capital. The *net worth* of a trader after deducting his liabilities from his assets; at the commencement of trading it is the amount invested by the owner in his business.

Carriage. The charge for conveying goods by rail or road.

Carriage Forward. This indicates that the carriage on the goods is to be paid by the consignee. (*Note.* When goods are sent *Carriage Paid*, the sender, or consignor, pays.)

Carriage Inwards. Carriage on purchases.

Carriage Outwards. Carriage on sales.

Cash Discount. An allowance made for prompt settlement of an account.

Commission. The charge made by a person for acting as agent to another, usually referred to as the 'principal.'

Composition. A part payment – i.e., a payment of so much in the pound – by an insolvent or bankrupt debtor to his creditors.

Consignee. The agent to whom goods are sent 'on consignment.'

Consignment. Goods sent to an agent to be sold on commission. The agent does not buy the goods, but merely holds them for his principal until they are sold. (See *Account Sales.*)

Consignment Note. A form that must be completed by the consignor when sending goods by rail.

Consignor. The sender of goods 'on consignment.'

Contingent Liability. A liability that depends on the happening of a specified event – e.g., the liability of an endorser upon a bill of exchange. (*Note.* Contingent liabilities usually appear as a footnote in the balance sheet.)

Contra. A book-keeping term meaning 'against,' 'on the opposite side.'

Contra Entries. A contra entry is made in the cash book to record (*a*) a payment of cash into the bank, *or* (*b*) a withdrawal of cash from the bank. The contra entry involves in each case an entry on both sides of the cash book, the letter 'C' (for 'contra') being inserted in the folio column against each entry as an indication that the double entry is completed on the opposite side.

Cost, Insurance and Freight (c.i.f.). When goods are quoted 'c.i.f.' this means that the price quoted covers also insurance and freight charges to the port or place of destination.

Credit Cards. Credit cards (e.g., Barclaycard) are used for day-to-day shopping as well as in hotels and restaurants, etc., and obviate the need to carry large sums of cash. Bills are settled monthly by cheque. (See p. 199.)

Credit Note. A document sent to a customer giving particulars of the amount he is entitled to be credited with in respect of overcharges, returned goods, allowances, etc. (See *Debit Note.*)

Creditor. One to whom something is owing; in book-keeping, the sender of the goods or the payer of the money.

Credit Sales. Those sales for which payment is made at a later date.

Crossed Cheque. One that has two parallel lines drawn across the face of the cheque with or without the words "& Co." written between them. A crossed cheque cannot be cashed over the counter but must be paid into a banking account. (See pp. 196 & 197.)

Current Account. In banking, a current account is one in which money previously lodged may be withdrawn or added to at any time. (See p. 190.) In partnership accounts, a current account is one which shows a partner's periodic drawings, interest, etc.

Current Assets. Those assets that are held by a trader for sale or conversion into cash in the ordinary course of business; e.g., stock-in-trade, book debts, bills receivable, etc. *Cash* itself is also a current asset. (Sometimes known as *Floating* or *Circulating* Assets.)

Days of Grace. The three extra days allowed for the payment of a bill of exchange.

Debenture. A certificate of indebtedness given by a company in respect of a loan.

Debit Note. A document giving particulars of the amount charged to another person's account. (See *Credit Note.*)

Debtor. One who owes; in book-keeping, the receiver of the goods or money.

Del Credere Agent. An agent who guarantees to his principal the due payment for goods sold on commission.

Del Credere Commission. An additional commission charged by the agent for guaranteeing payment for all goods that he may sell on behalf of his principal.

Delivery Note. Delivery notes contain brief particulars of the goods ordered, and are usually handed to the customer with the goods when delivery is made.

Demurrage. A charge made at so much a day for delay in loading and unloading ships, railway trucks, etc.

Depreciation. The gradual and permanent decrease in the value of an asset from any cause.

Direct Debiting. A banking service which combines the benefits of the cheque and the standing order services. (See p. 200.)

Discount a Bill. To receive cash in advance from a banker for a bill of exchange before it is due.

Dishonoured. A bill of exchange or a cheque that is not met when presented for payment is said to be 'dishonoured.' (See pp. 197 & 206.)

Dividend. That part of a company's profits which is divided among the shareholders. *Dividend* also refers to the payments made by a bankrupt estate to the creditors. (See *Composition.*)

Double Entry. This refers to the entry of each transaction *twice* in the ledger. (See p. 78.)

Draft. The name given to a bill of exchange *before* it is accepted.

Drawee. The person upon whom a bill of exchange is drawn, or the bank upon which a cheque is drawn.

Drawer. The person who *draws* (or signs) a bill or cheque.

Drawings. The sums withdrawn from the business by the owner for his own use.

Endorse. To sign one's name on the *back* of a bill of exchange or cheque in order to transfer it to another person.

Endorsee. The person to whom the bill or cheque has been transferred by endorsement.

Endorser. The person who endorses the bill or cheque thus.

Errors Excepted; Errors and Omissions Excepted (E.E., E. & O.E.). Often written on statements, invoices, etc., so that if any errors or omissions are subsequently discovered they may be corrected.

Executor. The person appointed by a *testator* (i.e., a person who makes a Will) to carry out his instructions.

Fiduciary Loan. A loan granted without security upon the confidence of the honour of the borrower.

Fixed Assets. Those assets that are held solely for use in the business and are not intended for resale – e.g., machinery, furniture and fittings, buildings, etc.

Folio. In book-keeping, *two* pages facing each other, both numbered alike.

Free on Board (f.o.b.). A price quoted for goods which includes all charges until the goods are placed on board the ship.

Free on Rail (f.o.r.). A price quoted for goods which includes all charges until the goods are placed in the railway trucks.

Free on Steamer. See *Free on Board.*

Freight. The charge made for transporting goods by water, land, or air.

Gilt-edged Securities. Securities of first-class standing (e.g., Government stock) which are readily convertible into cash.

Goodwill. The value of the connection and reputation of a business.

Gross Profit. The difference between the cost price and the selling price of goods.

Gross Weight. The *full* weight of the goods as packed – i.e., including the weight of the container in which they are packed.

Imprest System. The method by which a fixed sum is advanced and the expenditure from the amount at the end of, say, a week or a month is repaid, thus enabling the weekly (*or* monthly) balance to remain constant. (See pp. 83 & 84.)

Insolvent. Unable to pay one's debts in full.

Insurance. A contract by means of which an insurance company (the 'insurer') undertakes, in return for a sum of money called the 'premium,' to make good to the person insuring (the 'insured') any loss he may suffer as a result of fire, burglary, accident, etc. (*Note.* The written contract is called the 'insurance policy.')

Interest. The payment made by the borrower of money to the lender for the use of that money. Interest is usually charged at so much per cent per annum.

Interest on Capital. The amount charged against a business for the capital employed before distributing profit.

Inventory. A list of goods or property.

Invoice. A document sent to the customer by the supplier, giving full particulars of the goods sold including description, quantity, price, etc.

IOU (I owe you). A written acknowledgement of a debt.

Joint Account. Two or more persons or firms joining together to trade in some particular article or venture, and sharing the profits or losses.

Legal Tender. Any form of money that can be used in legal payment of a debt and that cannot be refused by the creditor. (See p. 209.)

Letter of Credit. A letter addressed by a banker to his agent or correspondent, either at home or abroad, authorizing the latter to pay to a particular person (i.e., the bearer of the L/C) a certain sum of money. (See p. 198.)

Liabilities. Debts of a person or firm. Liabilities may be *current* – i.e., those due for immediate or early settlement (e.g., trade creditors); *long-term* – i.e., those that do not have to be met in the immediate future; or *contingent* (see p. 297).

Limited Liability. A term meaning that the shareholders of a limited company are not liable for any sum in excess of the unpaid amount of the shares they have agreed to take.

Liquid Assets. Cash and those assets that are readily converted into cash. (Now usually termed *current* assets.)

Liquidation. The realization of the assets and the settling of the liability of a business.

Maturity. The date upon which bills, promissory notes, etc., legally become payable.

Mortgage. A transfer of property or land as security for money borrowed. (Such property is said to be *mortgaged*, and interest at an agreed rate is payable by the borrower.)

National Giro. A banking service operated by the Post Office and offering current account facilities. (For details see pp. 214–215.)

Net. After all deductions, discounts, etc., have been allowed.

Net Cash. This means that no deductions will be allowed when payment is made.

Net Proceeds. The amount remaining after all charges, expenses, and commission have been deducted.

Net Profit. The amount by which the gross profit exceeds the expenses of selling and of running the business.

Net Weight. This is the weight of the goods alone, and is obtained by deducting the 'tare' from the 'gross weight.' (See *Tare.*)

Oncost. (See *Overhead.*)

Open Account. An account which is outstanding or unsettled.

Open Cheque. A cheque that is not crossed and that may be cashed over the bank counter.

Optimum. The best, everything being taken into consideration.

Overdraft. An amount drawn in excess of the sum standing to one's credit at the bank, interest being charged on the day-to-day balance of the overdraft.

Overhead. A term used to express the indirect expenses of trading, such as rent, rates, lighting and heating, advertising, etc. Overheads are sometimes referred to as: burden, oncost, establishment charges, fixed charges, etc.

P.A.Y.E. (*Pay As You Earn*). The method used for deducting Income Tax from wages and salaries, etc.

Payee. The person named in a cheque (or bill of exchange) to whom the amount is directed to be paid.

Paying-in Slip. A form used when paying in money to a bank.

Per Contra. A book-keeping term meaning *on the opposite side.*

Personal Account. A record of transactions with persons or firms.

Policy (Insurance). The document setting out the conditions under which the person insured is compensated by the insurance company.

Post (*Posting*). A book-keeping term meaning to transfer items from the subsidiary books to the Ledger.

Post-date. To date *after* the current date.

Power of Attorney. A legal document appointing one person to act as the attorney (or agent) for another person, either generally or for some specific purpose.

Premium. The annual sum paid by the insured person to the 'insurer' under the terms of the insurance policy. (See *Insurance.*)

Price-list. A document issued by a supplier, giving particulars of and the prices at which he is prepared to sell his goods.

Pro Forma Invoice. An invoice sent for the purpose of giving details of goods a customer may wish to purchase.

Promissory Note (legal definition). An unconditional promise in writing made by one person to another, signed by the maker, engaging to pay on demand, or at a fixed or determinable future time, a sum certain in money to, or to the order of, a specified person or to bearer.

Proposal Form (Insurance). A printed form containing a number of questions that require to be answered before the contract with the insurance company can be entered into.

Purchases Day Book (or *Purchases Journal* or *Bought Day Book* or *Bought Journal*). Used in book-keeping to record particulars of goods bought on credit.

Quotation. An offer of goods at certain prices, sent usually in reply to an inquiry received. (See pp. 158 & 159.)

Rebate. An allowance or reduction.

Receipt. An acknowledgment in writing of the receipt of money or property.

Refer to Drawer. When a cheque is *dishonoured* (i.e., returned by the banker unpaid) it is usually marked "R/D," which means 'refer to the drawer' of the cheque for an explanation of the non-payment of the cheque.

Remittance. Money of any kind sent by one person to another.

Returns. Returned purchases, sales, empties, etc., which are recorded in the Returns Books.

Sale or Return. Goods "on sale or return" are those sent to a person or firm on the understanding that they may be returned to the supplier if unsold.

Sales Journal (or *Sales Day Book* or *Sold Book*). Used in book-keeping to record particulars of goods sold on credit.

Sequestration. The Scottish legal term for bankruptcy.

Shipping Note. A printed form that requires to be completed when goods are shipped.

Solvent. Able to pay all debts in full.

Stale Cheque. An out-of-date cheque. (Cheques usually become 'stale' if not cashed within six months.)

Standing Order. (See *Banker's Order.*)

Statement of Account. A periodical account showing the amount due by one person or firm to another for goods supplied. (Usually referred to as a 'statement.')

Stock-in-trade. The quantity and value of the goods and merchandise which a trader has in stock at any particular time.

Stock-taking. The term used when a trader periodically values his stock-in-trade in order to balance his books and ascertain his financial position.

Stop a Cheque. To instruct a banker not to pay a cheque when it is presented at the bank.

Sundries. A book-keeping term meaning 'more than one.'

Suspense Account. An account in which items are entered temporarily until their proper 'heading' is known.

Tare. The weight of the crate, box, or other container in which goods are packed when weighed separately from the goods themselves.

Term of a Bill. The time allowed for payment – e.g., "three months after date."

Trade Discount. Discount allowed off catalogue prices, and representing the difference between wholesale and retail prices.

Turnover. A trader's total sales for a given period; the net sales, or sales *less* returns inward.

Voucher. A receipt for cash paid, or any document supporting the accuracy of accounts; e.g., Petty Cash Voucher.

Working Capital. The amount of capital available for trading purposes; the amount by which the current assets exceed the current liabilities (i.e., the capital immediately available with which to 'work' the business).

Write Off. To close a Ledger account by posting a part or the whole of it to another account; e.g., to 'write off' a loss such as *Depreciation* or a *Bad Debt.*

Appendix D

Foreign Words and Phrases

ab initio (L.) – from the beginning
addendum (*pl.* addenda) (L.) – something to be added; appendix, addition
ad finem (L.) – to the end (abbr. *ad fin.*).
ad hoc (L.) – for this special purpose.
à deux (F.) – for two; between two.
ad infinitum (L.) – without limit; for ever (to infinity) (abbr. *ad inf.*).
ad interim (L.) – for the meantime; temporarily (abbr. *ad int.*).
ad libitum (L.) (abbr. *ad lib.*) – at pleasure; to any extent.
ad nauseam (L.) – to the point of disgust.
ad valorem (L.) – according to value (abbr. *ad val.*).
a fortiori (L.) – with stronger reason; more conclusively.
agent provocateur (F.) – person employed to provoke someone into doing some wrongful act (i.e., a 'provoking agent'; police or secret service spy.
aide-de-camp (*pl.* aides-de-camp) (F.) – officer assisting general by carrying orders, etc.
à la bonne heure (F.) – well and good; that's good.
à la carte (F.) – (of meals, etc.) ordered by separate items; picking from the bill of fare. (See *table d'hôte.*).
à la mode (F.) – in the fashion.
al fresco. (It.) – in the open air.
alias (L.) (*pl.* aliases) – assumed name.
alibi (L.) (*pl.* alibis) – plea of being *elsewhere.*
Alma Mater (L.) – bounteous (benign) mother; term used by former students in referring to their university.
alter ego (L.) – one's other self; a close friend.
amende honorable (F.) – public apology and reparation.
amour-propre (F.) – self-esteem.

anno Domini (L.) – in the year of our Lord, of the Christian era; (colloq.) advancing age.
ante (L.) – prefix meaning 'before.'
ante meridiem (L.) – before noon (abbr. *a.m.*).
anti (Gr.) – prefix meaning 'opposite', 'against.'
a posteriori (L.) – (reasoning) from effect to cause; inductive.
a priori (L.) – (reasoning) from cause to effect; deductively.
apropos (F.) – to the point or purpose; *apropos of* – in connection with, in respect of.
au courant (F.) – fully acquainted (with); well-informed.
au fait (F.) – conversant, instructed.
au pair (F.) – (of arrangement between two parties) paid for by mutual services (no money changing hands).
au revoir (F.) – good-bye; till we meet again.
auf wiedersehen (Ger.) – good-bye; till we meet again.
avant-garde (F.) – the pioneers or innovators in any art in a particular period.
avant-propos (F.) – preliminary matter; preface.
belles-lettres (F.) – studies, writings, of the purely literary kind.
bête noire (F.) – an object of special detestation; pet aversion.
bitte (Ger.) – if you please.
blasé (F.) – cloyed, tired of pleasure.
bona fide (L.) – in good faith; genuine, sincere.
bona fides (L.) – honest intention, sincerity.
bonhomie (F.) – geniality, good nature.
bon jour (F.) – good morning, good day.
bon marché (F.) – cheaply; a bargain.
bon mot (*pl.* bons mots) (F.) – witty saying.
bon soir (F.) – good evening, good night.
bon vivant (F.) – gourmand.
bon voyage! (F.) – a pleasant journey!
cadre (F.) – framework, scheme.
carte blanche (F.) – full discretionary power.
casus belli (L.) – act justifying war.
cause célèbre (*pl.* causes célèbres) (F.) – law-suit that excites much interest.
caveat emptor (L.) – let the buyer see to it (beware); disclaiming responsibility for buyer's disappointment.
ceteris paribus (L.) – other things being equal.
chargé d'affaires (*pl.* chargés d'affaires) (F.) – diplomatic agent; ambassador at minor level.
chef-d'oeuvre (F.) – masterpiece.
cherchez la femme (F.) – look for the woman; there is a woman at the bottom of the business.

ci-devant (F.) – former(ly); that has been (with the earlier name or state).
communiqué (F.) – official intimation or report.
compos mentis (L.) – sane; in one's right mind.
concierge (F.) – a porter or doorkeeper.
contra (L.) – against, opposite.
contretemps (F.) – unlucky accident; hitch.
cordon bleu (F.) – blue ribbon; first-class cook.
corpus delicti (L.) the substance of the offence; all that goes to make a breach of law.
corrigenda (L.) – things to be corrected (esp. errors in printed book).
coup de grâce (F.) – finishing stroke.
coup de main (F.) – a sudden, overpowering attack.
coup de maître (F.) – a master-stroke
coup d'état (F.) – violent or illegal change of government by ruling power.
cum (L.) – prep. meaning 'with'; e.g., *cum dividend* (abbr. *cum div.*), including dividend about to be paid.
cum grano salis (L.) – with a grain of salt; with reservations.
de facto (L.) – actually; in fact, whether by right (*de jure*) or not.
dei gratia (L.) – by the grace of God.
de jure (L.) – rightful, by right of law.
de luxe (F.) – luxurious; of superior kind.
de novo (L.) – afresh; once more.
Deo volente (L.) (abbr. *D. V.*) – God willing; if nothing occurs to prevent it.
de rigueur (F.) – indispensable; obligatory; required by etiquette.
de trop (F.) – not wanted; unwelcome; superfluous.
deus ex machina (L.) – an eleventh-hour solution (lit. a god from the machine).
dictum (*pl.* dicta, dictums) (L.) – formal saying; pronouncement; maxim.
dies non (L.) – a day on which no legal business is done.
distingué (F.) – having an air of distinction.
dossier (F.) – set of documents relating to a person or case.
double entendre (entente) (F.) – ambiguous expression; phrase with two meanings, one usually indecent.
dramatis personae (L.) – (List of) characters in a play.
emeritus (L.) – retired from office; e.g., *emeritus professor*.
en famille (F.) – at home, among one's family.
enfant terrible (F.) – (literally) a terrible child; one who asks awkward questions, repeats what he has heard, etc.
en masse (F.) – in a mass; all together.

en passant (F.) – in passing; by the way.
en rapport (F.) – in sympathy with.
en route (F.) – on the way (*to*, *for* a place, etc.).
entente (F.) – friendly understanding between States.
entrepreneur (F.) – person in effective control of commercial undertaking; contractor acting as intermediary.
erratum (*pl.* errata) (L.) – error in printing, etc.
esprit de corps (F.) – regard for honour and interests of body one belongs to.
et sequentes/et sequentia (L.) (abbr. *et seq(q.)* – (in reference to books, etc.) and the words, pages, etc., that follow.
ex (L.) – (prep. used in commerce) out of, sold from (warehouse, etc.); e.g., ex dividend (abbr. *ex div.* or *x.d.*) – not including next dividend.
ex adverso (L.) – from the opposite side; in opposition.
ex cathedra (L.) – authoritatively; from the (teacher's) chair.
exempli gratia (L.) (abbr. *e.g.*) – for example.
exeunt omnes (L.) – all leave the stage.
ex gratia (L.) – as an act of grace (e.g., an *ex gratia* payment).
ex-libris (L.) – book-plate, label with arms, crest, etc., and owner's name pasted into book.
ex officio (L.) – by virtue of one's office, as *ex-officio* members of committee.
ex toto (L.) – in part only, as distinct from *in toto* (entirely).
fait accompli (F.) – thing done and no longer worth arguing against; an accomplished fact.
faux pas (F.) – an offence against social convention; indiscreet speech or action (lit. 'false step').
flagrante delicto (L.) – during the crime; in the very act.
fons et origo (L.) – the source and origin (of).
force majeure (F.) – irresistible compulsion; circumstances beyond one's control.
furor scribendi (L.) – mania for writing.
habeas corpus (L.) – writ requiring person to be brought before judge or into court (lit., 'you must have the body').
habitué (F.) – frequenter (of); habitual visitor or resident.
hors de combat (F.) – disabled; no longer in a condition to fight.
ibidem (L.) – in the same place (abbr. *ibid.*).
ici on parle francais (F.) – here French is spoken.
idée fixe (F.) – a fixed idea; an obsession; monomania.
id est (L.) – that is (abbr. *i.e.*).
in camera (L.) – in the judge's private room, not in open court.
in extenso (L.) – at full length.

in extremis (L.) – at the point of death.
in flagrante delicto (L.) – in the very act of committing an offence.
infra (L.) – below, lower down, further on (in book). (*Vide infra*, see below.)
infra dig. (L.) (infra dignitatem) – beneath one's dignity, unbecoming.
in loco parentis (L.) – in the place of a parent.
in perpetuum (L.) – in perpetuity; for ever.
in re (L.) – in the matter of.
in situ (L.) – in its (original) place.
in statu quo (L.) – in the same state (as formerly).
inter alia (L.) – amongst other things.
in toto (L.) – entirely; completely.
ipso facto (L.) – by that very fact; obvious from the facts.
je ne sais quoi (F.) – an indescribable something ('I know not what').
laissez-faire (F.) – 'let alone'; policy of inaction; Government abstention from interference with individual action, esp. in commerce.
lapsus calami (L.) – a slip of the pen.
lapsus linguae (L.) – a slip of the tongue.
lèse-majesté (F.) – affront to sovereign or ruler; presumption.
lese-majesty – treason.
lex non scripta (L.) – unwritten law, i.e., common law.
lex scripta (L.) – written, i.e., statute law.
loco citato (L.) (abbr. *loc. cit.* or *l.c.*) – in the passage already quoted.
locum tenens (L.) – deputy acting esp. for clergyman or doctor; ('one occupying the place') a deputy or substitute.
locus (*pl.* loci, pr. losī) – locality or exact place of something.
locus sigilli (L.) (abbr. L.S.) – the place of the seal.
magnum opus (L.) – writer's or other artist's chief production.
maître d'hôtel (F.) – head-waiter; hotel manager.
mal de mer (F.) – sea-sickness.
mañana (Sp.) – tomorrow.
materia medica (L.) – remedial substances used in practice of medicine.
mens sana in corpore sano (L.) – sound mind in sound body (used esp. as expressing the ideal of education).
modus operandi (L.) – method of working.
modus vivèndi (L.) – mode of living; i.e., compromise pending settlement of dispute.
mot (F.) (*pl.* mots) – witty saying.
mot juste (F.) – the most precisely right expression.
multum in parvo (L.) – much in small compass; small but comprehensive.
mutatis mutandis (L.) – with necessary changes.
née (F.) – born (used in adding married woman's maiden name, as Mrs. Jones, née Smith).

nemine contradicente (L.) (abbr. *nem. con.*) } 'no-one contradicting/dissenting' (i.e., without a dissenting vote).
nemine dissentiente (L.) (abbr. *nem. diss.*) }

nihil ('nil') – nothing.

noblesse oblige (F.) – privilege entáils responsibility.

nolle prosequi (L.) – (legal) relinquishment by plaintiff or prosecutor of (part of) his suit; stay of proceedings.

nom de guerre (F.) – pseudonym, sobriquet; assumed name under which person fights, writes, etc.

nom de plume (F.) – pen-name; writer's pseudonym.

non compos mentis (L.) – of unsound mind; not responsible for one's actions.

non sequitur (L.) – (it does not follow) illogical inference; paradoxical result.

nota bene (L.) (abbr. N.B.) – mark well, note this.

nouveau riche (F.) – wealthy parvenu (lit. 'new rich').

obiter dictum (*pl.* dicta) (L.) – incidental remark; judge's expression of opinion uttered in arguing point but not binding.

onus probandi (L.) – burden of proof. (*Onus* – burden, duty, responsibility).

opere citato (L.) (abbr. *op. cit.*) – in the work cited.

outré (F.) – outside the bounds of propriety; eccentric; outraging decorum; in bad taste.

par excellence (F.) – above all others so called; by virtue of special excellence.

pari passu (L.) – with equal pace; simultaneously and equally.

passé (fem. passée) (F.) – past the prime; out of date.

passim (L.) (of allusions, phrases, etc.) – throughout, in every part (as: this occurs in Shakespeare *passim*).

per annum (L.) – by the year, yearly.

per caput (erroneously *per capita*) (L.) – a head, each.

per contra (L.) – (on) the opposite side (of an account, etc.).

per diem (L.) – by the day.

per mensem (L.) – by the month.

per procurationem (abbr. *per pro., p.p.*) – by proxy; by the action of (person signing document); for and on behalf of.

per se (L.) – by or in itself; intrinsically.

persona grata (L.) – acceptable person (especially diplomat).

persona non grata (L.) – unacceptable person.

pièce de résistance (F.) – most substantial dish; most important item.

poste restante (F.) – post-office department where letters are kept until applied for.

post meridiem (L.) – after noon.

post mortem (L.) – after death; examination made after death; (colloq.) discussion of game, etc. after its end.

prima facie (L.) – (arising) at first sight; (based) on first impression, as: he has *prima facie* a good case.

pro forma (L.) – as a matter of form; for form's sake; (of invoice) sent to purchaser before goods are dispatched.

pro rata (L.) – in proportion; at the same rate; proportional(ly).

pro tempore (L.) (abbr. *pro tem.*) – for the time, temporarily.

quasi (L.) – that is to say; as if, as it were; used with hyphen to denote 'not really,' 'almost,' 'seeming(ly),' as: engaged in a *quasi*-war.

quid pro quo (L.) – compensation; tit for tat.

qui vive (L.) (on the) – on the alert; watching for something to happen.

quod erat demonstrandum (L.) (abbr. *Q.E.D.*) – which was the thing to be proved.

quod vide (L.) (abbr. *q.v.*) – which see (in cross references).

quorum (L.) – number that must be present to constitute valid meeting.

raison d'être (F.) – what accounts for or justifies or has caused thing's existence.

rapprochement (F.) – a drawing together; establishment or renewal of cordial relations.

rendezvous (F.) – a place of meeting; an appointment.

répondez, s'il vous plait (F.) – please reply (abbrev. R.S.V.P.).

résumé (F.) – summary, epitome, abstract.

sang-froid (F.) – coolness, composure, in danger or difficulty.

savoir faire (F.) – quickness to see and do the right thing; address, tact.

savoir vivre (F.) – good breeding; being at home in society.

sequentes/sequentia (L.) (abbr. *seq.* or *seqq.*) – (&) the following, (&) what follows, appended to line or page numbers in references.

seriatim (L.) – one by one; point by point.

sic (L.) – so, thus. (Often used to call attention to some quoted mistake.)

sine die (L.) – without date; (of business) indefinitely adjourned.

sine qua non (L.) – indispensable condition or qualification.

sobriquet (soubriquet) (Fr.) – nickname, assumed name.

soi-disant (F.) – self-styled, pretended.

status quo (L.) – unchanged position.

status quo ante (L.) – previous position; pre-existing state of affairs.

sub judice (L.) – under judicial consideration; not yet decided.

subpoena (L.) – (noun) writ commanding person's attendance in court of justice; (verb) to serve subpoena on.

sotto voce (It.) – in an undertone, aside.

stet (L.) – let it stand.

sub rosa (L.) – in confidence, in secret.

supra (L.)– above; previously, before (in a book or writing).

table d'hôte (F.) – meal at a fixed price.
terra firma – solid earth; dry land.
tête-à-tête (F.) – private conversation or interview between two persons.
tour de force (F.) – feat of strength or skill.
tout de suite (F.) – immediately.
tout ensemble (F.) – taken together; thing viewed as a whole; general effect.
ubique (L.) – everywhere.
ultimo (L.) (abbr. *ult.*) – in the month preceding that now current (cf. proximo (abbr. *prox.*), of next month; instant (abbr. *inst.*), of the current month).
ultra vires (L.) – beyond one's power or authority.
vade-mecum (L.) – ('go with me'); handbook or other work of reference carried as a constant companion.
verbum (sat) sapienti (L.) (abbr. *verb. sap.*) – a word is enough to the wise.
versus (L.) (abbr. *v.*) – against, as: (law) Smith v. Jones; (cricket, etc.) England v. Australia.
via (L.) – by way of, through.
vice (L.) – in the place of, e.g., vice-chairman, vice-president, etc.
vice versa (L.) – the other way round.
vide (L.) – refer to, consult (in reference to passage in book, etc.)
vide infra (L.) – see below.
videlicet (abbr. *viz.*) (L.) – namely, to wit; that is to say.
vide supra (L.) – see above.
vis-à-vis (F.) – in a position facing one another; opposite (to).

Appendix E

Useful Addresses

Agriculture, Fisheries, and Food, Ministry of	
Cereals Economics and Statistics Eggs and Poultry Fisheries Meat, Livestock, and Fatstock Sugar and Tropical Foodstuffs	Whitehall Place, London SW1A 2HH
Advisory Service, Research, and Education Food Standards and Science Horticulture Land Drainage, Water Supply, and Machinery Land Use Milk and Milk Products	Great Westminster House, Horseferry Road, London SW1P 2AE
Animal Health Infestation Control	Hook Rise South, Tolworth, Surbiton, Surrey KT6 7NF
Co-operation and Labour	83–91 Artillery Mansions, Victoria Street, London SW1H OHZ
Fisheries Laboratory	Sea Fisheries Laboratory, Lowestoft, Suffolk
Plant Pathology	Hatching Green, Harpenden, Herts.
Agricultural Research Council	160 Great Portland Street, London W1N 6DT

Arts Council of Great Britain	105 Picadilly, London W1V 9FN
Automobile Association	P.O. Box 71, Fanum House, Leicester Square, London WC2H 7LY
Aviation, Civil	(see Department of Trade and Industry)
British Broadcasting Corporation	Broadcasting House, Portland Place, London W1A 1AA
Television Centre	P.O. Box 331, Television Centre, Wood Lane, London W12 7RJ
Regions:	
Midland	P.O. Box 361, 52 Carpenter Road, Birmingham B15 2JU
North	P.O. Box 27, 33 Piccadilly, Manchester M1 4BB
West	31 Whiteladies Road, Bristol BS8 2LR
Scotland	Queen Margaret Drive, Glasgow G12 8DG
N. Ireland	Ormeau Avenue, Belfast BT2 8HQ
Wales	Broadcasting House, Llantrisant Road, Cardiff CF5 2YQ
British Council	65 Davies Street, London W1Y 2AA
British European Airways Corporation	P.O. Box 7, Bealine House, Cavendish Avenue, Ruislip, Middlesex HA4 6QL
British Medical Association	B.M.A. House, Tavistock Square, London WC1H 9JR

British Railways Board	222 Marylebone Road, London NW1 6JJ
Area Boards	
Eastern	Station Road, York YO1 1HT
London Midlands	Euston House, Eversholt Street, London NW1 1DF
Scottish	Buchanan House, 48 Port Dundas Road, Glasgow G4 0HG
Southern	84 Tooley Street, London SE1 2TQ
Western	Paddington Station, London W2 1HA
British Standards Institute	2 Park Street, London W1Y 4AA
British Tourist Authority	64–65 St. James's Street, London SW1A 1NF
Commerce, Association of British Chambers of	68 Queen Street, London EC4N 1SN
Commonwealth Agricultural Bureaux, Executive Council	Farnham House, Farnham Royal, Bucks SL2 3BN
Commonwealth Development Corporation	33 Hill Street, London W1A 3AR
Commonwealth Office, Foreign and	Downing Street, London SW1A 2AL
India Office Library and Records	Orbit House, 197 Blackfriars Road, London SE1 8NG
Commonwealth Secretariat	Marlborough House, Pall Mall, London SW1Y 5HX
Commonwealth Telecommunications Board	28 Pall Mall, London SW1Y 5LP

Confederation of British Industry	21 Tothill Street, London SW1H 9LP
Cotton Growing Association, British	335 Royal Exchange, Manchester M2 7FL
Crown Estate Commissioners	13–15 Carlton House Terrace, London SW1Y 5AH
Customs and Excise, Board of	King's Beam House, 39–41 Mark Lane, London EC3R 7HE
Defence, Ministry of	
Main Building	Whitehall London SW1A 2HB
Adastral House	Theobalds Road, London WC1X 8RU
Norman Shaw Buildings South	Victoria Embankment, London SW1A 2JA
Old Admiralty Building	Whitehall, London SW1A 2BL
Meteorological Office	London Road, Bracknell, Berks. RG12 2UR
London Weather Centre	Penderel House, 284 High Holborn, London WC1V 7HP
Dock Labour Board, National	22–26 Albert Embankment, London SE1 7TE
Education and Science, Department of	2 Curzon Street, London W1Y 8AA
Electricity Authorities	
Area Boards	
London	County House, 46–49 New Broad Street, London EC2M 1LS

South-eastern	Queens Gardens, Hove, Sussex BN3 2LS
Southern	Southern Electricity House, Bath Road, Littlewick Green, Maidenhead, Berks. SL6 3QB
South-western	Electricity House, Colston Avenue, Bristol BS1 4TS
Eastern	P.O. Box 40, Ipswich IP9 2AQ
East Midlands	P.O. Box 4, 398 Coppice Road, Arnold, Nottingham N95 7HX
Midlands	Mucklow Hill, Halesowen, Birmingham
S. Wales	Newport Road, St. Mellons, Cardiff CF3 9XW
Merseyside & N. Wales	Sealand Road, Chester CH1 4LR
Yorkshire	Wetherby Road, Scarcroft, Leeds LS14 3HS
North-eastern	P.O. Box 1SE, Newcastle-upon-Tyne, NE99 1PG
North-western	P.O. Box 14, Cheetwood Road, Manchester M8 8BA
N. Scotland	16 Rothesay Terrace, Edinburgh EH3 7SE
S. Scotland	Cathcart Ho., Inverlair Avenue, Glasgow G44 4BE
Employment, Department of	8 St. James's Square, London SW1Y 4JB
Environment, Department of the Local Government and Development	2 Marsham Street, London SW1P 3EB

Housing and Construction	Lambeth Bridge House, Albert Embankment, London SE1 7SB
Building Research Station	Bucknalls Lane, Garston, nr. Watford, Herts. WD2 7JR
Transport Industries	St. Christopher House, Southwark Street, London SE1 0TE
Road Research Laboratory	Crowthorn, Berks, RG11 6AU
Export Credits Guarantee Department	P.O. Box 272, Aldermanbury, London EC2V 7HR
Fire Protection Association	Aldermary House, 10–15 Queen Street, London EC4N 1TJ
Fisheries	(see Ministry of Agriculture)
Foreign and Commonwealth Office	Downing Street, London SW1A 2AL
Passports	Clive House, Petty France, London SW1H 9HD
	India Buildings, Water Street, Liverpool L2 0QZ
	1st Floor, Empire House, 131 West Nile Street, Glasgow G1 2RY
	Olympia House, Dock Street, Newport, Mon. NPT 1XA
	Westwood, Peterborough PE3 6TG
	30 Victoria Street, Belfast BT1 3LY

Forestry Commission	25 Savile Row, London W1X 2AY
Forest Products Research Laboratory	Princes Risborough, Aylesbury, Bucks.
Friendly Societies, Registry of	17 North Audley Street, London W1Y 2AP
Fuel and Power	(see Department of Trade and Industry)
Gas Council	59 Bryanston Street, London W1A 2AZ
Government Chemist	Cornwall House, Stamford Street, London SE1 7NF
Health and Social Security, Department of	Alexander Fleming House, Newington Causeway, London SE1 6BY
Scottish Home and Health Department	St. Andrew's House, Edinburgh EH1 3DE
Welsh Board of Health	Cathays Park, Cardiff CF1 3NT
Social Security Central Records	Newcastle-upon-Tyne, NE98 1YT/1YU/1YX
Scotland	39 Drumsheugh Gardens, Edinburgh EH3 7SR
Wales	Block 2, Government Buildings, Gabalfa, Cardiff CF4 4YJ
National Insurance Commissioner	6 Grosvenor Gardens, London SW1W 0DN
Scotland	23 Melville Street, Edinburgh EH3 7PW
Wales	7 Park Place, Cardiff CF1 3DP
Home Office	Whitehall, London SW1A 2AP

Immigration Nationality	Princeton House, 271–277 High Holborn, London WC1V 7EW
Fire Department	Ruskin Avenue, Richmond, Surrey TW9 4DN
Scientific Adviser	Horseferry House, Dean Ryle Street, London SW1A 2AP
Community Relations Commission	Russell Square House, 10–12 Russell Square, London WC1B 5EN
Race Relations Board	5 Lower Belgrave Street, London SW1W 0NR
Hotels and Restaurants Association, The British	88 Brook Street, London W1Y 1YF
Housing and Local Government	(see Department of the Environment)
Independent Television Authority	70 Brompton Road, London SW3 1EY
Industrial Assurance Commissioner	17 North Audley Street, London W1Y 1WE
Industrial Court	1 Abbey Gardens, Great College Street, London SW1P 3SE
Industrial Tribunals, Central Office	93 Ebury Bridge Road, London SW1W 8RB
Information, Central Office of	P.O. Box 2, Hercules Road, London SE1 7DU
Regions: London and South-eastern	St. Christopher House Annexe, Sumner Street, London SE1 9LB

Southern	6/8 Market Place House, Reading RG1 2EH
Southern-western	The Pithay, Bristol BS1 2NF
Midland	Five Ways House, Islington Row, Birmingham B15 1SH
North Midland	Cranbrook House, Cranbrook Street, Nottingham NG1 1EW
Northern	Wellbar House, Gallowgate, Newcastle-upon-Tyne NE1 4TB
North-western	Sunley Building, Piccadilly Plaza, Manchester M1 4BD
East and West Ridings	City House, New Station Street, Leeds LS1 4JG
Eastern	Block A, Government Buildings, Brooklands Avenue, Cambridge CB2 2DF
Wales	42 Park Place, Cardiff CF1 2PY
Inland Revenue, Board of	Somerset House, London WC2R 1LG
Assessments	Barrington Road, Worthing
Estate Duty	Minford House, Rockley Road, London W14 0DF
Special Commissioners of Income Tax	Turnstile House, 94–99 High Holborn, London WC1V 6LQ
Stamps, Office of the Controller of	Bush House (S.W. Wing), Strand, London WC2B 4QN

Scotland	6/14 Waterloo Place, Edinburgh EH1 3YR
Labour	(see Department of Employment)
Land Registry, H.M.	32 Lincoln's Inn Fields, London WC2A 3PH
Land Charges Agricultural Credits	Kidbrooke, London SE3 3PN
Lloyds Register of Shipping	69–71 Fenchurch Street, London EC3M 4BS
London Transport	55 Broadway, London SW1H 0BD
Medical Research Council	20 Park Crescent, London W1N 4AL
National Institute for Medical Research	The Ridgeway, London NW7 1AA
Central Public Health Laboratory Food Hygiene	Colindale Avenue, London NW9 5HT
Mersey Docks and Harbour Board	Mersey Docks and Harbour Board Building, Pier Head, Liverpool L3 1BZ
Metrication Board	22 Kingsway, London WC2B 6LE
National Coal Board	Hobart House, Grosvenor Place, London SW1X 7AE
National Economic Development Office	Millbank Tower, 21–41 Millbank, London SW1P 4QX
Ordnance Survey	Romsey Road, Southampton SO9 4DF

Overseas Governments & Administrations, Crown Agents for	P.O. Box 357, 4 Millbank, London SW1P 3JD
Shipping	77 Gracechurch Street, London EC3V 0AS
Patent Office	25 Southampton Buildings, London WC2A 1ST
Pharmaceutical Society of Great Britain	17 Bloomsbury Square, London WC1A 2NN
Plastics Federation, British	47/48 Piccadilly, London W1V 0DN
Port of London Authority	P.O. Box 242, P.L.A. Building, Trinity Square, London EC3P 3BX
Red Cross Society, British	4 Grosvenor Crescent, London SW1X 7EQ
Research Development Corporation, National	P.O. Box 236, Kingsgate House, 66–74 Victoria Street, London SW1E 6SL
Scottish Office	Dover House, Whitehall, London SW1A 2AU
Scottish Departments Agriculture	St. Andrews House, Regent Street, Edinburgh EH1 3DA
Development	EH1 3DD
Education	EH1 3DB
Home and Health	EH1 3DE
Information	EH1 3DQ
Marine Laboratory	P.O. Box 101, Victoria Road, Torry, Aberdeen AB9 8DB

State Managements	30 George Square, Glasgow G2 1EW
Stationery Office, H.M.	P.O. Box 121, Atlantic House, 45–50 Holborn Viaduct, London EC1P 1BN
London Retail	P.O. Box 15, 49 High Holborn, London WC1V 6HB
Postal Orders	P.O. Box 569, Cornwall House, Stamford Street, London SE1 9NH
Belfast	12 Linenhall Street, Belfast BT2 8AZ
Birmingham	258 Broad Street, Birmingham B1 2HE
Bristol	33 Ashton Vale Road, Bristol BS3 2HN
Cardiff	109 St Mary Street, Cardiff CF1 1JW
Edinburgh	Government Buildings, Bankhead Avenue, Edinburgh EH11 4AB
Manchester	Brazenose House West, Brazenose Street, Manchester M60 8AS
Stock Exchange	P.O. Box 119, London EC2P 2BT
Timber Trade Federation	Clairville House, 47 Whitcomb Street, London WC2H 7DL
Transport	(see Department of the Environment)

Transport Tribunal	Watergate House, 15 York Buildings, London WC2N 6LB
Trade and Industry, Department of	P.O. Box 392, 1 Victoria Street, London SW1H 0ET
Regional Offices	
East Midlands	Cranbrook House, 47 Cranbrook Street, Nottingham N91 1ES
London and South-eastern	Cromwell House, Dean Stanley Street, London SW1P 3HY
Midland	Five Ways House, Islington Row, Birmingham B15 1SJ
Northern	Wellbar House, Gallowgate, Newcastle-upon-Tyne NE1 4TJ
North-western	Sunley Building, Piccadilly Plaza, Manchester M1 4BA
South-western	The Pithay, Bristol BS1 2NE
Yorkshire & Humberside	City House, New Station Street, Leeds LS1 4JQ
Scotland	314 St Vincent Street, Glasgow G3 8XF
Wales	Gabalfa, Cardiff CF4 4YL
Civil-Aviation	Shell Mex House, Strand, London WC2R 0DP
Divisional Organization	
Southern	Civil Aviation Divisional Office, Heston Aerodrome, Hounslow TW5 9NF

Northern	Civil Aviation Divisional Office, Mersey House, The Strand, Liverpool L2 7PZ
Scotland	Civil Aviation Office for Scotland, Broomhouse Drive, Edinburgh EH11 3XE
Fuel	Thames House South, Millbank, SW1P 4QJ
National Engineering Laboratory	Birniehill, East Kilbride, Glasgow G75 0QU
National Physical Laboratory	Teddington, Middx. TW11 0LW
Trades Union Congress	23–28 Great Russell Street, London WC1B 3LS
Treasury	South Block, Great George Street, London SW1P 3AG
Trinity House,	Trinity Square, London EC3N 4DH
United Nations Organization	London Information Centre, 14 Stratford Place, London W1N 9AF
Weather Centre, London	Penderel House, 284 High Holborn, London WC1V 7HP
Women's Royal Voluntary Service	17 Old Park Lane, London W1Y 4AJ

Index

Index